D1645072

B 22.2.66
B 1 /67

# CALDAY GRANGE GRAMMAR SCHOOL

| | ISSUE DATE | CAT. | ISSUED TO | FORM |
|---|---|---|---|---|
| 1 | 25/1/65 | A | P. K. Jones | U6 ScM |
| 2 | 2/9/66 | B | GB Egart | L6G |
| 3 | 6/9/68 | B | P. R. French | RUT(P) |
| 4 | 5-11-70 | B | J E Michel | L6B |
| 5 | 25/3/74 | BC | D. MacNiell | L6P |
| 6 | | | | |
| 7 | | | | |
| 8 | | | | |
| 9 | | | | |

# A SECOND
# COURSE OF HEAT

# A
# SECOND COURSE OF
# HEAT

BY

A. E. E. McKENZIE, M.A.

*Trinity College, Cambridge*

CAMBRIDGE
AT THE UNIVERSITY PRESS
1963

PUBLISHED BY
THE SYNDICS OF THE CAMBRIDGE UNIVERSITY PRESS

Bentley House, 200 Euston Road, London, N.W. 1
American Branch: 32 East 57th Street, New York 22, N.Y.
West African Office: P.O. Box 33, Ibadan, Nigeria

©

CAMBRIDGE UNIVERSITY PRESS
1963

*Printed in Great Britain at the University Press, Cambridge*
*(Brooke Crutchley, University Printer)*

# CONTENTS

My original decision to devote myself to science was a direct result of the discovery which has never ceased to fill me with enthusiasm since my early youth—the comprehension of the far from obvious fact that the laws of human reasoning coincide with the laws governing the sequences of the impressions we receive from the world about us.                                   MAX PLANCK

# PREFACE

Much thought has been devoted recently, in various countries, to a modernisation of school physics syllabuses. There has been a strong plea in this country for a reduction of factual content and a greater concentration on principles. It happens that the particular branch of physics in which sixth-form students are apt to penetrate not very far into the wood because of a too detailed study of outlying trees is Heat. Too much time is often spent on drill in answering questions on the apparent expansion of liquids or in applying elaborate cooling corrections, while the study of gases, which is the core of Heat, does not proceed very far, and the crowning achievements of Heat, the study of radiation, leading to the Quantum Theory, and thermodynamics, are scarcely touched upon.

In this book I have omitted much traditional detail, particularly details of elaborate experiments, and I have tried to bring into focus the fundamental principles of the subject by keeping the factual detail small.

I have adopted the spirit of the recommendations in the report of the Science Masters' Association, *Physics for Grammar Schools*, although I have not always followed the letter. I think, for example, that the sixth-form student should be introduced to van der Waals's equation, which the report omits. I realise the danger that, once the equation has been presented, there is a strong temptation to use it to calculate the critical constants. But this, for examination purposes, must be resisted.

I hope, too, that the expansion of solids and liquids will play no part, or at least a very small one, in future Advanced level examination syllabuses. In an elementary form, expansion will have been covered at Ordinary level. But once it is included at Advanced level the door is open to questions on clocks running too slow in hot weather, on the tension in steel tyres forced while hot on to wheels, on corrections to barometers made very slightly inaccurate by a change of temperature, and so on. Preparation for such questions requires time which should be spent on more rewarding topics. I found that treatment of the expansion of solids and liquids cluttered up the developing argument, and so I omitted it.

When considering methods of finding the mechanical equivalent of heat I decided to include the method of Laby and Hercus, although

I adhere to the principle that teachers should not multiply unnecessarily methods of measuring a particular quantity, because the other accurate methods rest upon absolute determinations of the ohm and of the e.m.f. of a standard cell.

While the main purpose of a course of Heat in sixth-form teaching is to present the principles of classical physics, each topic should, where possible, be related to the latest developments in science. I have therefore included something about solid-state physics, low-temperature physics, and the conservation of mass-energy.

Following the recommendation of the General Conference on Weights and Measures in 1948 I have introduced the term Celsius scale for Centigrade scale, although the older term will doubtless die hard. I have also adopted the symbols recommended by the Royal Society, e.g. $\theta$ for temperature, $t$ being reserved for time. As regards the unit of heat, I feel that the student must be given the calorie at first but he should be weaned to the joule.

I wish to express my indebtedness to Mr H. Tunley for reading the manuscript and making most valuable and stimulating criticisms.

I acknowledge with thanks the permission of the Institute of Physics and the Physical Society to reproduce Figure 3 from J. A. Hall's *Fundamentals of Thermometry* and of Messrs Constable and Co. Ltd to reproduce Figure 41 from J. B. Perrin's *Atoms*.

I am very grateful to the different Examining Bodies for allowing me to reproduce questions. The following is the key to the acknowledgements made after each question: (O.S.) Oxford Scholarship; (C.S.) Cambridge Scholarship; (O. & C.) Oxford and Cambridge, (O.) Oxford Local, (C.) Cambridge Local, (L.) London, (N.) Northern Universities, General Certificate, or Higher Certificate, Examination.

A. E. E. M.

CAMBRIDGE
*January 1963*

CHAPTER 1

# THERMOMETRY

The fundamental and characteristic measurement in the study of heat is that of temperature. The idea of temperature developed from man's physiological sensations of hotness and coldness; a body's temperature represents its degree of hotness.

The principle underlying the scientific measurement of temperature is that any system tends towards thermal equilibrium, i.e. to have a uniform temperature throughout. Thus, if we place a thermometer in thermal contact with one system and then with another, we can say that the two systems are at the same temperature if both are in thermal equilibrium with the thermometer and the thermometer in both cases gives the same reading.

### Single-fixed-point thermometers

The earliest thermometers, which appeared in the seventeenth century, measured temperature by utilising the expansion of a liquid when heated. These thermometers were graduated by means of a single fixed point of temperature, for example, the freezing point of aniseed oil. The thermometer was placed in the freezing aniseed oil and the position of the surface of the liquid in its stem was marked and assigned an arbitrary numerical value. The stem could then be graduated beyond the fixed point in, say, 100 equal divisions, each division representing an equal expansion of the liquid in the thermometer.

Calibration by means of one fixed point was unsatisfactory because no two thermometers agreed. It was therefore replaced by calibration at two fixed points, which is the basis of all practical scales today, although, as we shall see (p. 8), there is a move to return to what is virtually a single-fixed-point scale.

### Celsius and Fahrenheit scales of temperature

The two fixed points used to define a scale of temperature are as follows: (1) the melting point of pure ice under a pressure of 1 standard atmosphere (76 cm of mercury), called the *ice point*; (2) the boiling point of pure water under a pressure of one standard atmosphere, called the *steam point*. The temperature interval between the fixed points is called the *fundamental interval*.

The calibration of a mercury-in-glass thermometer is made by marking the positions of the mercury surface in the stem at the ice and steam points. If it is desired to use the Celsius or Centigrade scale these positions are assigned the values 0 and 100; each degree is determined by $\frac{1}{100}$th of the apparent expansion of the mercury (relative to the glass) between the two fixed points. In the case of the Fahrenheit scale the fixed points are given the values 32 and 212, and each degree is determined by $\frac{1}{180}$th of the apparent expansion of the mercury between the fixed points.

### General definition of the Celsius scale of temperature

We will express mathematically the method of defining the Celsius scale of temperature just described, giving a general definition which is not confined to the mercury thermometer. Let $X_0$ and $X_{100}$ be the values of a property of a substance (such as the apparent volume of mercury in a thermometer) at the ice and steam points. If $X$ is the value of the property at $\theta$ °C, we define $\theta$ by the equation

$$\theta = \frac{X - X_0}{X_{100} - X_0} \cdot 100.$$

We might be tempted to say that, when applying this equation to the mercury thermometer, we are merely assuming that mercury expands (relative to glass) uniformly with temperature. However, if we define temperature in terms of the relative expansion of mercury, we are arguing in a circle. Indeed when we compare scales of temperature based on the expansion of different liquids or gases, or even on the same liquid in different kinds of glass, we find that the scales are all slightly different. Regnault (1810–78) compared a mercury thermometer (constructed of the ordinary soft glass of his time) with an air thermometer. At the fixed points, of course, the scales agreed; but half-way between, when the air thermometer read 50·0 °C, the mercury thermometer read 50·2 °C.

### The mercury-in-glass thermometer

We shall discuss later the grounds on which one particular scale of temperature was chosen, to the exclusion of the rest. In the meantime we will consider the mercury thermometer, assuming that it is supposed to be reading on the mercury scale.

The mercury thermometer is the one most used in the teaching laboratory and was that employed by many of the pioneer investigators of heat. It is subject to serious errors but, if these are corrected or circumvented, its accuracy in the range 0–200 °C is second only to that of the platinum resistance thermometer and it is much the more convenient to use.

The errors of a mercury thermometer, apart from the error caused by any non-uniformity in its stem, spring from the imperfections of the glass bulb in which the mercury is contained. For example, a thermometer bulb, on being placed in ice after being removed from boiling water, may take some hours to return to its original volume at 0 °C. Also the bulb of a thermometer suffers a gradual permanent contraction. Joule found a rise in the ice point of one of his thermometers of about 1 °F over the course of 38 years. Since Joule's time, however, there has been a big improvement in the glass used for making thermometers.

The chief advantage of the mercury thermometer, and indeed of any liquid-in-glass thermometer, is that it is a simple direct-reading instrument.

## The gas thermometer

Gases expand about 20 times as much as mercury and about 120 times as much as thermometer glass. Hence, in a gas thermometer, errors due to erratic changes in the volume of the glass bulb are small. Another great advantage of the gas thermometer is its wide range, from about −270 to 1600 °C.

When gases are heated their pressure, as well as their volume, may increase. There are, in fact, three mutually dependent variables: pressure, volume and temperature. Gas thermometers are either of the constant-pressure type, in which the change of volume of the gas is used to measure temperature; or of the constant-volume type, when the change of pressure of the gas is utilised. The latter type has proved to be the more satisfactory mainly because it is more convenient to measure accurately a change of pressure than a change of volume.

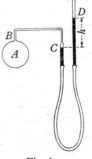

Fig. 1

A simple form of constant-volume gas thermometer, designed by Jolly, is shown in Fig. 1. $A$ is a bulb containing the gas; to measure the pressure of the gas the bulb is connected to a manometer consisting of two vertical glass tubes joined by rubber tubing and containing mercury. The pressure of the gas in the bulb is equal to $H+h$, where $H$ is the atmospheric pressure in cm of mercury and $h$ is the difference of levels of the mercury in the manometer as shown in Fig. 1. Before taking a reading the arm $D$ is moved up or down until the mercury level is at a fixed mark at $C$, thereby ensuring a constant volume of the gas.

For calibration, the bulb $A$ is surrounded by pure melting ice. The gas contracts, the level, $C$, of the mercury rises, and $D$ must be lowered to bring the mercury back to $C$. The bulb $A$ is then placed in steam from water boiling under 1 atmosphere pressure; the gas expands, pushing the mercury at $C$ down so that the arm $D$ must be raised to bring the mercury back to $C$. If $p_0$, $p_{100}$ and $p$ are the pressures of the gas in the bulb at the ice point, steam point and at an unknown temperature $\theta\,°\mathrm{C}$ respectively, we define the scale of temperature of the gas used as follows:

$$\theta = \frac{p-p_0}{p_{100}-p_0}.100.$$

The bulb $A$ should be large compared with the volume of the 'dead space' from $B$ to $C$, which contains gas at a temperature different from that in the bulb when the latter is immersed in, say, a water bath. To make the dead space as small as possible, most of the tube between $B$ and $C$ is capillary, but the tube must be wider at $C$; otherwise the mercury at $C$ would be appreciably depressed owing to surface tension.

Regnault, in the middle of the nineteenth century, realising that the gas thermometer is more accurate and reliable than the mercury thermometer, introduced the practice of comparing the readings of mercury thermometers with those of a gas thermometer, the latter being regarded as a standard. In the 1880's Chappuis, at the Bureau International des Poids et des Mesures, made accurate comparisons of mercury thermometers, constructed of an improved thermometer glass 'verre dur', with a constant-volume hydrogen thermometer, which he had elaborated to correct for the errors of the simple Jolly instrument of Fig. 1. In 1887 the International Committee of Weights and Measures adopted the hydrogen Centigrade scale as the standard scale and for 40 years the constant-volume hydrogen thermometer was the standard instrument in the laboratories of the world. The readings of mercury thermometers were converted to those of the constant-volume hydrogen thermometer for all experimental work of high accuracy.

Today helium is used for the lowest temperatures that a gas thermometer can measure (in the region of $-270\,°\mathrm{C}$), while at the highest temperatures (in the region of $1600\,°\mathrm{C}$) nitrogen is preferable because hydrogen and helium diffuse through the platinum-iridium bulb of the thermometer. The scales of temperature of hydrogen, helium and nitrogen are very nearly the same and their differences are known as a result of several very thorough investigations. The following are readings of the same temperature in degrees Celsius or Centigrade about midway between the fixed points on the scales of the three gases, in the cases both of the constant-volume and constant-pressure thermometers:

|                        | Hydrogen | Helium | Nitrogen |
|------------------------|----------|--------|----------|
| Constant-volume (°C)   | 50·003   | 50·001 | 50·010   |
| Constant-pressure (°C) | 50·004   | 50·000 | 50·032   |

The modern gas thermometer, capable of reading to this high degree of accuracy, is an elaborate instrument, cumbersome, and usable in one position only, so that it is quite unsuitable for anything but standardising other more convenient thermometers. The bulb normally has a volume of about a litre (to minimise the dead-space error); uniformity of temperature must be ensured in the comparatively large volume of gas. It is necessary also to keep the temperature of the mercury manometer constant. Corrections are made for the expansion of the bulb, for the dead space and for fluctuations in atmospheric pressure.

## The absolute scale

There is, at first sight, no apparent reason why the hydrogen scale of temperature should be regarded as any more fundamental than the mercury scale. The two scales differ by a fraction of a degree between the fixed points and by as much as 3 °C at about 350 °C. The hydrogen thermometer was selected as the standard because it is more sensitive than the mercury thermometer and because it has a much wider range. We shall now see that there are good theoretical reasons, as well as those of practical convenience, for basing the standard scale of temperature on gas thermometers.

The scales of the so-called permanent gases (which are difficult to liquefy), such as hydrogen, helium and nitrogen, are very nearly identical, both at constant volume and at constant pressure. It was known that this must be so from the early investigations on the expansion and contraction of gases with change of temperature, which were made in the days when temperature was measured on the mercury scale.

It was found that the increase in volume with rise in temperature at constant pressure of all permanent gases may be represented by the same straight line (Fig. 2), showing that all permanent gases expand by the same amount. If the graph is produced backwards the temperature corresponding to zero volume of any permanent gas is $-273\,°C$. Similarly, by plotting pressure against temperature at constant volume, another straight line is obtained and the temperature corresponding to zero pressure of the gas is also $-273\,°C$. This temperature of zero volume or of zero pressure is called the *absolute zero* and is believed to be the lowest possible temperature. According to classical (i.e. pre-quantum) physics, as the absolute zero is approached and reached, the molecules of the gas slow down and eventually come to rest with zero energy, but we shall see that this picture, although broadly true, requires slight modification (see p. 109).

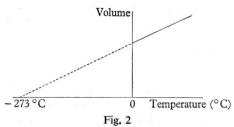

Fig. 2

Temperatures measured from the absolute zero in degrees Celsius are known as *absolute temperatures*. Since the absolute zero is approximately $-273\,°C$, the absolute temperature $T$ corresponding to a temperature of $\theta\,°C$ is normally taken as

$$T = (\theta + 273)\,°K,$$

where K denotes Kelvin. The present best value for the absolute zero is $-273.15\,°C$, so that, for accurate work,

$$T = (\theta + 273.15)\,°K.$$

### The perfect gas

We have imagined a gas shrinking to zero volume, if cooled sufficiently, although we know that, before this could happen, the gas would liquefy and probably solidify. Hence we must introduce the concept of a *perfect* or ideal *gas*, which is incapable of liquefying, because its molecules are supposed not to attract each other, and which can shrink to zero volume when its molecules come to rest because the molecules are imagined as mass points. We shall discuss the behaviour of the perfect gas in terms of molecules in chapter 5. Here we can define a perfect gas, in a complete and satisfactory manner, as a gas which obeys Boyle's law exactly at all pressures and which suffers no change of temperature when allowed to expand into a vacuum (because, unlike a real gas, there is no mutual attraction between the molecules and hence no energy is required to separate them).

A graph of volume, $v$, against absolute temperature, $T$, for a mass of perfect gas at constant pressure is a straight line through the origin (i.e. Fig. 2 with the origin shifted to where the graph cuts the temperature axis); hence $v/T$ is constant, the pressure remaining constant. Similarly, $p/T$ is constant when the volume remains constant.

The three laws governing the behaviour of a perfect gas can be expressed as follows.

(1) *Boyle's law*. The pressure of a given mass of gas is inversely proportional to its volume if the temperature remains constant:

$$pv = \text{constant, when } T \text{ is constant.}$$

(2) *Charles's law*. The volume of a given mass of gas increases by approximately $\frac{1}{273}$ of its volume at 0 °C for each degree C rise in temperature, if the pressure is kept constant:

$$v/T = \text{constant, when } p \text{ is constant.}$$

(3) *Law of pressures*. The pressure of a given mass of gas increases by approximately $\frac{1}{273}$ of its pressure at 0 °C for each degree C rise in temperature, if the volume is kept constant:

$$p/T = \text{constant, when } v \text{ is constant.}$$

These laws are obeyed almost exactly by real gases, at temperatures well above their liquefying points, such as hydrogen, helium, oxygen and nitrogen at normal laboratory temperatures. The three laws can be combined into the single equation

$$pv/T = \text{constant.}$$

## The perfect-gas scale of temperature

We must be clear, when stating the gas laws, what scale of temperature we are using. The discoverer of Charles's law (actually Gay-Lussac) used the mercury scale. Today Charles's so-called law is simply a definition of the perfect-gas scale of temperature, which is the ultimate scale to which all others are corrected. Each degree Celsius is defined as responsible for $\frac{1}{100}$th of the change of volume of a perfect gas between the ice and steam points, at constant pressure; or, alternatively, as responsible for $\frac{1}{100}$th of the change of pressure of a perfect gas between the ice and steam points at constant volume.

The readings of gas thermometers may be corrected to the perfect-gas scale from the results of investigations into the deviations from the gas laws of real gases. The smaller their pressure the more exactly do real gases obey Boyle's law and the more nearly do all gases expand or contract by the same amount, thus giving more exactly the same value for the absolute zero. If constant-volume gas thermometers are used with different initial pressures, their readings can be extrapolated to very low pressures and these will be readings on the perfect gas scale.

The corrections to the gas scales, to convert them to the perfect-gas scale, are not large: for the hydrogen scale the correction is $+0.06\,°C$ at $-200\,°C$ and for the nitrogen scale it is $+0.77\,°C$ at $1000\,°C$; between the ice and steam points the corrections are only a few thousandths of a degree.

### The thermodynamic scale

There is a theoretical scale of temperature, proposed by Lord Kelvin in 1854 and known as the thermodynamic scale (p. 183), which is independent of the properties of any substance. This scale is identical with the absolute scale of the perfect gas and provides a most satisfying theoretical basis for the definition of the ultimate scale of temperature. It enables us to interpret and estimate extremely high temperatures, at which gases cease to exist as elements, such as those of atomic explosions, of the order of 10 to 15 million $°C$, and of the interior of stars, between 10 and 100 million $°C$.

In the original thermodynamic scale the zero was the absolute zero and the size of the degree was defined by $\frac{1}{100}$th of the fundamental interval between the ice and steam points. But Lord Kelvin pointed out that the scale could be determined by using a single fixed point. At the Tenth General Conference of Weights and Measures in 1954 it was decided to define the thermodynamic scale by assigning the value $273.16\,°K$ to the triple point of water (see p. 123), which is more precise than the ice point and $0.010\,°C$ above it. The size of the degree is determined by the fact that there are $273.16$ degrees between the absolute zero and the triple point of water. The difference between this new scale, to be known as the Kelvin scale ($°K$), and the earlier thermodynamic scale, based on the ice point and the steam point, is at present undetectable. A difference would be revealed if more accurate experiments than are at present possible showed that the temperature of the triple point of water, on the earlier scale, is not exactly $273.16\,°K$.

### SUMMARY

We will summarise briefly the main argument in our discussion of temperature so far. Scales of temperature based on the expansion of liquids and gases are all different, although the scales of the permanent gases are nearly the same. The ultimate scale of temperature is that of the perfect gas; temperatures on this scale are measured by using a gas thermometer and making corrections for the deviations from the perfect-gas laws of the gas employed in the thermometer. Mercury thermometers required for accurate work are compared with gas thermometers so that the mercury readings can be converted to the perfect-gas scale.

There is a lowest limit of temperature, known as the absolute zero. The absolute scale of temperature utilises Celsius degrees and assigns to the temperature of the absolute zero the value 0 °K. To convert Celsius temperatures to absolute temperatures we must add 273 (or more exactly 273·15).

The absolute scale of the perfect gas is identical with the thermodynamic or Kelvin scale, based on theoretical considerations which will be discussed in chapter 10.

### The platinum resistance thermometer

The electrical resistance of platinum increases with rise of temperature; the phenomenon is utilised in the platinum resistance thermometer. If we define the platinum scale of temperature by applying the general formula on p. 2, then

$$\theta = \frac{R - R_0}{R_{100} - R_0} . 100,$$

where $R_0$, $R_{100}$ and $R$ are the resistances of the platinum wire at the ice point, steam point and temperature $\theta$ respectively, and we find that it differs slightly from the perfect-gas scale between the fixed points and quite considerably at higher and at lower temperatures.

In 1887 Callendar investigated how the resistance of a platinum wire varies between 0 and 600 °C, the temperatures being measured by a gas thermometer. He neatly avoided several serious experimental difficulties by sealing the platinum wire inside the bulb of the gas thermometer. He found that, if $R$ and $R_0$ are the resistances of the platinum wire at $\theta$ °C and at 0 °C on the perfect-gas scale,

$$R = R_0(1 + a\theta + b\theta^2),$$

where $a$ and $b$ are constants. This is an empirical relation (i.e. based on experimental observation and not on theory) which has been shown to hold more and more accurately with each subsequent investigation. The platinum resistance thermometer, first introduced by Sir William Siemens in 1871, was in disfavour when Callendar undertook his work; it is now regarded as the most accurate thermo-meter in the range −190 to 660 °C.

In order to determine the constants $a$ and $b$ in the above equation the resistance of the platinum wire must be determined at three fixed points. The third fixed point adopted, in addition to the ice and steam points, is the boiling point of sulphur (444·600 °C). Note that the equation gives temperatures on the perfect gas scale.

We shall not describe in detail the various practical forms of platinum resistance thermometers, but merely make a few general

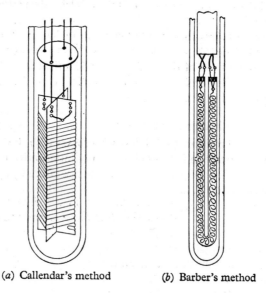

(a) Callendar's method          (b) Barber's method

Fig. 3

comments. The platinum wire is usually supported on a mica or quartz framework and it is enclosed in a protecting tube or sheath made of glass, porcelain or fused silica. Callendar wound the wire on a notched cross of mica (Fig. 3a); the form now used in the National Physical Laboratory, devised by Barber, consists of a helix of platinum wire in a fine U-shaped glass capillary (Fig. 3b). The important thing to avoid is straining of the wire, since this would affect its resistance, and in Barber's instrument the leads to the helix are sealed into the end of the capillary to prevent straining.

Callendar measured the resistance of the wire by a modified form of Wheatstone bridge, but today a potentiometer is used. The ends of the platinum wire are connected to four terminals, two of which are used for leading the current in and out, and the other two for measuring the potential difference across the wire. The resistance of the platinum wire in a precision instrument is usually about 25 $\Omega$ at the ice point; the potential drop across it is compared with the potential drop across a standard resistance of about the same value connected in series with it.

The small current which is passed through the platinum wire to measure its resistance heats it, and this heating must be taken into account in work of high accuracy. If the resistance is found using various currents, the resistance at zero current can be estimated by extrapolation.

Although platinum is always used for resistance thermometers in scientific work, copper and nickel are sometimes employed in industry because they are cheaper. Also employed in industry are certain semi-conductors, called thermistors, made of oxides of various metals such as iron, nickel, manganese and cobalt. The resistance of a thermistor decreases with increasing temperature; its most valuable characteristic is that the decrease is comparatively large, so that a thermistor thermometer has a much higher sensitivity than a platinum resistance thermometer (although a considerably lower accuracy).

### Thermocouples

When wires of two dissimilar metals are connected as in Fig. 4, and one of the junctions is heated while the other is kept cold, an e.m.f. is set up depending on the difference of temperature of the junctions. The arrangement is known as a thermo-couple and it can be used to measure temperature. The cold junction is usually kept in melting ice while the other junction is brought to the tem-perature to be measured. The simplest method of measuring the e.m.f. is to connect the free ends of the thermo-couple to a millivoltmeter, and the most accurate method is to use a potentiometer.

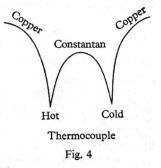

Thermocouple

Fig. 4

The commonest pair of metals employed for thermocouples in industry are iron and constantan (an alloy containing 57 % copper and 43 % nickel), since they give a comparatively high e.m.f. and are inexpensive. Other pairs of metals used are copper/constantan and platinum/alloy of platinum and rhodium.

The thermocouple consisting of platinum/platinum-rhodium is

regarded as the most accurate thermometer in the range 660 °C to 1000 °C. The relation between the e.m.f., $e$, of the thermocouple and the temperature $\theta$ on the perfect-gas scale in this range is

$$e = a + b\theta + c\theta^2.$$

The constants $a$, $b$ and $c$ are determined by finding the e.m.f. at the freezing points of antimony (630·5 °C), silver (960·5 °C) and gold (1063 °C).

Thermocouples have a big advantage over the platinum resistance thermometer in the measurement of rapidly varying temperatures. When there is no risk of contamination the junction of the thermocouple can be sealed into the body whose temperature is required and the time lag is then very small. Thermocouples will also measure the temperature almost at a point, which is impossible with a platinum resistance thermometer.

### Radiation pyrometers

Above the gold point (1063 °C) temperatures are determined by measuring the intensity of the radiation emitted by the hot glowing body and extrapolating Planck's radiation law, which states the mathematical relationship between the intensity of the radiation and the temperature. We shall describe the instruments used, known as radiation pyrometers, in chapter 9. The idea of using radiation to estimate the temperature of a body is, of course, common in everyday life; we speak of a body being red hot or white hot.

### APPENDIX

#### The International Temperature Scale

In 1927 the International Committee of Weights and Measures adopted a practical scale of temperature, known as the International Temperature Scale, and this was revised at their meeting in 1948. The scale was intended to be as accurate as possible a practical realisation of the thermodynamic scale, based on the ice point and the steam point, or, what amounts to the same thing, of the perfect-gas scale. Its purpose was to facilitate the task of standardising thermometers by the national physical laboratories of the world.

It took the form of a series of accurately reproducible fixed points, determined by the labours of a large number of investigators who measured them with gas and other thermometers. In order to realise temperatures between the fixed points, particulars of the instruments to be used were specified. This is obviously essential because if, say, a mercury thermometer were used for a certain range, its readings would not be exactly the same as those of a platinum resistance thermometer.

Table 1. *Summary of the chief instruments for measuring temperature*

| | Mercury thermometer | Gas thermometer | Platinum resistance thermometer | Thermocouple | Radiation pyrometer |
|---|---|---|---|---|---|
| Temp. limits ... | −39 to 600 °C | −270 to 1600 °C | −200 to 1100 °C | −250 to 1600 °C | |
| Remarks ... | A simple, direct-reading instrument. It has many errors but when they are corrected it is accurate between 0 and 200 °C. Must be compared with a gas thermometer for its readings to be converted to the perfect-gas scale | A standardising instrument only. The chief gases used are hydrogen, helium and nitrogen. Their deviations from the perfect-gas laws are used to correct the gas thermometer readings to those of the perfect-gas scale, which is identical with the thermodynamic scale | The most accurate of all thermometers in the range −190 to 660 °C. Its readings can be expressed as temperatures on the perfect-gas scale by means of formulae which are based on comparisons between it and the gas thermometer | A simple instrument, which can measure temperature almost at a point and also rapidly varying temperatures. Its readings are converted to temperatures on the perfect-gas scale as in the case of the platinum resistance thermometer. It is the most accurate thermometer in the range 660 to 1063 °C | Indispensable above the range of the other instruments. Can be directly compared with a gas thermometer up to about 1600 °C, and beyond that it is based on the radiation laws |

The primary fixed points of the 1948 scale are as follows:

| | |
|---|---|
| Boiling point of oxygen | $-182 \cdot 970$ °C |
| Melting point of ice | 0 °C |
| Boiling point of water | 100 °C |
| Boiling point of sulphur | $444 \cdot 600$ °C |
| Freezing point of silver | $960 \cdot 8$ °C |
| Freezing point of gold | $1063 \cdot 0$ °C |

In addition to these primary fixed points about a dozen secondary fixed points, not quite so accurately reproducible, were also given. We shall not list these secondary fixed points, although we have already mentioned one of them, the freezing point of antimony ($630 \cdot 5$ °C).

The scale was divided into the following four parts, temperatures below $-190$ °C being left undefined:

(1) *From* $-190$ °C *to the ice point*

Measurements in this range are made with a specified platinum resistance thermometer, using the formula

$$R = R_0 \{1 + a\theta + b\theta^2 + c(\theta - 100)\, \theta^3\},$$

the constants $a$, $b$ and $c$ being determined by means of the ice, steam, sulphur and oxygen points.

(2) *From the ice point to* 660 °C

Measurements in this range are made with a specified platinum resistance thermometer, using the formula

$$R = R_0 (1 + a\theta + b\theta^2),$$

the constants $a$ and $b$ being determined by means of the ice, steam and sulphur points.

(3) *From* 660 °C *to the gold point*

Measurements in this range are made with a platinum/platinum-rhodium thermocouple, the cold junction being kept at a temperature of 0 °C, using the formula

$$e = a + b\theta + c\theta^2,$$

the constants $a$, $b$ and $c$ being determined by means of the freezing point of antimony, the silver point and the gold point.

(4) *Above the gold point*

Above the gold-point temperatures are determined by radiation pyrometers (see pp. 164–6).

### Accuracy and reproducibility

Despite the fact that the best gas thermometer value for the sulphur point is $444 \cdot 6 \pm 0 \cdot 1$ °C, the sulphur point is given as $444 \cdot 600$ °C, since platinum resistance thermometers can measure it to $0 \cdot 002$ °C. We therefore say that the point has a reproducibility of $\pm 0 \cdot 002$ °C and an accuracy of

±0·1 °C. Specifying the sulphur point as 444·600 °C enables workers to compare their platinum resistance readings to a high degree of accuracy although their values may be incorrect on the thermodynamic scale.

## Realisation of the fixed points

Details of accurate methods of obtaining the fixed points are clearly as important as the specifications of the interpolation instruments. For example, to obtain the ice point, pure ice in the form of ice shavings is placed in a lagged vessel of glass or earthenware fitted with a drain cock. Distilled water is poured over the ice shavings, drained away, and then the ice is stirred. A reproducibility of 0·001 °C may be attained in this way. For methods of obtaining the other fixed points the student should refer to specialist books on Thermometry.

## QUESTIONS

1. (a) What is a scale of temperature?
   (b) Define the Celsius (or Centigrade) scale.
   (c) Will the scales for mercury and air thermometers necessarily agree at any temperatures? Is there any serious disagreement at other temperatures?

2. What are the advantages and disadvantages of the mercury-in-glass thermometer?

3. State the methods available for the measurement of temperature (a) above the boiling point, (b) below the freezing point, of mercury.

4. Describe a simple type of constant-volume air thermometer.

5. What are the advantages of a gas thermometer for use as a standard?

6. What is the ultimate scale of temperature to which all other scales are made to conform?

7. (a) What is meant by the absolute zero of temperature?
   (b) How did the conception arise?
   (c) What is its value on the Fahrenheit scale?

8. What part is played by absolute temperature in the statement of the gas laws?

9. (a) Explain the principle of (i) the platinum resistance thermometer, (ii) the thermocouple used as a thermometer.
   (b) How are readings with these thermometers made to agree with those on the perfect-gas scale?

10. What is the International Temperature Scale?

11. How are temperatures measured above the gold point (1063 °C)?

12. Discuss the measurement of temperature and explain how temperature is defined on the scale of a given type of thermometer.

When used to measure temperatures of about 300 °C the readings on the scale of an accurate mercury thermometer are about two degrees higher than those of an accurate air thermometer. Why is this, and what reasons, if any, are there for adopting one scale rather than the other?

(O. & C.)

13. Describe a simple electrical thermometer and outline the method by which you would calibrate and use it. What are the advantages and disadvantages of the thermometer you describe when compared with a mercury thermometer?

The e.m.f. of a certain thermocouple with one junction $A$ in melting ice and the other $B$ in the steam from water boiling at standard pressure is 4·40 mV. With $B$ still in the steam and $A$ in a boiling liquid the e.m.f. is 10·8 mV in the same direction as before. Calculate the temperature of the boiling liquid on the scale of this thermometer. $-145 °C$ (C.)

14. What exactly is meant by 70 °C on the scale of a mercury thermometer and by 343° absolute?

A constant-volume gas thermometer shows a pressure of 760 mm at 15 °C and a pressure of 773 mm at 20 °C. Calculate the absolute zero on the Centigrade scale for this gas. $-277 °C$ (O.)

15. What are the essential steps in defining a scale of temperature? What is meant by the absolute zero of temperature?

Write down expressions defining temperature on (a) the gas scale, (b) the platinum resistance scale.

The resistance, $R$, of platinum varies with the gas scale temperature, $t$ °C, according to the equation

$$R = R_0(1 + \alpha t + \beta t^2),$$

where $R_0$ is the resistance at 0 °C and $\alpha$ and $\beta$ are constants. For a certain platinum resistance thermometer the values of $\alpha$ and $\beta$ were $4·13 \times 10^{-3}$ and $-6·4 \times 10^{-7}$ respectively. Calculate the reading of the platinum thermometer when the gas scale temperature was 200 °C. (O. & C.)

16. Describe briefly the essentials of a constant-volume gas thermometer and a platinum resistance thermometer.

Discuss these two types from the point of view of (a) accuracy, (b) convenience, (c) consistency, (d) calibration. (O.S.)

## CHAPTER 2

# CALORIMETRY

### Units of heat

The commonest method of measuring heat, a subject known as calorimetry, is to cause the heat to be absorbed by water and to measure the rise in temperature of the water. The unit of heat, the *calorie (abbreviated to 'cal')*, is *the quantity of heat required to raise*

1 *gm of water through* 1 °*C*. If, say, 300 gm of water are raised through 20 °C, the quantity of heat absorbed is $300 \times 20 = 6000$ cal. This fact, that quantity of heat is given by the product of the mass of water and the rise in temperature, was established experimentally by mixing different masses of warm and cold water and finding the temperatures of the resulting mixtures, assuming that, on mixing, the heat lost by the warm water was equal to that gained by the cold water—a principle known as the conservation of heat.

Later more accurate experiments showed that the quantity of heat required to raise 1 gm of water through 1 °C varies slightly at different parts of the temperature scale. It therefore became necessary to define the calorie in terms of a specified temperature range: *the* 15 °*C calorie is the quantity of heat required to raise* 1 *gm of water from* 14·5 *to* 15·5 °*C*.

Other units which have been employed are the 20 °C calorie, defined in the range of 19·5 to 20·5 °C, and the mean calorie, which is $\frac{1}{100}$th of the heat required to raise 1 gm of water from 0 to 100 °C.

In experiments of the highest accuracy, which do not include those normally carried out in a teaching laboratory, it is necessary to specify which calorie has been employed. To avoid this complication the Ninth General Conference on Weights and Measures recommended in 1948 that the results of experiments involving the measurement of heat should be expressed, where possible, in a unit which is unaffected by the vagaries of water and which is constant at all temperatures, namely the *joule* (symbol 'J').

The joule is a unit of work and is defined as the work done when a force of 1 N (newton) acts through 1 m; or alternatively as $10^7$ ergs, where 1 erg is the work done when a force of 1 dyn acts through 1 cm. Heat can be measured in joules because work is convertible into heat and there is a fixed rate of exchange. We shall discuss this more fully in the next chapter.

The values of the three calories we have mentioned are as follows:

$$15 °C \text{ calorie} = 4·1852 \text{ J}$$
$$20 °C \text{ calorie} = 4·1813 \text{ J}$$
$$\text{Mean calorie} = 4·1832 \text{ J}.$$

It will be seen that these three calories differ by considerably less than 1 %: as 1 % is the kind of accuracy to be aimed at by the student in a calorimetric experiment, he can usually ignore the distinction between them.

The unit of heat on the British system is the British thermal unit (Btu), which is the quantity of heat required to raise 1 lb of water through 1 °F. If we wish to be more precise, the temperature range may be specified to be 59·5 to 60·5 °F.

Other units of heat are the *therm*, equal to 100000 Btu (used by gas companies), and the *Centigrade heat unit* which is the quantity of heat required to raise 1 lb of water through 1 °C.

## Specific heat

If equal masses of water at 20·0 °C and at 40·0 °C are mixed the resulting temperature is very nearly 30·0 °C. But if a mass of water at 20·0 °C is mixed with an equal mass of mercury at 40·0 °C, the temperature of the mixture is 20·65 °C. The mercury must cool through 19·35 °C to produce the heat needed to raise the temperature of the water through 0·65 °C. In general, different substances require different quantities of heat to raise equal masses of them through the same range of temperature.

*The specific heat of a substance is the quantity of heat required to raise unit mass of the substance by 1 degree.*

Mercury requires 0·033 cal to raise 1 gm of it through 1 °C and its specific heat is therefore 0·033 cal $\text{gm}^{-1}$ $\text{deg}^{-1}$ C. The prefix specific indicates that specific heat, like specific gravity, is really a ratio and represents a comparison of the heat capacity of the substance with that of water, because the calorie is defined in terms of the heat capacity of water. Hence specific heats are sometimes expressed without units; their numerical values are independent of the system of units employed (if the slight variation with temperature in the value of the heat unit is ignored). Thus the specific heat of mercury may be expressed as 0·033 cal $\text{gm}^{-1}$ $\text{deg}^{-1}$, 0·033 Btu $\text{lb}^{-1}$ $\text{deg}^{-1}$ F or 0·033.

In work of very high accuracy, when the variation in the value of the calorie with temperature must be taken into account, the least confusing units for expressing specific heats are joules $\text{gm}^{-1}$ $\text{deg}^{-1}$ C.

The quantity of heat $Q$ required to raise a mass $m$ of a substance specific heat $c$ from a temperature $\theta_1$ to a temperature $\theta_2$ is given by

$$Q = mc(\theta_2 - \theta_1).$$

It is worth noting that $c$ here represents the *mean* specific heat of the substance over the temperature range $\theta_1$ to $\theta_2$; the specific heats of all substances vary with temperature and are slightly different at, say, 0 and 100 °C.

Two other convenient concepts are as follows:

*The thermal capacity of a body is the quantity of heat required to raise the temperature of the body by 1 degree.*

*The water equivalent of a body is the mass of water having the same thermal capacity as the body.*

Thus a calorimeter weighing 100 gm, made of copper of specific heat 0·1 cal gm⁻¹ deg⁻¹ C, has a thermal capacity of 10 cal per °C and a water equivalent of 10 gm.

## Method of mixtures

The earliest and simplest method of measuring mean specific heats is known as the method of mixtures.

To find the specific heat of a solid, a lump of the solid is heated, say in boiling water, and then transferred, by means of a piece of thread tied to it, to cold water in a metal can, known as a calorimeter. The water is stirred and the rise in temperature caused by the hot solid is noted. Let $m_1$ and $m_2$ gm represent the masses of the solid and water respectively, $\theta_1$, $\theta_2$ and $\theta_3$ °C the initial temperature of the solid, the initial temperature of the water, and the final temperature of the mixture respectively, $c$ cal gm⁻¹ deg⁻¹ C the specific heat of the solid, and $w$ gm the water equivalent of the calorimeter. Heat lost by hot solid = heat gained by water and calorimeter:

$$m_1 c(\theta_1 - \theta_3) = (m_2 + w)(\theta_3 - \theta_2).$$

This is probably the most inaccurate of all the experiments performed in the teaching laboratory and it is instructive to consider the errors involved. Experiments in calorimetry are far more difficult to perform accurately than electrical measurements since there is no perfect insulator of heat and some escape of heat is inevitable. The errors are as follows:

(1) The hot solid will carry some of the hot water in which it has been heated to the cold water in the calorimeter. This can be avoided by keeping the solid dry, heating it in a copper vessel surrounded by a steam jacket.

(2) The hot solid will cool slightly during its transfer to the calorimeter. Hence this transfer must be as rapid as possible.

(3) The calorimeter and its contents will lose heat while rising to this final temperature, which will therefore not be as high as it should be. This error can be dealt with, as we shall show shortly, either by calculating its value or by preventing it from occurring.

(4) There will be a slight loss of heat as the result of evaporation from the water when its temperature rises.

The masses of the solid and of the water in the calorimeter should be such that a rise of about 10 °C results when mixing takes place. By estimating temperatures to 0·1 °C an accuracy of 1 % in the temperature rise can then be achieved. It is undesirable that the rise of temperature should be too large because this may result in serious loss of heat by evaporation of the water. If the masses of the solid and of the water are of the order of 100 gm it is a waste of time to measure them to an accuracy greater than 0·1 gm; an error of 0·1 gm in 100 gm is an error of 0·1 %, ten times smaller than the error in the rise in temperature.

### Methods of avoiding cooling corrections

There are two methods whereby a cooling correction can be avoided. The first is to arrange for the initial temperature of the calorimeter and its contents to be as much below the temperature of its surroundings as its final temperature is above. This may not entirely eliminate the cooling error, however. Suppose, in the experiment just described, room temperature is 15·0 °C and the temperature of the calorimeter and its contents rises from 10·0 to 20·0 °C. The rise from 10·0 to 15·0 °C, during which the calorimeter gains heat from its surroundings, occurs more rapidly than the rise from 15·0 to 20·0 °C, during which the calorimeter loses heat to its surroundings. Hence, on balance, the calorimeter loses a slight amount of heat.

The second method of avoiding cooling requires rather more elaborate apparatus but it has proved to be very satisfactory in investigations involving a slow transfer of heat. The jacket surrounding the calorimeter is kept always at the same temperature as the calorimeter itself by electrical heating. The calorimeter and jacket are known as an adiabatic calorimeter, the term 'calorimeter' being used to include the jacket. The heating of the jacket can be automatically controlled by means of a thermocouple having one junction soldered to the calorimeter and the other junction to the wall of the jacket; when there is a difference of temperature between the junctions an e.m.f. is set up which can be made to switch on the jacket's heating current.

### Cooling correction

There is a simple method of making a cooling correction, which is reasonably accurate when the hot body gives up its heat fairly rapidly on mixing, or when the heat is given up slowly but uniformly to the calorimeter and its contents, e.g. by an electric heater. The initial temperature of the calorimeter must be the same as that of the surroundings. The time for the calorimeter to reach its highest temperature is observed and then the temperature is recorded every ½ min for a few minutes as the calorimeter cools. The rate of cooling is roughly proportional to the difference in temperature between the calorimeter and its surroundings. Hence the average rate of cooling, while the calorimeter is reaching its highest temperature, is half the rate of cooling immediately after the calorimeter has reached its highest temperature. If $t$ minutes is the time taken by the calorimeter to reach its highest temperature and $r$ °C per minute is the rate of cooling immediately after, the cooling correction is $\frac{1}{2}rt$ °C, and this must be added to the observed rise in temperature of the calorimeter.

### Newton's law of cooling

The law we have just used, that the rate of cooling† of a body is proportional to the difference in temperature between the body and its surroundings, is only approximately true, and it holds only for a small difference in temperature. If, however, a body is cooled by forced convection, e.g. if it is placed near to an open window or to an electric fan, *its rate of loss of heat is proportional to its excess temperature over its surroundings*. This law is known as *Newton's law of cooling*, and it holds for considerable excesses of temperature (of the order of 50 °C or more). But what usually interests us in calorimetry is cooling under still conditions, and Newton's law, with its wider range, is of little practical use—except perhaps to designers of motor-car radiators.

### Modern development of the method of mixtures

The method of mixtures was investigated very thoroughly about 1840 by Regnault, who obtained high accuracy by careful correction and elimination of errors. The modern development of the method has been to replace the water and calorimeter by a hollow block of copper, silver or aluminium, contained in a vacuum flask to minimise cooling (Fig. 5). Such a calorimeter is known as an aneroid calorimeter (without liquid).

Water has the disadvantages that its large specific heat results in a small rise in temperature, and it confines the determination of specific heats to a narrow range of temperature because steam is formed if a very hot body is introduced. Copper has a specific heat only $\frac{1}{10}$th that of water and hence its rise in temperature is ten times as great. Metal-block calorimeters have been used for finding the specific heats of solids up to 1600 °C and also at very low temperatures.

The solid whose specific heat is required is usually shaped so as to

---

† The term 'rate of cooling' of a body is somewhat ambiguous because it may mean rate of loss of heat or rate of fall of temperature. So long as the specific heat of a particular body remains constant, however, its rate of fall of temperature is proportional to its rate of loss of heat.

fit snugly into the hollow in the block. It is heated (or cooled) to a known temperature and then dropped into the block, with which it rapidly shares its heat. The change in temperature of the block is measured by a thermocouple.

## Bomb calorimeter

For measuring heats of combustion of fuels the method of mixtures must be employed. A weighed sample of the fuel is ignited by an electrically heated wire and burnt in oxygen under pressure in a sealed steel 'bomb' (Fig. 6). The bomb is immersed in water and the heat generated is measured by the method of mixtures.

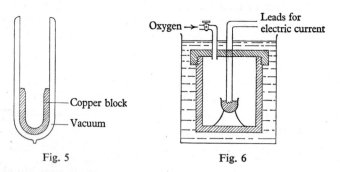

Fig. 5                    Fig. 6

Bomb calorimeters are sometimes used in an aneroid form, i.e. without fluid. They are made of silver so that they reach their equilibrium temperature within 10 min. They are usually calibrated by burning in them a substance like benzoic acid, whose calorific value has been accurately determined in an electrically calibrated calorimeter.

## Electrical method

The electrical method of determining specific heats is the most generally useful method and it is conveniently applicable over the whole range from low to high temperatures. The principle of the method is to raise the temperature of a known mass of the substance, whose specific heat is required, by a quantity of heat produced electrically and measured in joules.

The electrical method was first used to determine the mechanical equivalent of heat, i.e. the number of joules equivalent to a calorie. We will describe how the method can be employed to find the specific heat of a liquid, assuming the value of the mechanical equivalent of heat to be known.

A heating coil, connected to the electric circuit shown in Fig. 7, is immersed in the liquid contained in the calorimeter, whose details are not shown in Fig. 7, but are similar to Fig. 17, p. 35. A current, $i$ amp, measured by the ammeter, is passed through the coil, and the p.d., $V$ volts, across the coil is measured by the voltmeter. The liquid is stirred steadily, and its temperature is observed every minute. Suppose that the temperature of the liquid rises from $\theta_1$ °C to $\theta_2$ °C in $t$ sec, that the mass and specific heat of the liquid are $m$ gm and $c$ cal gm$^{-1}$ deg$^{-1}$ respectively, and that the water equivalent of the calorimeter is $w$ gm. For an experiment of this accuracy we can ignore the variation of the calorie with temperature and we will assume that 1 cal is equivalent to 4·18 J.

Heat produced by the electric current = $Vit$ J.

$$= \frac{Vit}{4\cdot18} \text{ cal.}$$

Heat gained by liquid and calorimeter = $(mc+w)(\theta_2-\theta_1)$ cal,

$$\therefore \quad (mc+w)(\theta_2-\theta_1) = \frac{Vit}{4\cdot18}.$$

Since the liquid is being heated for perhaps 10 min it is necessary to apply a cooling correction to allow for the heat lost during this period by the liquid and calorimeter. The heating occurs steadily and hence the simple method of obtaining the cooling correction, given on p. 20, may be applied. This cooling correction must, of course, be added to the rise in temperature $(\theta_2-\theta_1)$ in the above equation.

## The Nernst calorimeter

The decrease of the specific heats of substances at low temperatures is of great theoretical interest and has been the subject of much experimental investigation. Modern techniques of low-temperature calorimetry are based on those of Nernst, whose calorimeter is shown in Fig. 8. The block of metal, whose specific heat is required, serves as its own calorimeter and in it is embedded a platinum coil, insulated from the block, which is used both for heating and for measuring the temperature. The block is suspended by the wire leads in an evacuated glass vessel surrounded by a constant-temperature jacket which may contain, for example, liquid air or liquid hydrogen. This is an isothermal-jacket calorimeter, as opposed to the adiabatic calorimeter described on p. 20.

A small quantity of electricity is passed through the coil, sufficient to heat the block about 1 °C, and the rise in temperature is measured by the change in the resistance of the coil. In this way the specific heats at particular temperatures can be found. The insulation of the block is good and the cooling correction is small. When it is desired to bring the block to the temperature of the surrounding bath, hydrogen is admitted into the evacuated glass vessel. Non-metallic substances whose specific heats are required are contained in a silver calorimeter in which the platinum coil is embedded.

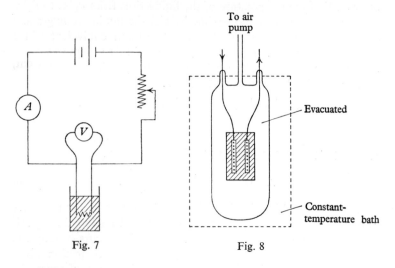

Fig. 7                    Fig. 8

## Microcalorimetry

It is sometimes necessary to measure very small quantities of heat, for example from minute quantities of radioactive materials, from germinating grain, from cement while it is setting, or from the metabolism of small animals, and special techniques have been perfected for this purpose.

One method is to employ twin calorimeters, $A$ and $B$, surrounded by the same jacket. Radioactive material, for example, is placed in calorimeter $A$ while calorimeter $B$ is heated electrically to keep it at the same temperature as $A$. Any transfer of heat to or from the jacket is the same for both calorimeters. Hence the heat generated in calorimeter $A$ is equal to that supplied electrically to $B$.

This is a neat way of compensating for heat leakage—the problem which faces all designers of calorimetric experiments.

## Continuous-flow method

When heat is produced continuously, for example by the burning of coal gas, it is convenient to arrange for the heat to be absorbed by a steady stream of water in what is called a continuous-flow (or constant-flow) calorimeter. For determining the calorific value of coal gas the gas flame is surrounded by a double spiral copper pipe (Fig. 9) carrying the flow of water, which is kept constant by a constant-head arrangement; the design of the calorimeter is such that all the heat of the flame is absorbed by the water and no appreciable heat is lost by the calorimeter to its surroundings. The water's rate of flow, $m$ lb/min, and its rise in temperature, $(\theta_2 - \theta_1)$ °F, are measured and also the rate of flow of the gas, $v$ cu ft/min, by means of a gas meter. The calorific value is $[m(\theta_2 - \theta_1)/v]$ Btu/cu ft.

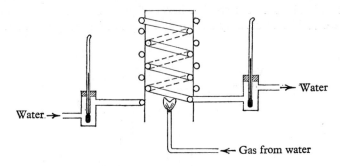

Fig. 9

The chief advantage of the method is that readings are taken when the calorimeter is in a steady state. It is unnecessary to consider the heat required to raise the temperature of the calorimeter itself; when the inflow and outflow temperatures of the water are steady, all the heat is being absorbed by the water (assuming no heat loss to the surroundings).

A continuous-flow calorimeter, with electrical heating, was developed into an instrument of high precision by Callendar and Barnes, who used it to find the mechanical equivalent of heat (see question 11, p. 37) and also the variation of the specific heat of water with temperature.

### Cooling correction with continuous-flow method

An effective way of eliminating the cooling correction in the electrical continuous-flow method is to take two sets of readings under identical conditions, except that the rates of flow of the fluid are different in the two cases, the rates of supply of heat being adjusted so that the temperatures of outflow are the same.

Let the cooling correction in both cases be $H$ cal sec$^{-1}$, the supplies of heat be $S_1$ and $S_2$ cal sec$^{-1}$, and the rates of absorption of heat by the fluid be $Q_1$ and $Q_2$ cal sec$^{-1}$. Then

$$S_1 = Q_1 + H,$$

$$S_2 = Q_2 + H.$$

Subtracting, $\qquad S_1 - S_2 = Q_1 - Q_2.$

### Determination of the specific heat of a gas at constant pressure

Electrical, continuous-flow calorimeters have been used in the best determinations of the specific heats of gases at constant pressure. The calorimeter used by Scheel and Heuse in 1912 is indicated in

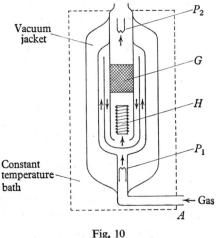

Fig. 10

Fig. 10, which has been drawn out-of-scale for the sake of clarity, the actual calorimeter being longer and narrower.

The gas, at the desired initial temperature, entered the calorimeter at $A$ and its temperature was measured by the platinum resistance thermometer $P_1$ (the leads from $P_1$, $P_2$, and $H$ are not shown in the figure). It then passed to the electric heater $H$, following a re-entrant route to ensure that it acquired all the heat given out by $H$. It was then thoroughly mixed to ensure uniformity of temperature, by passing through the gauze $G$, and its final temperature was measured by the platinum resistance thermometer $P_2$. The vacuum jacket, surrounded by a bath at the mean temperature of the gas, served to minimise heat leakage.

Let $V_1$ volts be the p.d. across the heating coil, $i_1$ amp the current through the heating coil, $m_1$ the mass of the gas flowing through the calorimeter per sec, $\theta$ the rise in temperature of the gas, $c_p$ the specific heat of the gas at constant pressure, and $h$ the heat leakage from the calorimeter per sec:

$$\frac{V_1 i_1}{J} = m_1 c_p \theta + h.$$

The small heat leakage $h$ was eliminated by repeating the experiment with a different rate of flow, the power supplied to the heater being adjusted so that the platinum resistance thermometers recorded the same temperatures as before. With obvious nomenclature,

$$\frac{V_2 i_2}{J} = m_2 c_p \theta + h.$$

Subtracting, $\qquad \dfrac{V_1 i_1 - V_2 i_2}{J} = (m_1 - m_2) c_p \theta.$

### Latent heat of fusion

When ice is heated its temperature remains constant until it is melted; about 80 cal of heat are required to convert 1 gm of ice at 0 °C to water at the same temperature. This large amount of heat is stored as potential energy in the water and is given out when the water changes back to ice. Joseph Black described it as 'latent heat'.

*The latent heat of fusion of a substance is the quantity of heat required to convert unit mass of the solid to liquid at the same temperature.*

The latent heat of fusion of ice can be determined by the method of mixtures. Small lumps of ice, dried with blotting paper, are dropped into a calorimeter containing warm water, the mixture is stirred and the temperature, when all the ice has melted, is observed. Suppose that $m_1$ gm of ice, of latent heat $L$ cal gm$^{-1}$, are added to $m_2$ gm of water in a calorimeter of water equivalent $w$ gm and that the initial and final temperatures of the water are $\theta_1$ and $\theta_2$ °C respectively:

Heat gained by ice = Heat lost by water and calorimeter,

$$m_1 L + m_1 \theta_2 = (m_2 + w)(\theta_1 - \theta_2).$$

By using sufficient ice to cool the calorimeter as much below room temperature as its initial temperature was above, the error due to heat loss to the surroundings can be kept reasonably small.

One of the difficulties of this method is to dry the ice completely before dropping it into the calorimeter. Hence there is much to be said for using ice at a temperature below 0 °C. It is then necessary to find the specific heat of ice, in order to calculate the heat required to raise the ice from its initial temperature to its melting point, and this can be done by repeating the experiment with ice at a different initial temperature.

The most accurate determination of the latent heat of fusion of ice was made at the Washington Bureau of Standards in 1913 by an electrical method. A calorimeter similar to that of Nernst (Fig. 8), containing ice initially below 0 °C, was employed. The latent heat of fusion of ice was found to be 333 J per gm.

### Latent heat of vaporisation

When water is heated its temperature rises until it reaches its boiling point; its temperature then remains constant as it is boiled away into steam. About 539 calories or 2250 joules of heat are required to convert 1 gm of water at 100 °C to steam at the same temperature.

*The latent heat of vaporisation of a liquid is the quantity of heat required to change unit mass of the liquid to vapour at the same temperature.*

The latent heat of vaporisation of a liquid varies with the external pressure, which affects the boiling point. Similarly, latent heat of fusion depends on the external pressure, which effects the melting point, but to a much smaller extent. We shall discuss the effect of pressure in chapter 8; in what follows we shall confine ourselves to normal atmospheric pressure.

There are two ways of finding the latent heat of vaporisation of a liquid: (1) measurement of the heat given out when a known mass of the vapour condenses, using the method of mixtures; (2) measurement of the heat absorbed when a known mass of the boiling liquid is vaporised, using the electrical method.

### Condensation method

In the condensation method for water, steam is blown into water in a calorimeter, the rise in temperature and the mass of steam condensed being measured. Suppose that $m_1$ gm of steam of latent heat $L$ cal gm$^{-1}$ are condensed and that the temperature of the steam is 100 °C. Let $m_2$ gm be the mass of water in the calorimeter, $w$ gm the water equivalent of the calorimeter, and $\theta_1$ and $\theta_2$ °C the initial and final temperatures of the water.

Heat lost by steam = Heat gained by water and calorimeter,

$$m_1 L + m_1(100 - \theta_2) = (m_2 + w)(\theta_2 - \theta_1).$$

The steam must be free from condensed water drops and hence a water trap (Fig. 11) is essential. Since the mass of condensed steam is small it cannot be determined very accurately from the difference in the two, comparatively large, masses of the calorimeter and its contents; moreover, there is a danger of loss of mass by evaporation before the second weighing is completed. Hence greater accuracy can be achieved by condensing the steam in a light, spiral, copper or aluminium tube (Fig. 12), a method employed by Berthelot.

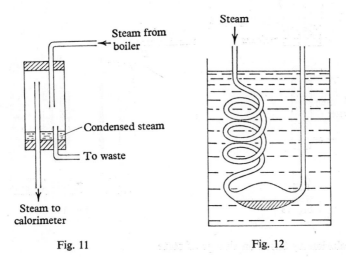

Fig. 11         Fig. 12

## Vaporisation method

The principle of the vaporisation method, as used by Henning (1906) and others, is shown in Fig. 13. The liquid is boiled away steadily by an electric heater, and the vapour is condensed and weighed. Suppose that a mass $m$ gm of the liquid of latent heat of vaporisation $L$ cal gm$^{-1}$ condenses from vapour in $t$ sec, and that the voltage across and the current through the heater are $V$ volts and $i$ amp respectively:

Heat generated by heater = Heat to boil liquid away,

$$\frac{Vit}{4 \cdot 18} = mL.$$

It is necessary to correct for loss of heat from the electric heater which does not serve to evaporate the liquid, and this may be done by the method of changing the power supplied by the heater.

Awberry and Griffiths (1924) combined the vaporisation and condensation methods. They measured the heat required to boil away water at a steady rate, passed the steam through a condenser and measured the rate of condensation of the steam—a method identical with that just described—and, in addition, they measured the heat absorbed on condensation of the steam, by the constant flow of water through the condenser, giving a second value for the latent heat.

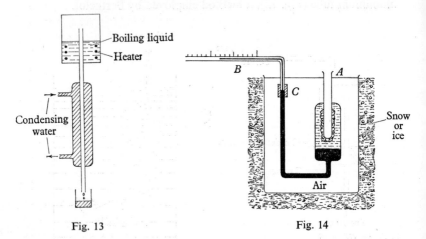

Fig. 13   Fig. 14

### Calorimetry based on change of state

Once latent heats of fusion or vaporisation are accurately known they can be utilised to make measurements of heat. We shall describe two types of calorimeter involving the melting of ice and the condensation of steam respectively. There is a third type, used by Dewar for finding specific heats at very low temperatures, which involved the evaporation of liquid oxygen. All three types are now very little used but they had the advantage, when they were first introduced, of avoiding accurate measurements of small changes of temperature, then found difficult. It should not be assumed, however, that these types of calorimeter will not, in the future, be found more convenient than others for particular purposes.

### Bunsen's ice calorimeter (1871)

In the earliest, crude form of ice calorimeter, used, for example, to measure the specific heat of a substance, a convenient mass, $m$ gm, of the substance was heated to a temperature $\theta$ °C and then placed in a cavity in a large block of ice. The mass, $M$ gm, of ice melted was absorbed by a sponge and weighed. If $c$ cal gm$^{-1}$ deg$^{-1}$ C is the specific heat of the substance and $L$ cal gm$^{-1}$ the latent heat of fusion of ice,

Heat lost by substance = Heat gained by ice,

$$mc\theta = ML.$$

A much more accurate ice calorimeter, utilising the change in volume of ice when it melts, was devised by Bunsen. In Fig. 14, $A$ is a test tube sealed into a glass vessel completely filled with pure water, free from dissolved air, and, at the bottom, mercury. A mantle of ice is formed round the outside of the test tube by evaporating ether in the test tube. Since water expands on freezing, the mercury is forced along the capillary tube $B$ and the position of its meniscus can be adjusted by some suitable arrangement represented by $C$. The whole instrument is in an air jacket surrounded by melting ice for some time before and during the experiment.

A mass $m_1$ gm of the substance whose specific heat, $c$ cal gm$^{-1}$ deg$^{-1}$ C, is required is heated to a suitable temperature $\theta_1$ °C and then transferred to $A$, a plug being inserted into the top of $A$ to prevent loss of heat. Some of the ice surrounding $A$ melts, and the consequent contraction causes the mercury meniscus to recede along $B$. The distance $d_1$ moved by the meniscus is measured. The instrument is calibrated by placing a known mass of water, $m_2$ gm, at room temperature, $\theta_2$ °C, in $A$. Suppose that the water causes a movement $d_2$ of the meniscus. Then

$$\frac{m_1 c \theta_1}{m_2 \theta_2} = \frac{d_1}{d_2}.$$

When 1 gm of ice melts there is a shrinkage of 0·0907 c.c. From this it can be calculated that, with a capillary tube $B$ of 0·5 mm diameter, the sensitivity of the calorimeter is about 6 mm per calorie. This is a high sensitivity and hence the calorimeter is suitable for measuring the specific heats of substances which are available only in small quantities, e.g. the rare earths. The drawback is that too much reliance cannot be placed on the accuracy of the results since the ice formed round the outside of $A$ may vary slightly in density, partly because it is impossible to remove all the dissolved air in the water, and partly because of strains set up on solidification. In some modern forms of the instrument the ice has been replaced by other substances, such as diphenylmethane, which do not suffer seriously from this defect.

### Joly's steam calorimeter (1886)

Joly's steam calorimeter measures heat in terms of the mass of steam condensed on a body. It involves very accurate weighing, since less than 2 mg of steam are condensed per calorie, and most investigators have found it far less convenient than other methods for finding the specific heats of solids and liquids. But its use by Joly, in a classic research in 1890, for finding the specific heats of gases at constant volume, has scarcely been improved upon.

For this investigation Joly employed a differential form of his calorimeter (Fig. 15). A differential instrument is one that measures differences in quantities rather than the quantities themselves. Two similar, hollow, copper globes were both evacuated and suspended from the arms of a balance in a chamber into which steam was passed. Small metal trays, attached to the globes, served to catch the steam condensed on the globes. One side of the balance was suitably loaded until the globes were in equilibrium. The globes were then dried and one of them was filled with, say, hydrogen at a pressure of 20 atm. When steam was readmitted to the chamber, more steam condensed on the gas-filled globe than before, because of the heat required to raise the temperature of the gas. If $m$ gm is the mass of steam condensed by the gas, $L$ cal gm$^{-1}$ the latent heat of steam, $M$ gm the mass of the gas, $c_v$ cal gm$^{-1}$ deg$^{-1}$ C the specific heat of the gas at constant volume, $\theta$ °C the initial temperature of the gas, and 100 °C the temperature of the steam,

$$mL = Mc_v(100 - \theta).$$

Joly found that the most troublesome experimental difficulty was condensation of steam at the small holes in the steam chamber through which passed the wires supporting the globes; this was serious because it caused a drag on the wires and affected the delicate weighing. He overcame it by inserting an absorbent plaster of Paris plug in each hole and by surrounding each wire with a platinum coil, heated by an electric current to evaporate any water which was not absorbed by the plaster of Paris.

### The variation of specific heat with temperature

In 1819 Dulong and Petit discovered the empirical law that the product of the specific heat and atomic weight, known as the *atomic heat*, of most elements in the solid state at ordinary temperatures is about 6·4 cal/gm atom/°C or 27 joule/gm atom/°C. However, some substances, like diamond, have a much smaller atomic heat than this at ordinary temperatures.

Atomic heats diminish with decreasing temperature, becoming very small indeed near the absolute zero. The curve in Fig. 16 applies to all solid elements so long as the temperature scale is suitably adjusted in each case. The almost flat part at the top of the curve represents ordinary temperatures for most elements and corresponds to Dulong and Petit's law. Diamond at ordinary temperatures is represented by the steep part of the curve. Its atomic heat varies more rapidly with temperature at ordinary temperatures than is the case with most other substances and it must be raised to a high temperature to reach its maximum atomic heat.

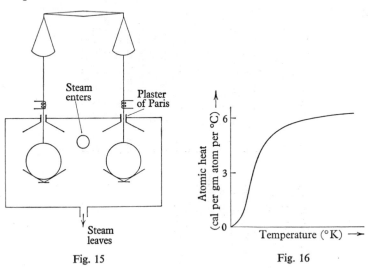

Fig. 15                       Fig. 16

According to classical (i.e. pre-quantum) physics, atomic heats should remain constant at all temperatures. The explanation of their variation with temperature is provided by the quantum theory (p. 83).

Example. *A body initially at 50 °C cools to 45 °C in 5 min, the temperature of the surroundings being 15 °C. What will be its temperature after another 5 min, assuming Newton's law of cooling to hold?*

If $\theta$ is the temperature of the body at time $t$, and $\theta_0$ is the temperature of the surroundings, Newton's law may be expressed as follows:

$$-\frac{d\theta}{dt} = k(\theta - \theta_0),$$

where $k$ is a constant,

$$\therefore \quad \frac{d\theta}{\theta - \theta_0} = -k\,dt.$$

Table 2. *Summary of calorimetric methods*

| Method of mixtures | Electrical method | Change-of-state methods | Continuous-flow methods |
|---|---|---|---|
| The earliest method, which has been used successfully for finding the specific heats of solids, liquids, and gases at constant pressure; also latent heats. It is the only suitable method for finding the calorific value of a fuel. In its modern form water has been replaced by copper, silver or aluminium, thereby giving a higher temperature rise and a wider temperature range | The most generally useful and the most accurate method. It has the advantage of being applicable over a wide temperature range. It has been used for finding the specific heats of solids, liquids and gases and also latent heats of fusion and vaporisation | These include Bunsen's ice calorimeter, Joly's steam calorimeter and Dewar's liquid-oxygen calorimeter. They are seldom used today. Bunsen's ice calorimeter is sensitive but not completely accurate; Joly's steam calorimeter is troublesome to use but valuable for finding the specific heats of gases at constant volume; and Dewar's liquid-oxygen calorimeter, which he used for finding specific heats at low temperatures, has been superseded by the electrical method | Continuous-flow methods can be employed with or without electric heating. They are accurate and, in their electrical form, have been employed in some of the best determinations of the mechanical equivalent of heat, of the variation of the specific heat of water with temperature, and of the specific heat of gases at constant pressure |

Integrating,                  $\log_e(\theta - \theta_0) = -kt + C,$

where $C$ is a constant of integration.
    When $t = 0$, $\theta = 50$

$$\therefore \quad \log_e(50 - 15) = 0 + C,$$

$$C = \log_e 35.$$

When $t = 5$, $\theta = 45$

$$\therefore \quad \log_e(45 - 15) = -5k + \log_e 35,$$

$$k = \tfrac{1}{5}(\log_e 35 - \log_e 30).$$

When $t = 10$,

$$\log_e(\theta - 15) = -10 \cdot \tfrac{1}{5}(\log_e 35 - \log_e 30) + \log_e 35$$

$$= 2 \log_e 30 - \log_e 35.$$

We can take logs to base 10 since this is equivalent to multiplying each term by the same factor.

$$\log_{10}(\theta - 15) = 2 \cdot 9542 - 1 \cdot 5441$$

$$= 1 \cdot 4101.$$

$$\theta - 15 = 25 \cdot 7,$$

$$\theta = 41 \, °C.$$

## QUESTIONS

1. How is a unit of heat defined?
Why does the specific heat of a substance have the same numerical value whether expressed in cal $gm^{-1}$ $deg^{-1}$ C or in Btu $lb^{-1}$ $deg^{-1}$ F?

2. State and discuss critically the precautions taken in determining a specific heat by the method of mixtures, with particular reference to (i) the reduction of heat losses, (ii) the relative amounts of substances to be mixed, (iii) sensitivity of thermometers, (iv) stirring, (v) weighing.

3. Fig. 17 represents a form of calorimeter for use in the method of mixtures. List the important features in its design and the errors they are designed to minimise.

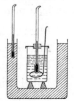

4. A copper calorimeter of weight 100 gm contains 10 gm of water at 15 °C. 50 gm of water initially at 95 °C are poured into the calorimeter, and the final temperature is found to be 72·7 °C. Calculate the specific heat of copper.                    (O.S.)

Fig. 17

5. (a) What is meant by latent heat?
    (b) An aluminium electric kettle weighing 500 gm contains 1 kg of water at 10 °C. It is fitted with a 1 kW heating element. How long

will it take the kettle to come to the boil, and how much longer will it take to boil dry? Assume that there is no heat loss. (Specific heat of aluminium = 0·22 cal gm$^{-1}$ deg$^{-1}$ C. Latent heat of steam = 540 cal gm$^{-1}$. 1 cal = 4·2 J.)                                                                    (O.S.)

6. 10 gm of copper initially at 0 °C is dropped into liquid oxygen at − 183 °C. The volume of gas evolved is 1800 c.c. measured at s.t.p. The copper is then transferred to water at 0 °C and 1·6 gm of ice form on the copper. Find the latent heat of evaporation of oxygen and the mean specific heat of copper.

(Latent heat of ice = 80 cal gm$^{-1}$. Density of oxygen at s.t.p. = 1·43 gm l.$^{-1}$.)                                                            (O.S.)

7. State the relative advantages and disadvantages of the following methods of determining specific heat: (i) method of mixtures, (ii) electrical method, (iii) method of continuous flow, (iv) methods involving change of state.

8. Heat is supplied at a rate of 8·0 W to 200 gm of a liquid in a calorimeter until the temperature of the liquid becomes constant. The rate of cooling at this temperature, when the supply of heat is stopped, is 0·95 °C per minute. If the thermal capacity of the calorimeter is 12 cal per °C, what is the specific heat of the liquid?                                        (N.)

9. (a) Distinguish between rate of loss of heat and rate of fall of temperature.

(b) Fig. 18 represents cooling curves for equal volumes of water and of another liquid cooling in similar calorimeters under identical conditions. How would you use the curves to find the specific heat of the liquid?

(c) A copper calorimeter of mass 100 gm, containing 150 gm of water at 70 °C, loses heat at the rate of 88 cal/min. If the water is replaced by an equal volume of turpentine at 70 °C, what will be (i) the rate of loss of heat, (ii) the rate of fall of temperature?

(Density of turpentine = 0·87 gm cm$^{-3}$. Specific heat of turpentine = 0·42 cal gm$^{-1}$ deg$^{-1}$ C. Specific heat of copper = 0·1 cal gm$^{-1}$ deg$^{-1}$ C.)
                                                                          (Partly C.)

10. Define specific heat and latent heat of fusion.

A student performs a simple calorimetry experiment for finding the latent heat of fusion of ice, recording the following experimental figures:

Mass of copper calorimeter empty           = 52·46 gm
Mass of copper calorimeter + water          = 194·7 gm
Mass of copper calorimeter + water + melted ice = 202·2 gm
Initial temperature of water                  = 16 °C
Final temperature of water                   = 12 °C
Room temperature                          = 15 °C.

(The heat required to raise the temperature of 1 gm of copper through 1 °C is 0·1 cal.)

(a) State the precautions that you would take in such an experiment to ensure accuracy, and criticise the readings recorded.

(b) Use the figures to calculate the latent heat of fusion of ice.

(c) Make an estimate of the accuracy that the result should have, assuming that the readings are correct to the number of figures given. (C.)

11. Fig. 19 represents the apparatus of Callendar and Barnes in their determination of the number of joules equivalent to 1 cal (the mechanical equivalent of heat).

Water flowed at a steady rate through the central tube and was heated by an electric current in the platinum wire $R$. The current was led in and out of $R$ by the leads $CC$ and it was measured by a potentiometer; the p.d. across $R$ was measured, using the leads $PP$, also by a potentiometer. The temperatures of the inflowing and outflowing water were measured by the platinum resistance thermometers, $T_1$ and $T_2$.

To avoid calculating the heat leakage during the experiment, the rate of flow of the water and the electric current were changed in such a way that the temperatures recorded by $T_1$ and $T_2$ remained the same.

Using symbols for the various quantities measured, derive an expression for the number of joules equivalent to 1 cal.

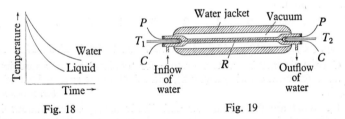

Fig. 18                    Fig. 19

12. Water in a vacuum flask is boiled steadily by passing an electric current through a coil of wire immersed in the water. When the potential difference across the coil is 5·25 V and the current through it is 2·58 A, 6·85 gm of water evaporate in 20 min. When the potential difference and the current are maintained at 3·20 V and 1·57 A respectively, 2·38 gm of water evaporate in 20 min, all the other conditions being the same. Calculate the latent heat of vaporisation of water in joules per gm. (N.)

13. (a) Describe the Bunsen ice calorimeter and explain how you would use it to find the specific heat of a diamond.

(b) 4 gm of a substance at 50 °C dropped into the ice calorimeter caused the mercury thread in the capillary tube to move through 5·4 cm. The cross-sectional area of the tube was 0·005 cm². 1 gm of ice occupies 1·09 c.c. and the latent heat of fusion of ice is 80 cal/gm. Calculate the specific heat of the substance. (O.)

14. (a) Describe how the specific heat of a gas at constant volume may be determined by Joly's differential steam calorimeter.

(b) In an experiment with this calorimeter, one of the spheres contained 4·285 gm of air. The initial temperature of the sphere was

16·0 °C and the temperature of the steam was 100·0 °C. The extra condensation of steam on the sphere, caused by the air inside the sphere, was 0·116 gm. Calculate the specific heat of air at constant volume.
(Latent heat of steam = 2253 J gm⁻¹.)

15. (a) Fig. 20 represents the cooling curve of a substance, originally liquid, which solidifies. Explain its shape.

(b) Find the latent heat of fusion of the substance from the following data, assuming Newton's law of cooling to hold: temperature of surroundings 15 °C; temperature at $BC$ 65 °C; time interval along $BC$ 20 min; specific heat of the liquid 0·050 cal gm⁻¹ deg⁻¹ C; the slope of a tangent to the curve $AB$ at temperature 75 °C is 5 °C min⁻¹.

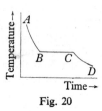

Fig. 20

16. A calorimeter of mass 40·0 gm, made of copper of specific heat 0·095, contains 92·4 gm of liquid which is initially at the air temperature, 12·0 °C. Immersed in the liquid is a heating coil, carrying a current of 2·0 A under a p.d. of 7·0 V. The current is passed for 5 min, and temperature readings as tabulated below are taken at intervals of 1 min for a total time of 8 min.

| Time from start (min) | 0 | 1 | 2 | 3 | 4 | 5 | 6 | 7 | 8 |
|---|---|---|---|---|---|---|---|---|---|
| Temp. (°C) | 12·0 | 15·8 | 19·3 | 22·7 | 26·1 | 29·5 | 28·5 | 27·5 | 26·5 |

Correct the maximum temperature for 'cooling' by an approximate method (without drawing a graph), and calculate the specific heat of the liquid. (O. modified.)

17. What are the advantages and disadvantages of continuous-flow calorimetry? Describe how this method has been applied to determine either (a) the latent heat of steam, or (b) the specific heat of a gas at constant pressure.

A liquid flows at a steady rate along a tube containing an electric heating element. When the power supplied to this heater is 10 W and the rate of flow of the liquid is 50 gm/min, the outflow temperature of the liquid is 5 °C higher than the inflow temperature. When the rate of flow is doubled, the power supplied to the heater must be increased to 19 W for the outflow temperature to be unchanged. If the inflow temperature is the same in each experiment, calculate a value for the specific heat of the liquid. (Assume that 4·2 J = 1 cal.) (N.)

18. Define *specific heat, latent heat*. Describe how you would find the latent heat of melting ice experimentally, mentioning possible sources of error and the methods of avoidance or correction.

A litre of water is supercooled to −3 °C. A very small fragment of ice is dropped in and freezing begins. If the water is thermally insulated, how much water will freeze and what will be the final volume of the mixture of ice and water?

(Latent heat of fusion of ice is 80 cal/gm; the specific gravity of ice is 0·917.)

19. If 5 gm of ether are placed in the inner tube of a Bunsen ice calorimeter and evaporated by connecting the tube to a vacuum pump, the mercury index is found to move a distance of 10 cm. Assuming that the density of ice is 0·91 gm/c.c. and its latent heat of fusion 80 cal/gm, what is the latent heat of evaporation of ether? The area of cross-section of the tube containing the mercury is 0·066 cm². Give a sketch of the apparatus, and indicate by an arrow the direction of motion of the index. (O. & C.)

20. Describe an electrical method of measuring the latent heat of steam. What advantages has it over the method of mixtures?

What becomes of the energy absorbed by a liquid when it vaporises without change of temperature?

7·5 gm of copper at 27 °C were dropped into liquid oxygen at its boiling-point ($-183$ °C) and the oxygen evaporated occupied 1·89 l. at 20 °C and 750 mm pressure. Calculate the latent heat of vaporisation of oxygen.

(Specific heat of copper = 0·08. Density of oxygen at s.t.p. = 1·429 gm l.⁻¹.) (O. & C.)

21. What is Newton's law of cooling?

A calorimeter containing a hot liquid is placed inside an enclosure whose walls are at 10 °C, and cools from 80 to 60 °C in 10 min; how long will it take to cool from 60 to 40 °C if Newton's law of cooling holds?

15·2 (C.S.)

CHAPTER 3

# THE MECHANICAL EQUIVALENT OF HEAT AND THE CONSERVATION OF ENERGY

## The caloric theory

The early researches into the measurement of heat in the eighteenth century were guided by the theory that heat is a weightless, invisible, *indestructible* fluid, called caloric. It was assumed that, when hot and cold bodies are mixed, a quantity of caloric leaves the hot body and enters the cold body unchanged in amount. The automatic flow of caloric from a higher to a lower temperature was explained by assuming that caloric is self-repellent. This self-repulsion also accounted for the expansion of bodies when they are heated.

Latent heat was regarded as an association or combination of caloric with matter, so that when a body is heated and changes from solid to liquid without rise of temperature, the body's stock of 'free' caloric, responsible for its temperature, does not increase.

The production of a motive force by heat, for example in a steam engine, was thought to be caused by caloric falling from a higher to a lower temperature, by analogy with the motive force of water, falling from a higher to a lower level in a water-mill. Just as no water is destroyed in passing through a water-mill, so, it was thought, no caloric is destroyed on passing through a steam engine, the same quantity of heat leaving the engine as enters it, but at a lower temperature.

The fact that a piece of soft iron can be rendered red hot by hammering was interpreted (not very satisfactorily) as the squeezing of caloric from the pores of the iron by the blows of the hammer.

### The kinetic theory of heat

An entirely different theory of heat had been held in the seventeenth century. Heat was regarded as the energy of motion of the particles of which a body is composed—what we should now call the kinetic energy of its particles. This theory gave a direct and convincing explanation of the heating of iron by hammering; the kinetic energy of the hammer is transferred to the particles of the iron, causing them to vibrate more quickly.

The inability of the caloric theory to account for the production of heat by mechanical means was strikingly illustrated by the experiments in 1798 of Count Rumford, who demonstrated that a blunt borer, pressed against the barrel of a cannon which was continuously rotated, produced an apparently inexhaustible supply of heat.

The experiments of Rumford did not make much impression but, about forty years later, a completely different line of investigation pointed strongly to the kinetic theory of heat. This was the investigation of the heat which reaches us from the sun in the form of thermal radiation. Could thermal radiation be a flow of caloric through space, or did it consist, like light, of vibrations in the ether? Experiment showed that thermal radiation behaves like light; hence, it was argued, when thermal radiation falls upon a body, the vibrations of the ether must be communicated to the particles of the body.

### The experiments of Joule

If heat is the energy of vibration of the particles of a body it can be called into existence by mechanical means, such as friction. The most convincing test of the theory is to find experimentally whether the quantity of mechanical work which produces unit quantity of heat, known as *the mechanical equivalent of heat*,† is always the same, whatever the mechanical method of producing the heat. This was done by James Prescott Joule (1818–89) and his work provided the chief experimental basis on which the kinetic theory of heat was established. We will first list his experiments and results (Table 3), and then describe one experiment in some detail. The mechanical equivalent of heat is denoted by $J$ and it was expressed by Joule as the number of foot-pounds equivalent to one British thermal unit of heat.

### Table 3

| Year | Method | $J$ (ftlb/ Btu) |
|------|--------|-----------------|
| 1843 | Measurement of the work done in driving a dynamo and of the heat generated in wires by the current | 838 |
| 1843 | Measurement of the work done in driving water through fine tubes and of the heat produced | 770 |
| 1845 | Measurement of the work done in compressing air and of the heat produced; also of the work done by air in expanding and of the heat absorbed | 798 |
| 1845 | Measurement of the work done in stirring water with a paddle-wheel and of the heat produced | 890 |
| 1847 | Improved paddle-wheel experiment | 782 |
| 1849 | Measurement of the work done in turning a bevel-edged cast-iron wheel against a bevel-edged cast-iron disc (slipping-clutch arrangement) and of the heat produced | 777 |
| 1867 | Electrical method (as on p. 22) | 783 |
| 1878 | Paddle-wheel with friction balance | 773 |

### Joule's paddle-wheel experiment, with a friction balance

Joule's final paddle-wheel experiment of 1878 is shown, in principle, in Fig. 21. Water in a calorimeter was churned, and thereby heated, by rotating a paddle-wheel between vanes fixed to the wall of the calorimeter. In the earlier experiments the paddle was driven by falling weights and the work done was the product of the weights and the total distance they fell (the weights were alternately raised and allowed to fall twenty times). This resulted in a very small rise of temperature of the calorimeter and its contents, of the order of $\frac{1}{2}$ °F, estimated by Joule to $\frac{1}{200}$ °F. It is perhaps not surprising that Joule's early critics were sceptical of the validity of his results.

† Some physicists dislike the term mechanical equivalent of heat because heat is itself mechanical. They prefer to speak of the conversion factor between ftlb and Btu or between joules and calories.

In the final version of the experiment shown in Fig. 21, the calorimeter was not rigidly fixed in position but was suspended so that it was free to rotate with the paddle. Rotation of the calorimeter was prevented by cords passing round the calorimeter and supporting the masses $MM$. The paddle was rotated by a handwheel at a rate just sufficient to keep $MM$ steady in mid-air.

This arrangement for measuring the work done by the paddle is known as a friction balance. Suppose that the radius of the calorimeter where the cords pass round it is $r$ (Fig. 22). The hanging weights exert a couple $2Mgr$ on the calorimeter. Since the calorimeter does not rotate, the friction between the paddle and the water

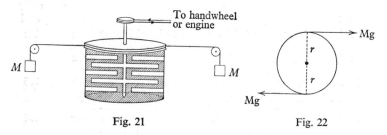

Fig. 21                              Fig. 22

must exert an equal and opposite couple on the calorimeter. Hence, for each complete revolution of the paddle, the work done is $2\pi \cdot 2Mgr$. Suppose that, when the paddle rotates $n$ times, the temperature rise is $\theta$, that the water equivalent of the calorimeter and its contents is $W$, and that the specific heat of water is $c$ (taken by Joule as unity).

$$\text{Heat produced} = Wc\theta.$$

$$\text{Work done} = 4\pi nMgr.$$

$$\therefore J = \frac{Wc\theta}{4\pi nMgr}.$$

Joule's experiment was repeated in 1879 by Rowland, who designed the paddle and vanes to produce heat at a much faster rate and drove the paddle with a steam engine. He obtained a rate of rise of temperature of about 1 °F per minute as compared with Joule's 1 °F per hour. Hence his cooling correction was of far less importance and his result more reliable.

Rowland claimed that his result was correct to 2 parts in 1000 and indeed it differs by less than this from the best modern value. Nevertheless, his result is disregarded because the mercury thermometer which he used could not be compared with the standard hydrogen thermometer under conditions of rapidly rising temperature. All of Joule's careful determinations are now of historical interest only because his temperature readings, made with mercury thermometers, cannot be converted into modern absolute temperatures.

## Modern methods for $J$

The most accurate determinations of the mechanical equivalent are given in Table 4. Birge takes as the most probable value $J = 4\cdot1855$ J/15 °C cal.

### Table 4

| Year | Method | $J$ (joules $cal_{15}^{-1}$) |
|------|--------|------------------------------|
| 1921 | Jaeger and Steinwehr (electrical) | 4·1841 |
| 1927 | Laby and Hercus (mechanical, continuous flow) | 4·1853 |
| 1939 | Osborne, Stimson and Ginnings (electrical) | 4·1858 |

In two of the above three methods the work was measured in terms of electrical energy. When an electric current $i$ amp flows through a p.d. of $V$ volts for a time $t$ sec the work done is $Vit$ joules. This is because the volt is defined in terms of the joule; two points are at a p.d. of 1 V if 1 J of electrical energy is transformed during the passage of 1 A for 1 sec between the points. Since it is possible to measure $V$ and $i$ very accurately, by means of a potentiometer, a standard resistance and a standard cell, the electrical energy $Vit$ can be obtained in joules. The determination rests upon accurate absolute measurements of the standard resistance and of the e.m.f. of the standard cell.

In all of the above three methods the temperatures were measured with platinum resistance thermometers, which have none of the vagaries and uncertainties of mercury thermometers. The cooling correction, that bugbear in all heat experiments, was kept small and estimated as accurately as possible.

## The experiments of Jaeger and Steinwehr and of Osborne, Stimson and Ginnings

The determinations of $J$ by Jaeger and Steinwehr at the Reichsanstalt in Berlin (the national physical laboratory of Germany) and by Osborne, Stimson and Ginnings at the U.S. Bureau of Standards in Washington were made by the electric heating of water in a calorimeter, represented in principle by Fig. 7 on p. 24. As already stated, the rise in temperature of the water was measured with a platinum resistance thermometer and the electrical energy was obtained by measuring the current through, and the p.d. across, the coil by means of a potentiometer, a standard resistance and a standard cell. The differences in the design of the apparatus arose from different methods of minimising and estimating the cooling corrections.

### Variation of the specific heat of water with temperature

By repeating their experiments over small temperature ranges, Jaeger and Steinwehr, and Osborne, Stimson and Ginnings, investigated the variation of the specific heat of water with temperature, the heat input being measured in joules. They found that the temperature of minimum specific heat was about 33·5 °C (Fig. 23).

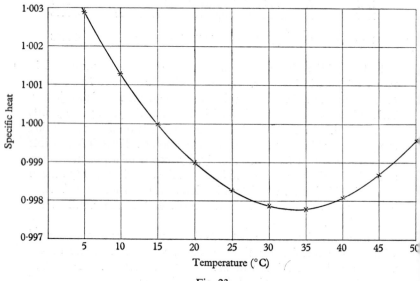

Fig. 23

### The experiments of Laby and Hercus

In the experiments of Laby and Hercus to determine $J$, performed in Melbourne, Australia, the work producing the heat was measured mechanically, by means of a friction balance similar to that used by Joule and Rowland, although the heat was produced electrically. A continuous-flow method was adopted, and the heat generated was measured when the apparatus reached a steady state.

The apparatus is indicated in Fig. 24. $C$ is a metal calorimeter supported by ball-bearings (not shown in the figure) and a torsion wire. The poles, *NS*, of an electromagnet were rotated round *C* and they set up eddy currents in *C*, producing the heat to be measured. The forces on the eddy currents exerted by the rotating magnetic field of the electromagnet tended to rotate *C* and this was prevented by the hanging masses *MM*. The reaction on the electromagnet acted like a brake, making it necessary to do work to rotate the electromagnet. As explained on p. 42, the work done on *C* by the electromagnet during *n* revolutions is $4\pi n M g r$, where *r* is the radius of the disc round which pass the cords supporting *MM*.

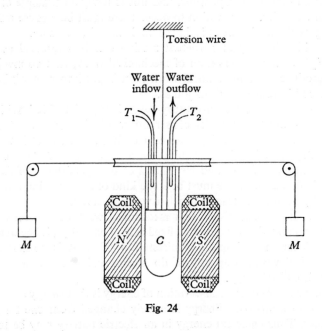

Fig. 24

The calorimeter *C* consisted of fourteen copper tubes passing through slots in stalloy stampings, rather like the armature of an induction motor. The stalloy increased the magnetic field. Through the copper tubes, in which the greater part of the eddy currents flowed, a steady stream of water was passed and its temperatures at inflow and outflow were measured by the platinum resistance thermometers, $T_1$ and $T_2$. The outer covering of *C* was a vacuum flask to reduce heat losses.

Suppose that the mass of water passing through *C* while the electromagnet made *n* revolutions was *m*; that the temperature of the water rose from $\theta_1$ to $\theta_2$; and that the mean specific heat of water in the temperature range $(\theta_2 - \theta_1)$ is $c$.

$$\text{Heat produced} = mc(\theta_2 - \theta_1),$$

$$\therefore J = \frac{4\pi n M g r}{mc(\theta_2 - \theta_1)}.$$

## The principle of the conservation of energy

The founders of mechanics took as a fundamental axiom that perpetual motion is impossible, and this is really an example of the law of causality. For motion to occur there must be a cause and in a perpetual machine there is, in the final analysis, no cause.

The impossibility of perpetual motion can be expressed as the principle of the conservation of mechanical work, that no machine can produce more mechanical work than is put into it, work being measured in foot-pounds or joules.

In the early nineteenth century several physicists felt intuitively that there must be a wider conservation principle than this which holds in the interrelated phenomena of heat, light, electricity and chemistry, as well as in mechanics. Faraday spoke of the 'law of the conservation of force' and Helmholtz of the 'persistence of force'. They believed that there must be some kind of conservation but they were by no means clear as to what was conserved.

When it was established that mechanical work can be converted into heat, and vice versa, with a fixed rate of exchange, it began to be realised that the simplest manifestation of what is conserved is mechanical work. Capacity to do mechanical work, whatever its form, is called *energy*.

The principle of the conservation of energy is that *energy cannot be created or destroyed*. Energy is merely changed from one form to another. Thus chemical energy in an electric battery may be transformed into an equivalent amount of electrical energy in a circuit, and thence into an equivalent amount of heat and light in a lamp, or into an equivalent amount of mechanical energy in an electric motor.

Planck stated the principle in terms of a model heat engine: it is impossible to construct an engine which will work in a cycle (such that the initial and final states are the same) and produce continuous work from nothing.

## Internal energy

Heat is a form of energy, but what is the exact form of this energy? When a gas is heated there may be an increase in the kinetic energy of translation of its molecules and also in their rotational energy; the potential energy may increase because the molecules attract each other and work must be done to separate them as the gas expands; also the vibrational energy of the atoms in each molecule may increase. Is the sum of all these energies, i.e. the total energy contained by a body, equal to the total heat which a body contains? We shall see that such an idea leads to confusion. It is better to reserve the term heat for energy in transition from a hot to a cold body as a result of a difference of temperature; once the energy is inside a body it is called *internal energy*. As Zeemansky has put it, heat is like rain which ceases to be rain when it enters a lake.

The necessity for the distinction between heat and internal energy becomes most clearly apparent when we consider the case of a gas. The temperature of a gas may be raised either by putting heat into it or by doing work upon it in compressing it. Hence we might just as well talk about the total work in a gas as by the total heat in it.

### The first law of thermodynamics

Suppose that heat $Q$ is supplied to a gas and that the gas expands, doing work $W$ equivalent to heat $W/J$. Then the increase in the internal energy of the gas, $\Delta E$, is defined by the equation

$$\Delta E = Q - W/J.$$

If work is done *on* the gas (by compression) instead of *by* the gas (on expansion), $W$ is negative and the term $-W/J$ becomes positive.

The equation defining $\Delta E$ embodies the principle of the conservation of energy and it is known as the *first law of thermodynamics*. It states that the increase of internal energy of a system is equal to the sum of the heat put into the system and of the work done upon the system. It enables us to calculate the *change* of internal energy but not the total value of the internal energy in the system.

We shall discuss internal energy further on pp. 57–8.

### Mass and energy

The principles of the conservation of mass and of the conservation of energy were combined by Einstein into the single principle of the conservation of mass-energy. Mass can be annihilated and converted into energy and vice versa. From the special theory of relativity Einstein deduced that $E = mc^2$, where $E$ is the energy equivalent of a mass $m$ and $c$ is the velocity of light.

When coal is burnt energy is liberated and there is an annihilation of mass which is so small as to be undetectable. For a loss of mass of 1 mg about 3 tons of coal must be burnt.

The energy liberated when an atomic nucleus is disrupted, however, is enormously greater than that released in chemical reactions and Einstein's theory of mass-energy equivalence has been abundantly confirmed by accurate measurements of the masses of atomic nuclei, by means of the mass spectroscope, and of the velocities of the nuclei produced at a disintegration. A particularly accurate confirmation is provided by a comparison of the energy of the $\alpha$-particles released with the mass lost when the isotope of lithium, $_3Li^7$, is disintegrated by proton bombardment (Fig. 25):

$$_3Li^7 + {}_1H^1 = 2\,_2He^4$$
$$\text{proton} \quad \alpha\text{-particles}$$

The superscripts represent approximate nuclear masses and the subscripts nuclear charges.

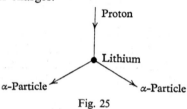

Fig. 25

Perhaps the most striking demonstrations of Einstein's theory are what are known as pair annihilation and pair production. A positive and a negative electron can annihilate each other and produce $\gamma$-radiation; conversely $\gamma$-radiation can be converted into a positive and a negative electron.

When a neutron and a proton combine to form a deuteron (the nucleus of heavy hydrogen, $_1H^2$) there is an annihilation of mass and the emission of $\gamma$-radiation of equivalent energy. The mass of the deuteron is about 0·002 atomic mass units† less than the sum of the masses of the proton and neutron and this is equivalent to an energy of two million electron-volts,‡ 2 MeV. By comparison the energy released in the oxidation of one atom of carbon (in the burning of coal) is very small—about 4 eV.

---

† The atomic mass unit is defined so that the most abundant oxygen isotope, $_8O^{16}$, has a mass of 16 atomic mass units. The masses of the proton and of the neutron are each approximately 1.

‡ An electron-volt is the energy gained by an electron in falling through a p.d. of 1 V and it is equal to $1·602 \times 10^{-12}$ erg.

The same quantity of energy must be added to break up a deuteron as is released when a deuteron is formed and hence it is called the binding energy of the deuteron.

Some radioactive substances exhibit what is known as $\beta$-decay; they emit $\beta$-rays which consist of negative electrons with different velocities. It would be expected that the electrons should all have the same velocity and, to account for the disappearance of energy in the cases of some of the electrons, Pauli suggested in 1931 that the total available energy is shared between an electron and a new particle, now called a neutrino, with zero charge, zero rest mass and a half unit of spin. The neutrino, in fact, was introduced to save three conservation laws: the conservation of mass-energy, the conservation of angular momentum and the conservation of linear momentum. Incidentally, the other conservation law is the conservation of charge.

The postulate of the neutrino would seem to support the contention of Poincaré that the principle of the conservation of energy is merely a definition of energy. If the principle breaks down we invent a new form of energy to save it. The criticism is hardly valid, however, because when a new particle like the neutrino is postulated experiments are performed to detect it.

The existence of the neutrino was confirmed experimentally in 1956 by Reines and Cowan, who showed that neutrinos in a nuclear reactor could reverse a $\beta$-decay reaction: neutrinos striking protons gave rise to neutrons and positive electrons.

$$\beta\text{-decay} \quad n \;\rightarrow\; p \;+\; e^- \;+\; \nu$$
$$\text{neutron} \;\; \text{proton} \quad -\text{ve} \;\; \text{neutrino}$$
$$\text{electron}$$

$$\textit{Reverse reaction} \quad \nu \;+\; p \;\rightarrow\; n \;+\; e^+$$
$$\text{neutrino} \;\; \text{proton} \;\; \text{neutron} \quad +\text{ve}$$
$$\text{electron}$$

## QUESTIONS

*Take J as 778 ft lb/Btu or 4·2 J/cal, unless otherwise stated.*

1. (*a*) State the kinetic theory of the nature of heat.

(*b*) Define the mechanical equivalent of heat.

(*c*) Explain why a piece of lead can be warmed more easily than a piece of steel by hammering it on an anvil.

2. In one of his experiments on the boring of cannon, Rumford found that the work done by one horse raised the temperature of 26·6 lb. of water from 32 to 212 °F in 2·5 h. Ignoring heat losses, calculate the work done by the horse per second.

3. How high must a waterfall be for the difference in temperature of the water at the bottom and at the top to be $\frac{1}{2}$ °C?

4. A car weighing 2000 lb travelling at 60 m.p.h. is braked and brought to rest. How much heat is developed in the brake drums, assuming that it is equivalent to the whole of the kinetic energy of the car?

5. The fly-wheel of an engine is 100 cm in diameter and rotates at 600 rev/min. A belt brake, acting on the circumference, supports a weight of 25 kg on one side and a spring balance on the other side reads 5 kg. Calculate the heat generated per sec.

6. A jet aircraft weighing 20000 kg uses paraffin as fuel. Estimate the fuel consumption required to maintain a rate of climb of 50 m sec⁻¹. Energy losses due to imperfections in the engine, or to wind resistance, may be neglected.

(Heat of combustion of paraffin = 10000 cal gm⁻¹.)     (C.S.)

7. Assuming that all the heat generated by the stopping of a bullet in a target enters the bullet, calculate the speed at which a lead bullet at 40 °C must strike the target in order that it shall just all be melted.

(Melting point, specific heat and latent heat of fusion of lead are 327 °C, 0·03 cal deg⁻¹ C gm⁻¹ and 5·9 cal gm⁻¹ respectively.)     (O.S.)

8. Assuming that a man eats food equivalent to 3000 kg cal a day, and that he can exert 0·1 h.p. for 8 h a day, calculate his efficiency considered as a machine.

(1 h.p. = 0·75 kW.)

9. A current of 1·5 A is passed through a coil of wire having a resistance of 1·3 Ω immersed in 40 gm of water, contained in a lagged calorimeter which has a water equivalent of 10 gm. The temperature of the water rises 6 °C in 7 min. Find the mechanical equivalent of heat.     (O.S.)

10. Describe briefly a modern accurate method of determining the mechanical equivalent of heat in which the work is measured (i) electrically, (ii) mechanically.

11. (a) State the principle of the conservation of energy.

(b) Give three examples to illustrate the law.

12. (a) Distinguish between heat and internal energy. State and explain the first law of thermodynamics.

(b) Explain why the specific heat of a gas at constant pressure is greater than the specific heat at constant volume.

13. In the light of the concepts of heat as energy in process of transfer because of a temperature difference, and of internal energy, discuss one example of each of the following: (a) heat is transferred to a substance without causing its temperature to rise; (b) the temperature of a substance changes although no heat is transferred to or from the substance.

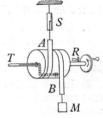

14. Fig. 26 represents an apparatus devised by

Fig. 26

Callendar for determining the mechanical equivalent of heat in the teaching laboratory. A silk band $AB$ is wrapped round a hollow copper drum; it is supported at its upper end by a spring balance $S$ and kept taut by the hanging mass $M$. The drum contains a little water whose temperature is measured by the bent thermometer $T$. The drum is rotated by hand, so that the reading of $S$ remains steady, and the number of revolutions of the drum is measured by the counter $R$. The friction between the silk band and the drum generates heat, causing the temperature of the drum and the water inside it to rise.

Deduce an expression for the mechanical equivalent of heat, using symbols for the various quantities measured.

How would you eliminate the need for a cooling correction?

15. Two brass cones fit one inside the other. The outer one is rotated about a vertical axis at 720 rev/min, and the inner one is held fixed by an arm whose length, measured from the axis of rotation, is 15 cm, and to which a horizontal pull of 200 gm wt. is applied at right angles to the arm. The total mass of the two cones together is 250 gm, and the inner one contains 25 gm of water. Assuming that the initial temperature is 20 °C and that there are no heat losses, find the temperature at the end of 5 min.

(Take $J$ to be 4·2 J per cal, and the specific heat of brass to be 0·10.)

(O.)

16. Explain the term *mechanical equivalent of heat* and describe an experiment to find its value when heat is generated by friction between two solid surfaces.

Oil at 15·6 °C enters a long glass tube containing an electrically heated platinum wire and leaves at 17·4 °C, the rate of flow being 25 c.c./min and the rate of supply of energy 1·34 W. On changing the rate of flow to 15 c.c./min and the power to 0·76 W the temperature again rises from 15·6 to 17·4 °C. Calculate the mean specific heat of the oil between these temperatures. Assume that the density of the oil is 0·87 gm/c.c. (N.)

17. Describe very briefly one mechanical method of measuring the mechanical equivalent of heat, and comment fully on its merits and inherent errors.

In a commercial X-ray tube, a current of 15 mA of electrons strikes a target which is at a potential of 100 kV positive with respect to the filament. What flow of water is required to keep the target cool assuming that all the heat is conducted away by the water, and that its rise in temperature should not be greater than 30 °C?

(You may assume that the entire kinetic energy of the electrons is converted into heat in the target.) (O. & C.)

18. The anode of a wireless valve is bombarded by a stream of electrons each of mass $9 \times 10^{-28}$ gm moving with a velocity of $10^9$ cm/sec. If the mass of the anode is 0·5 gm, its specific heat is 0·1 and $3 \times 10^{17}$ electrons hit it per second, calculate the rate at which its temperature rises on the assumption that all the energy of the electrons is converted into heat at the anode.

In actual practice it is found that the anode reaches a steady temperature. How do you account for this? (C.)

19. Discuss the caloric theory of heat, and give a critical survey of the evidence which led to its replacement by the theory that heat is a form of energy. In the familiar equation

$$\text{Work} = J \times \text{Heat}, \tag{1}$$

do you consider that the factor $J$ does, or does not, play a role identical with the factor 2·54 in the equation

$$\text{Length in cm} = 2\cdot 54 \times \text{length in inches}?$$

Is equation (1) to be taken to mean that heat and mechanical energy are completely interconvertible? (C.S.)

20. (a) What experimental evidence is there for Einstein's theory of mass–energy equivalence?

(b) The following measurements, in atomic mass units (a.m.u.), have been made with a mass spectrograph:

$_3\text{Li}^7$, 7·01818 a.m.u.   $_1\text{H}^1$, 1·00813 a.m.u.   $_2\text{He}^4$, 4·00388 a.m.u.

Calculate the energy, in electron-volts, released when an atom of $_3\text{Li}^7$ is hit by a proton and disintegrates into two $\alpha$-particles.

(1 a.m.u. $= 1\cdot 66 \times 10^{-24}$ gm;   velocity of light $= 3 \times 10^{10}$ cm sec$^{-1}$; 1 eV $= 1\cdot 60 \times 10^{-12}$ erg.)

21. When the uranium isotope $_{92}\text{U}^{235}$ undergoes fission the energy released is 200 MeV. Calculate the corresponding loss of mass. (Use data at the end of question 20.)

## CHAPTER 4

# THE THERMAL BEHAVIOUR OF A PERFECT GAS

The core of the theory of heat is based upon the concept of a perfect gas (p. 6) and in this chapter we shall consider how real gases would behave if they were perfect. In chapter 5 we shall see how the behaviour can be explained in terms of atoms and molecules, and in chapter 6 we shall discuss the deviations of real gases, particularly when close to their liquefying points, from this behaviour.

### The equation of state

The expansion of a perfect gas is used to define the ultimate scale of temperature, to which all other scales are reduced, and the defining equation may be taken as

$$pv/T = \text{constant} \quad \text{(p. 7)}.$$

Real gases, at temperatures well above their liquefying points, also conform to this equation except at high pressures.

The numerical value of the constant clearly depends on what mass of gas we are considering. We shall see that, if we take 1 *mole*, i.e. the molecular weight in grams, of gas the constant is the same for all gases. The constant is denoted by $R$ and is called the *gas constant*. The equation, known as the *equation of state*, becomes

$$pV = RT.$$

Note that we have used capital $V$ for the volume of 1 mole, a convention to which we shall adhere.

The universality of $R$ follows from *Avogadro's principle*, that equal volumes of all gases at the same temperature and pressure contain the same number of molecules. The molecular weight of oxygen, $O_2$, is 32, and 1 mole or 32 gm occupies 22·4 l. at 0 °C and 76 cm of mercury (standard temperature and pressure). Hence 1 mole of all other gases, e.g. 2·016 gm of hydrogen, $H_2$, occupies the same volume at s.t.p.

We will calculate the value of $R$, taking the density of mercury at 0 °C as 13·6 gm cm$^{-3}$, so that a pressure of 76 cm of mercury is 76 × 13·6 × 981 dynes cm$^{-2}$.

$$R = \frac{p_0 V_0}{T_0} = \frac{76 \times 13\text{·}6 \times 981 \times 22400}{273}$$

$$= 8\text{·}32 \times 10^7 \text{ ergs mole}^{-1} \text{ deg}^{-1} \text{ C},$$

$$= 8\text{·}32 \text{ joules mole}^{-1} \text{ deg}^{-1} \text{ C}.$$

When we are dealing with 1 gm of gas, of molecular weight $M$, instead of with 1 mole, the equation of state becomes

$$pv = \frac{RT}{M}.$$

The form of equation which we shall use for any other mass of gas than 1 mole or 1 gm is

$$pv = nRT,$$

where $n$ is the number of moles of gas under consideration. For example, if the gas consists of 0·1 gm of oxygen, $n = 0·1/32$ moles, since the molecular weight of oxygen is 32.

Example. *Two bulbs of volumes 20 and 30 c.c. are connected by a capillary tube of negligible volume. They contain air at a pressure of 76 cm of mercury and temperature 17 °C. When the smaller bulb is placed in ice and the larger bulb in water at 100 °C, what is the pressure of the air?*

The mass of the air in the two bulbs can be represented by $n$ moles of air:

$$pv = nRT,$$

$$76 \times 50 = nk(273 + 17),$$

writing $k$ for $R$ since $p$ is not expressed in dyne cm$^{-2}$.

When the bulbs are at 0 and 100 °C let the masses of air they contain be $n_1$ and $n_2$ moles, and let the common pressure be $p$ cm of mercury.

$$p \times 20 = n_1 k\, 273,$$

$$p \times 30 = n_2 k\, 373.$$

But

$$n_1 + n_2 = n,$$

$$\therefore \quad \frac{20p}{273} + \frac{30p}{373} = \frac{76 \times 50}{300},$$

$$p = 82·4 \text{ cm of mercury.}$$

## Isothermals

If we plot pressure against volume of a fixed mass of gas at constant temperature we obtain curves similar to those in Fig. 27, and they are known as *isothermals*. Their equations are $pv = nRT_1$, $pv = nRT_2$, and $pv = nRT_3$, where $n$ is the number of moles of gas to which they refer.

## Work done when a gas expands

A gas can be heated by compressing it, e.g. with a bicycle pump. Hence the temperature of a gas can be raised either by doing work in compressing it or by heating it. Likewise the temperature can be lowered either by making the gas do work in expanding or by extracting heat from it.

When heat was thought to consist of a fluid, caloric, which was supposed to be conserved, the rise in the temperature of a gas on compression and its fall in temperature on expansion were very difficult to explain. We now realise that the work done in compressing a gas causes an increase in the velocity of the gas molecules and that the gain in the kinetic energy of the molecules represents a rise in temperature. Similarly, when a gas does work in expansion the velocity of its molecules is reduced.

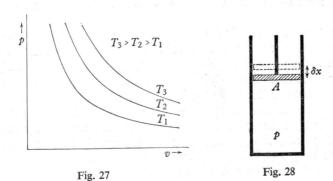

Fig. 27          Fig. 28

We will derive an expression for the work done by a gas when it expands very slightly. Suppose that a gas at pressure $p$ is contained in a cylinder fitted with a weightless frictionless piston of area $A$ (Fig. 28). The piston must be held down by force $pA$ to keep it in position. Let this force be infinitesimally reduced so that the piston is pushed up by the gas a distance $\delta x$, which is so small that the pressure of the gas is virtually unchanged by the expansion.

Work done by gas $= pA\,\delta x$.

$A\delta x$ is the very small change in volume of the gas, which we will represent by $\delta v$,

$$\therefore \text{ work done by gas } = p\,\delta v.$$

When a gas expands considerably, say from volume $v_1$ to $v_2$, there is one simple case. Suppose that the pressure is kept constant during the expansion, by supplying the gas with heat at a sufficient rate. The work done is $p(v_2 - v_1)$.

But when the pressure changes during the expansion we must add the many small quantities of work $p\,\delta v$, $p$ being different in each case; the total work done may be represented by $\sum\limits_{v_1}^{v_2} p\,\delta v$. The calculation is possible only if the relation between $p$ and $v$ is known, when the work done is $\int_{v_1}^{v_2} p\,dv$.

## Principal specific heats of a gas

The specific heat of a gas is the heat required to raise unit mass of it through 1 degree of temperature. The molar specific heat is the heat required to raise 1 mole, i.e. 1 gm molecular weight, through 1 degree.

Heat causes not only the temperature of a gas to change but also its pressure and volume. If the volume increases the gas will do work against the pressure of the atmosphere and its temperature will, in consequence, be lowered. There are innumerable specific heats of a gas, each depending on how much the volume is allowed to change—depending, in turn, on how the pressure is controlled. Only two specific heats are of importance; they are known as the *principal specific heats* of a gas and they are the specific heat at constant volume, $c_v$, and the specific heat at constant pressure $c_p$. We will denote the molar specific heats by $C_v$ and $C_p$ cal mole$^{-1}$ deg$^{-1}$ C and derive a relation between them which holds for all gases.

To raise the temperature of 1 mole of gas from $T_1$ to $T_2$ at constant volume the heat required is $C_v(T_2-T_1)$. The pressure of the gas will increase but, since the volume remains unchanged, no work is done by the gas. All the heat supplied serves to increase the kinetic energy of the molecules of the gas.

If the gas is heated through the same range of temperature at constant pressure, its volume will increase, and it will do work. Taking $V_1$ and $V_2$ as the initial and final volumes and $p_1$ as the constant pressure, the work done is $p_1(V_2-V_1)$. The heat supplied to the gas, $C_p(T_2-T_1)$, must produce the same increase of the kinetic energy of the molecules as occurred at constant volume, and also provide the energy for the work done by the gas.

$$\therefore C_p(T_2-T_1) = C_v(T_2-T_1)+\frac{p_1(V_2-V_1)}{J},$$

where $J$ is the mechanical equivalent of heat.

If $T_1$ and $T_2$ represent absolute temperatures,

$$p_1V_1 = RT_1, \quad \text{(p. 53)}$$
$$p_1V_2 = RT_2.$$

Subtracting, $\quad p_1(V_2-V_1) = R(T_2-T_1),$

$$\therefore C_p(T_2-T_1) = C_v(T_2-T_1)+\frac{R}{J}(T_2-T_1),$$

$$C_p = C_v+\frac{R}{J}$$

or $$C_p = C_v + R,$$

where all are expressed in joules mole$^{-1}$ deg$^{-1}$ C.

The corresponding equation for specific heats referred to 1 gm of gas is

$$c_p = c_v + \frac{R}{MJ},$$

where $M$ is the molecular weight of the gas.

The equation is strictly true only for a perfect gas (because we ignored the *internal* work done, in the expansion at constant pressure, against the mutual attraction of the molecules) but it is very nearly true for real gases well above their liquefying points.

If we know $c_p$, $c_v$, $R$ and $M$ we can calculate $J$. Indeed the first determination of the mechanical equivalent of heat was made in this way by Robert Mayer in 1842. For hydrogen $c_v = 2\cdot40$ and $c_p = 3\cdot42$ cal gm$^{-1}$ deg$^{-1}$ C. The gas constant, $R$, is 8·32 joules mole$^{-1}$ deg$^{-1}$ C (p. 53), and the molecular weight, $M$, of hydrogen is 2·016.

$$c_p = c_v + \frac{R}{MJ},$$

$$3\cdot42 = 2\cdot40 + \frac{8\cdot32}{2\cdot016J},$$

$$J = 4\cdot05 \text{ joules cal}^{-1}.$$

## Internal energy

The fact that a gas has an infinite number of specific heats (p. 56) is one way of stating the remarkable fact that we can effect a given change in the state of a gas by putting into it just as much heat as we feel inclined.

To illustrate this consider Fig. 29 in which $A$ and $B$ are two points on an isothermal, representing two states of a fixed mass of perfect gas, $(p_1 v_1 T)$ and $(p_2 v_2 T)$. There are innumerable ways in which state $A$ can be changed to state $B$. We will consider two ways, namely routes $ACB$ and $ADB$.

From $A$ to $C$ the gas increases in volume from $v_1$ to $v_2$ at constant pressure $p_1$. The gas does work $p_1(v_2 - v_1)$, which is represented by the area under the line $AC$. Now $C$ is at a higher temperature than $A$ because it is on a higher isothermal (Fig. 27) and heat must be supplied to the gas along $AC$. From $C$ to $B$ the volume is constant and no work is done; but the temperature falls and heat must be extracted from the gas. Since $B$ is at the same temperature as $A$, the kinetic energies of the molecules of the gas in states $B$ and $A$ are the same. Hence the net heat supplied along $ACB$, by the principle of the conservation of energy, must be equivalent to the work done by the gas, i.e. $[p_1(v_2-v_1)]/J$.

Now let us consider the route $ADB$. From $A$ to $D$ the volume is unchanged and no work is done; the temperature falls and heat must be extracted from the gas. From $D$ to $B$ the gas expands at constant pressure $p_2$ from volume $v_1$ to $v_2$ and the work done by the gas is $p_2(v_2-v_1)$, which is represented by the area under the line $DB$; the temperature rises and heat must be supplied to the gas. The net heat supplied along route $ADB$ is $[p_2(v_2-v_1)]/J$, which is different from that supplied along route $ACB$.

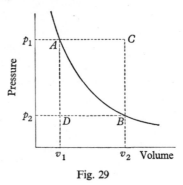

Fig. 29

We have thus shown that the quantity of heat which must be supplied to the gas in passing from state $A$ to state $B$ depends upon the intermediate states, and that this is so because different amounts of work are performed by the gas when the intermediate states are different. It is therefore convenient to introduce the concept of the *internal energy* of the gas, which takes account both of the heat supplied to the gas and of the work done by the gas. As we have already seen (p. 47), if $Q$ is the heat supplied to a gas and $W$ is the work done by the gas, equivalent to heat $W/J$, then the increase in the internal energy of the gas, $\Delta E$, is defined by the equation

$$\Delta E = Q-(W/J).$$

The internal energy of a perfect gas is equal to the kinetic energy of its molecules (both translational and rotational) and depends only upon the temperature. In the case of a real gas, since the molecules attract each other, they have potential energy when they have been separated, and hence the internal energy depends upon the volume of the gas as well as upon the temperature.

## Isothermal and adiabatic changes

Any of the three terms of the equation

$$\Delta E = Q - (W/J)$$

can separately be made zero and this gives rise to three special cases:

(1) When $W = 0$, the gas remains at constant volume. If the increase in temperature is $\Delta T$, $\Delta E = Q = C_v \Delta T$. This important fact, expressed in words, is that *the increase in internal energy is equal to the product of the specific heat at constant volume and the rise in temperature*.

(2) When $\Delta E = 0$, the gas remains at constant temperature. This is known as an *isothermal* change and

$$Q = W/J.$$

In the changes $ACB$ and $ADB$ in Fig. 29 there is no ultimate change in temperature, although there are intermediate changes in temperature. We shall normally confine the term isothermal change to one in which the temperature remains the same throughout the change, such as the change from $A$ to $B$ made along the isothermal curve.

(3) When $Q = 0$, the gas neither gains nor loses heat. This is known as an *adiabatic* change and

$$\Delta E = -W/J.$$

## Work done in an isothermal change

We will now consider how to calculate the work done during an isothermal expansion when the state of the gas remains always on the isothermal.

We have shown (p. 55) that the work done by a gas at pressure $p$ expanding through a small volume $\delta v$ is $p\delta v$; this is represented by the area of the narrow strip in Fig. 30. The total work done in the isothermal expansion from $A$ to $B$ is represented by the sum of the areas of the many narrow strips which make up the area under the curve $AB$. Since we know the equation of an isothermal we can calculate this area.

First, however, it must be pointed out that the expansion must take place extremely slowly if the intermediate states of the gas are to remain always on the isothermal. While the gas is doing work, heat must be supplied at a rate which exactly compensates the tendency to a fall of temperature. Such a change is called a *reversible* or *quasi-static* change. The change is said to be reversible because precisely the same change could be carried out in the reverse direction by making an infinitesimal increase in the counter-pressure on the gas, thereby compressing the gas, instead of allowing it to expand, and extracting heat from the gas instead of supplying it.

Work done by the gas in expanding from volume $v_1$ to $v_2$

$$= \int_{v_1}^{v_2} p\,dv$$

$$= \int_{v_1}^{v_2} \frac{k}{v}\,dv \quad \text{where} \quad k = p_1 v_1 = p_2 v_2$$

$$= k \log_e \frac{v_2}{v_1}.$$

Since the gas, supposed perfect, remains at constant temperature, an amount of heat must be supplied equal to $(k/J) \log_e(v_2/v_1)$.

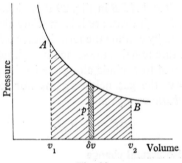

Fig. 30

Example. *A litre of gas at 1 atmosphere pressure $(10^6$ dynes cm$^{-2})$ is compressed isothermally and reversibly to half its volume.  Calculate the work done.*

Work done by the gas $= k \log_e(v_2/v_1)$,

where $\qquad\qquad k = p_1 v_1 = 10^6 \times 1000.$

$\therefore$ Work done by the gas $= 10^9 \log_e \frac{1}{2}$

$$= 10^9(-2\cdot303 \log_{10} 2)$$

$$= -6\cdot92 \times 10^8 \text{ ergs.}$$

## Adiabatic changes

We have seen that, besides an isothermal change, when the temperature remains constant, there is another special case, known as an adiabatic change, when no heat is supplied to, or extracted from, the gas. Any compressions and expansions which take place so quickly that there is no time for the gas to gain or lose heat are adiabatic. Examples are the sudden bursting of a bicycle tyre and the compressions and rarefactions in a sound wave.

The graph of pressure and volume, under *reversible* adiabatic conditions, of a fixed mass of gas is called an *adiabatic*. In Fig. 31 an isothermal is drawn and also an adiabatic. The adiabatic is steeper than the isothermal where they cross because, when the volume of the gas is increased adiabatically, the gas does work and its temperature falls but, if the same increase in volume occurs isothermally, the temperature remains constant, and hence the reduction in pressure is less than in the adiabatic change.

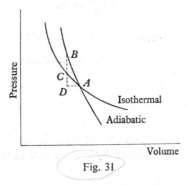

Fig. 31

Assuming that the curves in Fig. 31 refer to unit mass of perfect gas, we will derive the equation of the adiabatic. Suppose that the temperature of the gas on the isothermal is $T$ and that the temperature at $D$, which is situated on a lower isothermal, is $T - \delta T$. Consider the heat exchanges when the gas is taken along the route $ADCB$. From $A$ to $D$ the heat extracted from the gas is $c_p \delta T$. From $D$ to $C$ the heat supplied to the gas is $c_v \delta T$. From $D$ to $B$ as much heat must be restored to the gas as was extracted from $A$ to $D$, i.e. $c_p \delta T$, since the change is adiabatic. The changes of pressure $BD$ and $CD$ are proportional to the heats supplied because the volume is constant,

$$\therefore \frac{BD}{CD} = \frac{c_p \delta T}{c_v \delta T} = \frac{c_p}{c_v}.$$

We will denote $c_p / c_v$, which is a constant, by $\gamma$.

If $A$ and $B$ are extremely close together $CD/DA$ is the slope of the isothermal and $BD/DA$ is the slope of the adiabatic.

$$\therefore \frac{\text{Slope of adiabatic}}{\text{Slope of isothermal}} = \frac{BD/DA}{CD/DA} = \frac{BD}{CD} = \gamma.$$

The equation of the isothermal is

$$pv = RT/M \quad \text{(p. 53)}.$$

Differentiating,

$$p\,dv + v\,dp = 0 \quad (RT/M \text{ is constant}).$$

$$\therefore \text{ Slope of isothermal} = \frac{dp}{dv} = -\frac{p}{v}.$$

$$\text{Slope of adiabatic} = \frac{dp}{dv} = -\gamma\frac{p}{v}.$$

Hence, for the adiabatic,

$$\frac{dp}{p} + \frac{\gamma\,dv}{v} = 0.$$

Integrating, $\qquad \log_e p + \gamma\log_e v = constant$

or $\qquad\qquad\qquad\qquad pv^\gamma = constant.$

### Work done in adiabatic change

The work done in a reversible adiabatic change from volume $v_1$ to $v_2$ is represented by the area under the adiabatic, shown with single shading in Fig. 32. The extra work done in the isothermal change from volume $v_1$ to $v_2$ is shown by cross-hatch shading.

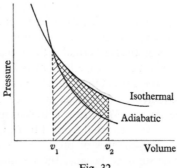

Fig. 32

To make quite clear that the work done is equal to the area under the curve only when the change is made extremely slowly, i.e. reversibly, consider the adiabatic expansion of a perfect gas into a vacuum. Here no work is done and consequently, unlike all other adiabatic changes, there is no change of temperature. Expansion into a vacuum may be regarded also as an isothermal change, without the usual accompaniment of absorption of heat, and it is clear that the expression for the work done on p. 60 applies only to a reversible isothermal change.

Some writers use the term *adiathermal* for sudden expansions or contractions without loss or gain of heat, reserving the term adiabatic for reversible changes only. We shall insert the adjective 'reversible' whenever we wish to emphasise the reversibility of a change.

Let the work done when a gas expands adiabatically and reversibly from volume $v_1$ to $v_2$ be $W$.

$$W = \int_{v_1}^{v_2} p\, dv.$$

But $pv^\gamma = C$, where $C$ is a constant.

$$\therefore W = \int_{v_1}^{v_2} \frac{C\, dv}{v^\gamma}$$

$$= \frac{C}{1-\gamma} (v_2^{1-\gamma} - v_1^{1-\gamma}).$$

But 
$$C = p_1 v_1^\gamma = p_2 v_2^\gamma,$$

$$\therefore W = \frac{1}{\gamma-1} (p_1 v_1 - p_2 v_2).$$

If the mass of gas contains $n$ moles and the temperature of the gas changes from $T_1$ to $T_2$,

$$p_1 v_1 = nRT_1 \quad \text{and} \quad p_2 v_2 = nRT_2 \quad \text{(p. 54)}.$$

$$\therefore W = \frac{nR}{\gamma-1} (T_1 - T_2).$$

*Example. A litre of air at 76 cm pressure is expanded adiabatically and reversibly to twice its volume. Find the work done.*

($\gamma$ *for air* $= 1\cdot4$.)

Taking the initial and final values of the pressure and volume as $p_1$, $v_1$ and $p_2$, $v_2$ respectively,

$$p_1 = 76 \text{ cm of mercury}, \quad v_1 = 1000 \text{ c.c.}, \quad v_2 = 2000 \text{ c.c.}$$

$$p_1 v_1^\gamma = p_2 v_2^\gamma,$$

$$\therefore 76 \times 1000^\gamma = p \times 2000^\gamma,$$

$$p_2 = \frac{76}{2^{1\cdot4}} = 29 \text{ cm of mercury}.$$

Work done $= \dfrac{1}{\gamma-1}(p_1 v_1 - p_2 v_2)$

$$= \frac{1}{1\cdot4-1} (76 \times 1000 - 29 \times 2000)$$

$$= 4\cdot5 \times 10^4 \text{ ergs.}$$

## Temperature change in an adiabatic

We will now derive an expression for the fall in temperature when a gas undergoes a reversible adiabatic expansion.

Let the volume of $n$ moles of gas at pressure $p$ and absolute temperature $T$ be $v$.

$$pv = nRT,$$

$$\therefore p = \frac{nRT}{v}.$$

In an adiabatic change,

$$pv^\gamma = \text{constant},$$

that is,

$$\frac{nRT}{v} . v^\gamma = \text{constant},$$

$$Tv^{\gamma-1} = \text{constant} \quad \text{(since } n \text{ and } R \text{ are constants).}$$

Alternatively, substituting for $v$ in the equation $pv^\gamma = \text{constant}$,

$$p\left(\frac{nRT}{p}\right)^\gamma = \text{constant},$$

$$\frac{T^\gamma}{p^{\gamma-1}} = \text{constant}.$$

Example. *A mass of air at 15 °C is expanded adiabatically and reversibly to twice its volume. Find the fall in temperature. ($\gamma$ for air = 1·4.)*

Taking the initial and final values of the volume and absolute temperature as $v_1$, $v_2$, and $T_1$, $T_2$, respectively,

$$T_1 v_1^{\gamma-1} = T_2 v_2^{\gamma-1},$$

$$T_1 = 288 \quad \text{and} \quad \frac{v_2}{v_1} = 2,$$

$$\therefore \quad T_2 = \frac{288}{2^{1\cdot4-1}}$$

$$= 218 \text{ °K.}$$

$$\therefore \quad \text{Fall of temperature} = 288 - 218$$

$$= 70 \text{ °C.}$$

## Determination of $\gamma$ by the method of Clément and Desormes

The value of $\gamma$ is of fundamental importance, as we shall show further in the next chapter. It can be calculated by determining $c_p$ and $c_v$ separately; then $c_p/c_v = \gamma$. But it can also be determined direct by a method devised by Clément and Desormes. We shall describe a simple form of apparatus (Fig. 33) suitable for use in the teaching laboratory.

A carboy (a large globular glass vessel used normally for holding acids) is fitted as shown with a bicycle valve and bung, and connected to a manometer containing paraffin. The carboy contains a little concentrated sulphuric acid in order to dry the air inside it.

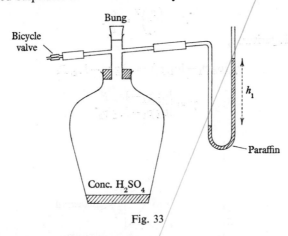

Fig. 33

Air is pumped into the carboy by means of a bicycle pump. This causes the air inside the carboy to become heated; it is left for about half an hour until it is at the temperature of the room. The reading, $h_1$, of the paraffin manometer is then taken. The bung is removed, causing the air to expand adiabatically, and it is replaced after 1 sec, this interval being allowed for the oscillations of the air in and out of the carboy to die down.

The states of the air in the carboy, before and after the removal of the bung, are represented by $A$ and $B$ respectively in Fig. 34. The air in the carboy was cooled by the adiabatic expansion and it gradually warms up to room temperature when its state will be represented by $C$. The reading of the manometer, $h_2$, is then taken. It should be noted that the curves in Fig. 34 relate to that portion of the air which remains in the carboy after the bung has been removed.

Since the pressure changes are small (paraffin having a low density) the graphs $AB$ and $AC$, which are an adiabatic and an isothermal respectively, are nearly straight lines.

$$\therefore \gamma = \frac{slope\ of\ adiabatic}{slope\ of\ isothermal} = \frac{AM/MB}{AN/NC} = \frac{h_1}{h_1 - h_2}.$$

A more accurate method of calculating $\gamma$, which does not assume the graphs to be straight, is as follows. Let the pressures and volumes at $A$, $B$, $C$ be $(p_1, v_1)$, $(P, v_2)$ and $(p_2, v_2)$ respectively, $P$ being atmospheric pressure.

$$p_1 v_1 = p_2 v_2,$$

$$p_1 v_1^\gamma = P v_2^\gamma.$$

$$\therefore \left(\frac{p_1}{p_2}\right)^\gamma = \frac{p_1}{P}.$$

Taking logarithms,

$$\gamma(\log p_1 - \log p_2) = \log p_1 - \log P,$$

$$\gamma = \frac{\log p_1 - \log P}{\log p_1 - \log p_2}.$$

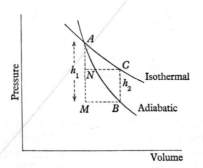

Fig. 34

Using this method of calculation it is necessary to read the barometer to find $P$ and to convert $h_1$ and $h_2$ cm of paraffin to the equivalent heights of mercury.

Example. *Obtain a relation between the pressure of the atmosphere and the height above the ground, assuming that the temperature of the atmosphere is uniform. Discuss the form of the relation.*

Let the pressure of the atmosphere at height $h$ be $p$ and at height $h + dh$, $p - dp$. Considering the thin layer of air shaded in Fig. 35, of unit cross-section, thickness $dh$ and density $\rho$:

$$-dp = g\rho \, dh.$$

The equation of state is

$$pV = RT$$

and $\qquad\qquad \rho = \dfrac{M}{V}$, where $M$ is the molecular weight

$$= \dfrac{Mp}{RT}.$$

$$\therefore \quad -dp = g\dfrac{Mp}{RT}\,dh,$$

$$\dfrac{dp}{p} = -\dfrac{Mg}{RT}\,dh.$$

Integrating, $\qquad \displaystyle\int_{p_0}^{p} \dfrac{dp}{p} = -\dfrac{Mg}{RT}\int_{0}^{h} dh,$

$$\log_e \dfrac{p}{p_0} = -\dfrac{Mgh}{RT}.$$

$$\therefore \quad p = p_0 e^{-Mgh/RT}.$$

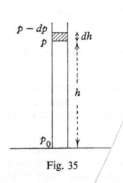

Fig. 35

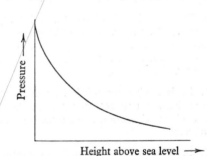

Fig. 36

The relation between $p$ and $h$ is shown in Fig. 36. The quantity $p$ is said to be an *exponential* quantity with respect to the independent variable $h$. Such quantities are quite common in physics and the independent variable is usually time; examples are the decay in activity of a radioactive substance, the decrease in amplitude of a pendulum, and the fall in voltage of a charged condenser leaking through a high resistance. In general, if

$$y = y_0 e^{-at} \quad \text{where } a \text{ is a constant,}$$

$$\dfrac{dy}{dt} = -ay_0 e^{-at}$$

$$= -ay.$$

Hence the rate of decrease of $y$ is proportional to itself.

## QUESTIONS

1. (*a*) Explain what is meant by the *gas constant*.

(*b*) Calculate the value of the gas constant, given that oxygen, of molecular weight 32, has a density $1\cdot429$ gm l.$^{-1}$ at s.t.p. (Density of mercury at 0 °C $= 13\cdot6$ gm cm$^{-3}$.)

2. (*a*) State *Boyle's law*.

(*b*) A little air has leaked into a barometer tube 100 cm long. The mercury stands at the 70 cm mark when the tube is vertical, and at the 78 cm mark when the tube is inclined at 30° to the vertical. What is the atmospheric pressure in mm of mercury? (O.S.)

3. A uniform capillary tube sealed at one end contains dry air enclosed by a pellet of mercury. If the length of the air column is 50 cm at 27 °C what will be its length at 100 °C?

4. The pressure of the air in a sealed bulb is 80 cm of mercury at 27 °C. What will be its pressure at 127 °C?

5. Two vessels, of volume 1 l. and 3 l. respectively, are connected by a long capillary tube. Initially they contain a perfect gas at 27 °C and pressure *p*. Calculate the new pressure of the whole system if the temperature of the 3 l. vessel is raised to 227 °C, while the temperature of the 1 l. vessel remains at 27 °C. (C.)

6. Fuels having combustion products of small molecular weight are more suitable for rockets than those of larger molecular weight, provided that the heat of reaction is the same for a given mass of fuel in each case. Comment. (C.S.)

7. In a poorly constructed constant-volume air thermometer, the volume of the bulb and stem immersed in the heating bath is 130 c.c. while the 'dead space' between this and the constant volume mark is 14 c.c. The pressure in the thermometer when it is all at 15 °C is 75 cm of mercury. Find the pressure when the bulb is immersed in a bath at 159 °C, while the 'dead space' remains at 15 °C. Calculate also the apparent temperature of the bath as deduced from this pressure. (O.)

8. Explain what is meant by the absolute zero of temperature on the gas scale. Describe how its value is determined.

A 'fire-balloon' consists of a spherical envelope, 2 m in diameter, filled with air at atmospheric pressure. A brazier placed below heats the air inside the envelope, the air being allowed to escape so that its pressure remains atmospheric. Assuming that the balloon and its fittings weigh 2 kg, to what temperature must the air be raised in order that the balloon may rise? The density of air at atmospheric pressure and temperature (assumed to be 0 °C) is $1\cdot29$ gm/l. (O. & C.)

9. Estimate approximately the total mass of the earth's atmosphere, assuming the values of well-known constants. (C.S.)

10. Calculate the external work done when 1 l. of air at 0 °C is heated at a constant pressure of 1 atm to 100 °C.

(Take 1 atm pressure to be $10^6$ dynes $cm^{-2}$.)

11. Prove that the external work done when a gas expands from volume $v_1$ to $v_2$ is $\int_{v_1}^{v_2} p\,dv$.

12. A rocket motor burns 100 gm of fuel per second and the combustion product is of molecular weight 18. If the combustion chamber is maintained at 1000 °K estimate the thrust exerted by the motor. ($R = 8 \times 10^7$ ergs $deg^{-1}$ K $mole^{-1}$.)      (C.S.)

13. (a) What are the two principal specific heats of a gas?

(b) Derive an expression for the difference between them.

(c) Calculate the value of this difference for helium, given that the density of helium at s.t.p. is 0·179 gm per l., and 1 atmosphere = $10^6$ dynes $cm^{-2}$.

14. The difference between the specific heats of a gas at constant pressure is approximately $2/M$ calories, where $M$ is the molecular weight of the gas. From this result deduce an approximate value of the mechanical equivalent of heat. (1 gm molecular weight occupies 22·4 l. at s.t.p. and 1 atmosphere = $10^6$ dynes $cm^{-2}$.)      (O.S.)

15. Explain how it is possible for a gas to have more than one specific heat. Calculate the difference of the principal specific heats of hydrogen given that the density of hydrogen is $9 \times 10^{-5}$ gm per c.c. at n.t.p.

(Density of mercury = 13·6 gm/c.c.; 1 cal = 4·2 J.)

Describe a method of measuring the specific heat of a gas either at constant pressure or at constant volume, and point out the principal sources of error.      (O. & C.)

16. Calculate the difference, in calories, between the quantities of heat required to raise 10 gm of oxygen from 0 to 10 °C when (a) the volume, (b) the pressure, is kept constant.

(Density of mercury = 13·6 gm $cm^{-3}$; mol.wt. of $O_2$ = 32; gm molecular volume at n.t.p. = 22·4 l.; $J = 4·18 \times 10^7$ ergs $cal^{-1}$.)      (O. & C.)

17. A mixture of one volume of oxygen and two volumes of hydrogen at n.t.p. is exploded in a container. What is the maximum pressure, in atmospheres, developed in the container?

($C_v$ for water vapour, 6·48 cal/gm mol. per °C. Heat of formation of water vapour 60000 cal/gm mol.)      (C.S.)

18. Assuming that the temperature of the atmosphere does not vary with the height, obtain a formula for the dependence of the barometric pressure on altitude. If the pressure is 76 cm of mercury at ground level, and 70 cm of mercury at a height of 800 m, estimate the pressure at 12000 m.      (O.)

19. Assuming that the temperature of the atmosphere is constant at 300 °K, and the gas constant for 1 gm of air is $2 \cdot 87 \times 10^6$ ergs/gm/degree, find the altitude at which the boiling point of water is 97 °C, given that the change in pressure required to lower the boiling point by one degree in the neighbourhood of 100 °C is 27 mm of mercury, and that the barometric pressure at sea level is 760 mm of mercury.     (O.)

20. (a) What is meant by (i) an isothermal, (ii) an adiabatic?

(b) Why is the slope of an adiabatic at a point on a $p–v$ diagram greater than that of the isothermal passing through the point?

21. A certain compressor has an intake of 10 m³/h and compresses to 300 atm. On the assumption that the compression is isothermal, calculate the horse-power necessary to drive the machine. (1 atm = $10^6$ dynes cm$^{-2}$, 1 h.p. = 746 W.)     (O. & C.)

22. A quantity of air at 10 °C and a pressure of ~~15 lb wt./sq.in.~~ 1 atmos. is compressed adiabatically to one-third of its volume. What is the resulting temperature and pressure? ($\gamma$ for air = 1·40.)

23. (a) Give the theory of an experimental method for determining the ratio of the principal specific heats of air.

(b) Suggest a reason why the velocity of sound in a gas should depend on the ratio of the principal specific heats of the gas.

24. Distinguish between an *isothermal* and an *adiabatic* change, and derive an expression for the relationship between the pressure and the volume of a fixed mass of gas while it is being compressed adiabatically.

Calculate (a) the rise in temperature, (b) the work done during the adiabatic compression of 1 mole of helium to half its volume, the gas being initially at n.t.p.

How can adiabatic expansion be made use of during the liquefaction of a gas?

($\gamma$ for helium = $\frac{5}{3}$; density of mercury = 13·6 gm cm$^{-3}$.)     (O. & C.)

25. A fixed mass of an ideal gas occupying 400 cm³ at 15 °C is expanded adiabatically until its temperature is 0 °C. What is the new volume if the ratio of the principal specific heats of the gas is 1·40? It is then compressed isothermally until the pressure is restored to its original value. Calculate the final volume of the gas and represent the changes on a $(p, v)$ diagram.     (N.)

26. Calculate the temperature of the air which a bicycle pump forces into a bicycle tyre.

(Make reasonable estimates of the values of any quantities involved.)     (C.S.)

27. In a rising current of dry air in the atmosphere the temperature and pressure near the base of the current are 10 °C and 75 cm of mercury respectively. What will be the temperature of the air when it has reached a region where the pressure is 60 cm of mercury, assuming that the changes occur under adiabatic conditions? ($\gamma$ for air = 1·4.)     (C.S.)

28. What is the change of temperature of the gas in an empty wine bottle if a cork is pushed in quickly? Make reasonable estimates of the quantities involved. (C.S.)

29. Some gas in a glass bulb fitted with a tap and a manometer is initially at a pressure of 79·55 cm of mercury. The tap is opened so that the pressure falls to atmospheric, 75·80 cm of mercury, and is quickly closed again. After the gas has warmed up to its initial temperature the pressure is 76·85 cm of mercury. What can you deduce from these results? (C.S.)

30. Give reasons for the temperature changes you would expect when a gas expands adiabatically (a) against a piston which is slowly withdrawn, (b) into another cylinder previously evacuated, (c) slowly through a valve into the surrounding atmosphere.

A vessel of low thermal conductivity containing air at 0 °C and at a pressure of 2 atm is opened and then quickly closed when the excess pressure has been released. What will be the final pressure in the vessel if its surroundings are maintained at 0 °C?

$(C_p/C_v$ for air $= 1·4.)$ (C.S.)

31. A simple air-gun consists of a uniform tube of cross-sectional area $a$ and length $l$, to one end of which is attached a closed chamber of volume $V$ containing air at a pressure $p$ greater than atmospheric pressure $p_0$. In the tube, immediately next to the chamber, a close-fitting pellet is placed, and the gun is discharged by making connection between the compressed air chamber and the tube. Assuming no leakage of air and no friction between the pellet and the tube, derive expressions for the value of $l$ which allows the greatest kinetic energy to be imparted to the pellet, and for the magnitude of this energy. (C.S.)

32. What is meant by a reversible adiabatic change?
How can the rise of temperature during an adiabatic compression be explained on the kinetic theory?
A cylinder of negligible thermal capacity and non-conducting walls is fitted with a frictionless piston. The cylinder contains 2·24 l. of nitrogen at s.t.p. A small explosion is fired inside the cylinder, producing 250 cal of heat; the gas is then allowed to expand reversibly and adiabatically down to atmospheric pressure. Calculate the final temperature of the gas.
In the final state, is all the energy of the explosion present as heat in the gas? If not, what has happened to any difference?

$(C_v$ for nitrogen $= 4·9$ cal °C$^{-1}$ per gm molecule; $C_p/C_v$ for nitrogen $= 1·40.)$ (C.)

CHAPTER 5

# THE KINETIC THEORY OF MATTER

The properties of matter which we recognise with our senses—for example the pressure, volume and temperature of a gas—are known as *macroscopic* properties. It is the fundamental aim of physics to explain such properties in terms of *microscopic* properties, which are the properties of atoms, molecules, electrons and other fundamental particles. This, in a nutshell, is what modern physics is about.

In this chapter we shall be concerned mainly with the explanation of the macroscopic behaviour of a perfect gas in terms of molecules,[†] and we shall find that the gas laws and the concepts of heat and temperature assume a new significance. We shall consider briefly also the microscopic properties of solids and liquids.

### The kinetic theory of gases

A volume of a perfect gas consists of millions of molecules, each molecule being regarded as a sphere of negligible volume. The molecules are moving at high speed and it is their continual bombardment of the walls of the containing vessel which constitutes the pressure of the gas. The molecules are continually colliding with each other and they are assumed to be perfectly elastic so that, at each collision, no kinetic energy is lost. They are also assumed to exert a negligible force of attraction on each other, with the result that the duration of the collisions is negligible and, between the collisions, a molecule travels in straight lines.

### Expression for *pv* (elementary treatment)

Consider a gas consisting of *n* molecules, each of mass *m*, in a cubical vessel of side *l*. The millions of molecules will be travelling with random motion, zigzagging as a result of collisions, and they will strike the faces of the cube at all angles. In order to calculate the

---

† A molecule is defined as the smallest portion of a substance capable of existing independently and retaining the properties of the substance. A monatomic molecule consists of a single atom, e.g. He (helium) and A (argon). A diatomic molecule consists of two atoms, e.g. $H_2$ (hydrogen), $O_2$ (oxygen) and $N_2$ (nitrogen). An atom is defined as the smallest part of an element which can take part in a chemical reaction.

pressure exerted by the gas we can imagine that the chaotic motion of the molecules is equivalent to three streams, each of $n/3$ molecules, travelling in three mutually perpendicular directions, normal to the faces of the cube. This is a reasonable assumption because the pressure on each of the faces of the cube is the same.

Let $c$ be velocity of the molecules (assumed to be the same for each molecule). A molecule, on striking one face of the cube perpendicularly, with velocity $c$, will rebound with velocity $c$, because it is perfectly elastic. Since its direction is reversed, its change of momentum is $mc - (-mc) = 2mc$.

Now a molecule travels backwards and forwards along one dimension of the cube $c/l$ times per second, so that it strikes each of the two faces $c/2l$ times per second. There are $n/3$ molecules travelling along each dimension, and hence the force exerted on each face of the cube which, by Newton's second law of motion, is equal to the total change of momentum per second, is

$$\frac{n}{3}\frac{c}{2l}2mc = \frac{1}{3}\frac{nmc^2}{l}.$$

The area of each face of the cube is $l^2$; hence the pressure, $p$, of the gas is given by

$$p = \frac{1}{3}\frac{nmc^2}{l \times l^2}.$$

The volume, $v$, of the gas in the cube is $l^3$.

$$\therefore pv = \tfrac{1}{3}nmc^2.$$

## Variation in velocities of the molecules

We have assumed that the velocities of all the molecules are the same, but this cannot be true since, when two perfectly elastic spheres travelling at the same velocity collide their velocities (or more strictly, their speeds, since we are ignoring directions) do not remain unchanged unless the collision is direct or symmetrical. Maxwell deduced from the laws of chance an expression showing that the distribution of velocities among the molecules, as a result of their collisions, is like the distribution of shots round the bull's eye of a target. The majority of the molecules travel with approximately the mean velocity, but there are a few which travel distinctly more quickly or more slowly than the average. When a faster-moving molecule hits a slower-moving one they exchange velocities approximately, so that the velocity of a particular molecule is continually changing. It is the statistical distribution of velocities which remains constant.

Maxwell's expression has been confirmed by experiment. In 1920 Stern allowed a metallic vapour from an oven to pass through a slit in a screen and then through a slit in a hollow rotating drum (Fig. 37). The drum was rotating so quickly that it turned through an appreciable angle while the molecules travelled across its diameter and the metallic deposit $AB$ on the interior of the drum was the spectrum of the molecular velocities.

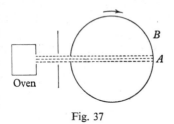

Fig. 37

### Expression for $pv$ (more rigorous treatment)

Consider a gas consisting of $n$ molecules each of mass $m$ in a cubical vessel of side $l$. The millions of molecules will strike the faces of the cube at all angles. The force exerted by the molecules on the face of a cube is, by Newton's second law of motion, the total change of momentum per second, perpendicular to the face, of the molecules striking it. We will therefore resolve the velocities of the molecules into components in the three directions of the sides of the cube. If $c_1$ is the velocity of a molecule and $u_1$, $v_1$ and $w_1$ are its three components,

$$c_1^2 = u_1^2 + v_1^2 + w_1^2.$$

The molecule, on striking one face of the cube with a perpendicular velocity $u_1$, will rebound with perpendicular velocity $u_1$ because it is perfectly elastic. Since its direction is reversed, its change of momentum is $mu_1 - (-mu_1) = 2mu_1$.

If there were no collisions the molecule would traverse the width $l$ of the cube and back $u_1/2l$ times per second and hence its change of momentum per second at the face under consideration would be

$$2mu_1 \frac{u_1}{2l} = \frac{mu_1^2}{l}.$$

However, the molecule is bound to collide with many other molecules and it will not itself traverse the width of the cube $u_1/2l$ times per second, although its momentum will, the momentum being passed on at each collision without any loss of time during the collision, since the molecules are perfectly elastic and do not attract each other.

Considering all the molecules in the cube, the total force on the face of the cube is the sum of the changes of momentum, perpendicular to the face, of the molecules striking it per second,

$$\Sigma \frac{mu_1^2}{l}.$$

But
$$\Sigma c_1^2 = \Sigma u_1^2 + \Sigma v_1^2 + \Sigma w_1^2.$$

Since there is no preferred direction in the cube,

$$\Sigma u_1^2 = \Sigma v_1^2 = \Sigma w_1^2 = \tfrac{1}{3}\Sigma c_1^2.$$

Let $\overline{c^2}$ represent the average of the squares of the velocities of all the $n$ molecules, i.e.

$$\overline{c^2} = \frac{\Sigma c_1^2}{n}.$$

$\therefore$ Force on face of cube $= \dfrac{\Sigma m u_1^2}{l}$

$$= \frac{m}{l}\tfrac{1}{3}\Sigma c_1^2$$

$$= \frac{nm}{3l}\overline{c^2}.$$

The area of each face of the cube is $l^2$; hence the pressure $p$ of the gas is given by

$$p = \frac{1}{3}\frac{nm\overline{c^2}}{l \times l^2}.$$

The volume, $v$, of the gas in the cube is $l^3$.

$$\therefore pv = \tfrac{1}{3}nm\overline{c^2}.$$

Note that the important velocity is not the mean velocity but the square root of the mean of the squares of the velocities, which is the velocity of the molecule whose kinetic energy is the average of the kinetic energies of all the molecules. The mean velocity is about 12/13 of the root mean square velocity.

### Velocity of the molecules

The total mass of the molecules in the equation $pv = \tfrac{1}{3}nm\overline{c^2}$ is $nm$ and hence the density, $\rho$, of the gas is $nm/v$. The equation can be written

$$p = \tfrac{1}{3}\rho\overline{c^2}.$$

Knowing $p$ and $\rho$ we can calculate $\overline{c^2}$.

A mole of hydrogen has a mass of 2·016 gm, and at s.t.p. it occupies 22·4 l. The density of hydrogen at s.t.p. is therefore

$$\frac{2\cdot016}{22400} \text{ gm cm}^{-3}.$$

Standard pressure is 76 cm of mercury; the density of mercury is 13·6 gm cm$^{-3}$, so that this pressure is equivalent to $76 \times 13\cdot6 \times$

981 dynes cm$^{-2}$. The root mean square velocity of the hydrogen molecules at 0 °C is given by

$$\sqrt{\bar{c}^2} = \sqrt{\frac{3p}{\rho}}$$

$$= \sqrt{\left(\frac{3 \times 76 \times 13 \cdot 6 \times 981}{2 \cdot 016/22400}\right)}$$

$$= 1 \cdot 84 \times 10^5 \text{ cm sec}^{-1}$$

$$\simeq 4000 \text{ m.p.h.}$$

The molecular weight of oxygen is 16 times that of hydrogen and hence the square root of its density is 4 times that of hydrogen. The root mean square velocity of molecules of oxygen at 0 °C is therefore about 1000 m.p.h. As a comparable figure, the velocity of sound in air is about 750 m.p.h.

### The significance of temperature

Suppose that 1 mole of a gas has a volume $V$ at absolute temperature $T$ and pressure $p$. Let the number of molecules in 1 mole be $N$, known as *Avogadro's number*, and let the mass and mean square velocity of the molecules be $m$ and $\bar{c}^2$.

$$pV = \tfrac{1}{3}Nm\bar{c}^2 \quad \text{(Kinetic theory).}$$

Also
$$pV = RT \quad \text{(Equation of state).}$$

$$\therefore \tfrac{1}{3}Nm\bar{c}^2 = RT$$

$$\tfrac{1}{2}m\bar{c}^2 = \frac{3}{2}\frac{R}{N}T,$$

i.e. *mean kinetic energy of translation per molecule* $= \tfrac{3}{2}kT$, where $k = R/N$, known as *Boltzmann's constant*.

Both $R$ and $N$ are universal constants, and therefore $k$ is a universal constant. Hence *the mean kinetic energy of translation of a molecule at any given absolute temperature is the same for all gases* (*assumed perfect*). We could, if we wished, define absolute temperature in terms of the kinetic energy of a molecule of a perfect gas: *the absolute temperature is proportional to the mean kinetic energy of translation of the molecules.*

### Avogadro's principle

In the above argument to establish the significance of temperature we assumed the equation of state, which is our definition of absolute temperature. We assumed also that Avogadro's number is a universal constant, which is equivalent to assuming Avogadro's principle, that equal volumes of all gases at the same temperature and pressure contain the same number of molecules. We can make an alternative approach to the meaning of temperature, however, which enables us to deduce Avogadro's principle from the Kinetic Theory.

Suppose that two different gases, having molecules of masses $m_1$ and $m_2$ and not necessarily at the same temperature, are mixed. The molecules will exchange kinetic energy. When a steady state is reached, how will the kinetic energy be divided between the two gases? Maxwell, treating the problem purely as one of statistical mechanics, showed that the mean kinetic energies of the molecules in the two gases will become the same: i.e.

$$\tfrac{1}{2}m_1\overline{c_1^2} = \tfrac{1}{2}m_2\overline{c_2^2}.$$

This is a special case of Maxwell's *principle of the equipartition of energy* which we shall define later (p. 80). A tiny particle of dust suspended in a gas acquires the same kinetic energy as the molecules; its velocity is very much less than those of the molecules because its mass is so much greater.

When gases are mixed their temperatures are equalised, as well as the mean kinetic energies of their molecules. Hence we can conclude that, at the same temperature, the mean kinetic energies of the molecules of all perfect gases are the same.

To deduce Avogadro's principle, suppose that equal volumes, $v$, of two gases at the same pressure, $p$, and at the same temperature, contain $n_1$ and $n_2$ molecules of masses $m_1$ and $m_2$ and of mean square velocities $\overline{c_1^2}$ and $\overline{c_2^2}$ respectively.

$$pv = \tfrac{1}{3}n_1 m_1 \overline{c_1^2} = \tfrac{1}{3}n_2 m_2 \overline{c_2^2}.$$

Since the temperatures are equal,

$$\tfrac{1}{2}m_1 \overline{c_1^2} = \tfrac{1}{2}m_2 \overline{c_2^2}.$$

$$\therefore n_1 = n_2.$$

## Determination of Avogadro's number and of the mass and size of an atom

Avogadro's number can be calculated from the known values of the charge of the electron (measured by Millikan's oil-drop experiment) and of the faraday, which is the charge carried by 1 gm of hydrogen in electrolysis.

$$\text{Charge of electron} = 1 \cdot 60 \times 10^{-19} \text{ coulomb,}$$

$$\text{Faraday} \qquad\quad = 96\,500 \text{ coulombs.}$$

∴ Number of atoms in 1 gm of hydrogen

$$= \frac{96\,500}{1 \cdot 60 \times 10^{-19}} = 6 \cdot 03 \times 10^{23}.$$

Avogadro's number is the number of molecules in 1 mole and this also is $6 \cdot 03 \times 10^{23}$ since 1 mole of hydrogen weighs 2 gm and contains half as many molecules as atoms.

From Avogadro's number the mass of an atom can be calculated.

$$\text{Mass of hydrogen atom} = \frac{1}{6 \cdot 03 \times 10^{23}} = 1 \cdot 66 \times 10^{-24} \text{ gm.}$$

To deduce an approximate size of an atom we can assume that, when a gas is liquefied, there is very little space between the atoms, because a liquid is almost incompressible. The density of liquids is of the order of 1 gm/c.c. and, if we assume this approximate value for liquid hydrogen, each hydrogen atom, of mass $1 \cdot 66 \times 10^{-24}$ gm, has a volume of about $1 \cdot 66 \times 10^{-24}$ c.c.

$$\therefore \text{Radius of hydrogen atom} = \left( \frac{1 \cdot 66 \times 10^{-24}}{\frac{4}{3}\pi} \right)^{\frac{1}{3}}$$

$$\simeq 10^{-8} \text{ cm.}$$

Another interesting calculation is that of the value at room temperature, say 15 °C, of $3/2\,kT$, the mean kinetic energy of translation of the molecules:

$$R = 8 \cdot 32 \text{ joules mole}^{-1} \text{ deg}^{-1} \text{ C (p. 53)}, \quad N = 6 \cdot 03 \times 10^{23}$$

and

$$T = 288 \text{ °K.}$$

Hence

$$\tfrac{3}{2}kT = \frac{3}{2} \frac{8 \cdot 32}{6 \cdot 03 \times 10^{23}} 288 = 5 \cdot 96 \times 10^{-21} \text{ joule;}$$

this is equal to 0·037 electron-volt (see footnote, p. 48).

**Other deductions from $pv = \frac{1}{3}nm\overline{c^2}$**

*Boyle's law*, that $pv = $ constant at constant temperature, follows directly from the above equation since $\frac{1}{3}nm\overline{c^2}$ is constant at constant temperature.

So also does *Dalton's law of partial pressures*, that the total pressure of a mixture of gases is equal to the sum of the pressures that each gas would exert if it were present alone in the complete volume of the mixture. If we worked out the pressure exerted by a mixture of two gases by the method on p. 74 we should obtain (with obvious nomenclature)

$$pv = \tfrac{1}{3}n_1 m_1 \overline{c_1^2} + \tfrac{1}{3}n_2 m_2 \overline{c_2^2},$$

and this is Dalton's law.

*Graham's law of diffusion* states that the rate of diffusion of a gas (e.g. through the porous wall of an unglazed vessel) is inversely proportional to the square root of the density of the gas. Consider unit volume of two gases at the same pressure having densities $\rho_1$ and $\rho_2$ and mean square velocities $\overline{c_1^2}$ and $\overline{c_2^2}$.

$$p = \tfrac{1}{3}\rho_1 \overline{c_1^2} \quad \text{and} \quad p = \tfrac{1}{3}\rho_2 \overline{c_2^2}$$

$$\sqrt{(\overline{c_1^2}/\overline{c_2^2})} = \sqrt{(\rho_2/\rho_1)}.$$

This is Graham's law, so long as we assume that the rate of diffusion of a gas is proportional to the velocity of the molecules. The diffusion rate is, of course, much slower than the velocity of the molecules because of the continual collisions as the molecules pass through the pores through which the gas is diffusing. The rate of diffusion is really proportional to the arithmetic mean of the velocities of the molecules, and not to the root mean square velocity, but the ratio of the arithmetic means is the same as the ratio of the root mean squares.

### Specific heat at constant volume of a monatomic gas

We have seen (p. 76) that the mean kinetic energy of the molecules of a gas is $\tfrac{3}{2}kT$, where $k$ is Boltzmann's constant. When the temperature of a gas rises by one degree the mean kinetic energy of each molecule increases by $\tfrac{3}{2}k$ and hence the molar specific heat of the gas at constant volume is $\tfrac{3}{2}k$ times the number of molecules, $N$, in 1 mole of the gas.

Molar specific heat of gas at constant volume

$$= \tfrac{3}{2}kN \text{ joules mole}^{-1} \text{ deg}^{-1} \text{ C}$$

$$= \tfrac{3}{2}R \text{ joules mole}^{-1} \text{ deg}^{-1} \text{ C} \quad (k = R/N)$$

$$= \tfrac{3}{2} \times 8\cdot 32 = 12\cdot 48 \text{ joules mole}^{-1} \text{ deg}^{-1} \text{ C}.$$

This expression agrees very well with the experimental values for monatomic gases. Argon, for example, has atomic weight 40, and the experimental value of the specific heat at constant volume is 0·312 joule gm$^{-1}$ deg$^{-1}$ C. Hence the molar specific heat is 40 × 0·312 = 12·48 joules mole$^{-1}$ deg$^{-1}$ C.

For the diatomic gases, having two atoms in each molecule, the expression does not hold. Hydrogen ($H_2$), of molecular weight 2, has a specific heat at constant volume of 10·0 joules gm$^{-1}$ deg$^{-1}$ C, giving a molar specific heat at constant volume of 20·0 joules mole$^{-1}$ deg$^{-1}$ C.

### Specific heat at constant volume of a diatomic gas

A monatomic molecule has three degrees of freedom corresponding to translational motion in three directions mutually at right angles. Maxwell's *law of the equipartition of energy* states that *the average energy of each degree of freedom of a system in equilibrium is the same for all the degrees of freedom*. The translational kinetic energy of a molecule is $\frac{3}{2}kT$ and this is $\frac{1}{2}kT$ for each degree of freedom.

Clausius suggested that the internal energy of a diatomic gas consists not only of the translational kinetic energy of the molecules but also of the rotational energy of the atoms composing the molecules. A diatomic molecule would be expected to have six degrees of freedom, three for translational motion and three for rotational motion about axes $OX$, $OY$ and $OZ$ in Fig. 38. The energy should be shared equally between these six degrees of freedom.

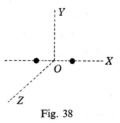

Fig. 38

But to explain the experimental values of the specific heats of diatomic gases, as we shall see, there can be only five degrees of freedom and this was regarded by Maxwell as one of the main weaknesses of the kinetic theory of gases. When, however, Rutherford put forward the nuclear theory of the atom in 1911 it was realised that, because of the minute size of the nucleus and the fact that nearly all the mass of each atom is contained in its nucleus, the moment of inertia of the molecule about the axis $OX$ in Fig. 38 is very much smaller than about the axes $OY$ and $OZ$. The quantum theory later explained why rotational motion should not occur at ordinary temperatures with so small a moment of inertia.

The pressure exerted by a diatomic gas is the result of the translational motion of the molecules. We have seen that the kinetic energy of translation of the molecules is $\frac{3}{2}kT$, which is $\frac{1}{2}kT$ for each degree of freedom. The total kinetic energy of translation and rotation of a diatomic molecule, with its five degrees of freedom, is therefore $\frac{5}{2}kT$.

Hence the molar specific heat at constant volume of a diatomic gas is $\frac{5}{2}R = 20\cdot8$ joules mole$^{-1}$ deg$^{-1}$ C. This agrees reasonably well with the experimental value for hydrogen of $20\cdot0$ joules mole$^{-1}$ deg$^{-1}$ C.

## Explanation of the value of $\gamma$

The experimental value of $\gamma$, the ratio of the principal specific heats, is about $1\cdot67$ for monatomic gases and about $1\cdot40$ for diatomic gases. This can be given a satisfying explanation as follows:

$$C_p = C_v + R \quad \text{(p. 57)}.$$

For a monatomic gas,

$$C_v = \tfrac{3}{2}R \text{ joules mole}^{-1} \text{ deg}^{-1} \text{ C},$$

$$C_p = \tfrac{3}{2}R + R = \tfrac{5}{2}R \text{ joules mole}^{-1} \text{ deg}^{-1} \text{ C}.$$

$$\therefore \gamma = \frac{C_p}{C_v} = \frac{5}{3} = 1\cdot67.$$

For a diatomic gas,

$$C_v = \tfrac{5}{2}R \text{ joules mole}^{-1} \text{ deg}^{-1} \text{ C},$$

$$C_p = \tfrac{5}{2}R + R = \tfrac{7}{2}R \text{ joules mole}^{-1} \text{ deg}^{-1} \text{ C}.$$

$$\therefore \gamma = \frac{C_p}{C_v} = \frac{7}{5} = 1\cdot40.$$

## Derivation of $pv^\gamma = $ constant for the adiabatic expansion of a monatomic gas

Consider a mass of monatomic gas containing $n$ molecules, at pressure $p$ and volume $v$, and let it expand adiabatically to a volume $v + dv$. The work done by the gas in expanding, $p\,dv$, is equal to the change in the internal energy, $-dE$, of the gas:

$$p\,dv = -dE.$$

But
$$pv = \tfrac{1}{3}nm\bar{c^2} \quad \text{(p. 75)}$$

$$= \tfrac{2}{3}\cdot\tfrac{1}{2}nm\bar{c^2}$$

$$= \tfrac{2}{3}E,$$

assuming that the internal energy, $E$, of the gas is equal to the total kinetic energy of translation of the molecules, $\tfrac{1}{2}nm\bar{c^2}$.

Differentiating, $\qquad p\,dv + v\,dp = \tfrac{2}{3}\,dE$

$$= -\tfrac{2}{3}\,p\,dv.$$

$$\therefore \frac{5}{3}\frac{dv}{v} + \frac{dp}{p} = 0.$$

Integrating, $\qquad \tfrac{5}{3}\log_e v + \log_e p = \text{constant},$

$$pv^{\frac{5}{3}} = \text{constant}.$$

## Atomic heats of solids

The kinetic theory explains the law, discovered by Dulong and Petit in 1819, that the product of the specific heat and atomic weight, known as the atomic heat, for most elements in the solid state at ordinary temperatures, is about 27 joules/gm atom/°C (p. 32).

The atoms in a solid may be pictured as vibrating about mean positions in a crystal lattice (see p. 86). Each atom has kinetic energy by virtue of its motion and potential energy by virtue of its position in the lattice. The atoms are analogous to heavy particles connected by light spiral springs and their potential energies to the work done in stretching or compressing the springs. The average value of an atom's potential energy is the same as the average value of its kinetic energy.

An atom has three degrees of freedom, in three directions mutually at right angles, for its kinetic energy, and three degrees of freedom for its potential energy, making six in all.

By the law of the equipartition of energy, when a solid is in equilibrium with a gas such as the air at the same temperature $T$, the energy associated with each degree of freedom of an atom of the solid is $\tfrac{1}{2}kT$. Hence the energy associated with six degrees of freedom is $3kT$ per atom. The atomic heat is $3k$ times the number of atoms in a gram atomic weight, namely $N$.

$\therefore$ Atomic heat

$$= 3kN \text{ joules/gm atom/°C}$$

$$= 3R \text{ joules/gm atom/°C} \quad (k = R/N)$$

$$= 25 \text{ joules/gm atom/°C}.$$

This agrees reasonably well with the law of Dulong and Petit but there are certain anomalous substances, such as diamond, for which the atomic heat is lower than 25. Moreover, the atomic heat of a substance should be the same at all temperatures whereas, in fact, the atomic heats of all substances become smaller with decreasing temperature and vanish at the absolute zero.

According to the quantum theory (p. 163) atoms do not take up energy continuously but in discrete amounts called quanta, of value $h\nu$ where $h$ is a universal constant and $\nu$ is a frequency of vibration of the atom. For most atoms at ordinary temperatures the quanta are small enough to be provided easily by the thermal vibrations of the surroundings. But in the case of a hard body like a diamond the quanta are so large, because of the high values of $\nu$, that equipartition of energy is not established at ordinary temperatures. At very low temperatures equipartition of energy breaks down for all substances because the energy available becomes comparable with the quanta of the atomic vibrations.

## The viscosity of gases

We will conclude this account of the kinetic theory of gases by discussing briefly two more of its triumphs: the explanations of the viscosity and of the thermal conductivity of a gas.

When a gas (or a liquid) flows in a tube there is a velocity gradient perpendicular to the axis of the tube as indicated in Fig. 39. The gas may be regarded as a series of layers, moving relative to each other, and each layer exerts forces on its two neighbouring layers, tending to slow down the faster-moving layer and accelerate the slower moving one. The phenomenon, known as *viscosity*, is the result of the transfer of momentum by molecules moving between the layers at right angles to the direction of flow. Molecules passing into a faster-moving layer gain momentum, while molecules passing into a slower-moving layer lose momentum, thereby causing the viscous drag between the layers.

The magnitude of the viscous drag between two layers, by Newton's second law of motion, is equal to the net rate of transfer of momentum between them. The mean distance between successive collisions of the molecules, known as the *mean free path*, $\lambda$, determines the distance between interacting layers of gas and, if $dv/dx$ is the velocity gradient in the gas, the difference in velocity of flow between interacting layers is $\lambda(dv/dx)$. The rate of transfer of momentum between layers is therefore proportional to $\lambda(dv/dx)$; it is proportional also to the number of molecules per unit volume, $n$, and to their mean velocity of translation, $\bar{c}$, which together determine the rate of interchange of molecules between the layers. Hence the viscous drag is proportional to $n\bar{c}\lambda(dv/dx)$.

If the pressure of the gas is increased at constant temperature, the mean free path, $\lambda$, diminishes in proportion as the number of molecules per unit volume, $n$, increases and hence $nc\lambda(dv/dx)$ is unchanged. The surprising deduction is reached that the viscosity of a gas should be the same at all pressures.

Although no one had shown much anxiety to investigate the viscosity of gases before the publication of this theory it was now seen to be of great interest. Maxwell devoted himself in the attic of his house in Kensington to observing the rate of decrement of the oscillations of circular plates suspended between fixed plates by a fine torsion wire under varying pressures (Fig. 40) and thereby confirmed the theory.

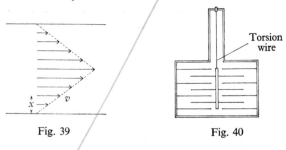

Torsion wire

| Fig. 39 | Fig. 40 |

It is significant that there comes a point, as the pressure of the gas is reduced, when the viscosity decreases; this occurs when the mean free path of the molecules is comparable with the distance between the plates.

A further prediction, also confirmed by experiment, was that the viscosity should increase as the temperature rises, because of the increase in velocity of translation $\bar{c}$ of the molecules. This too is surprising, in view of the fact that the viscosity of oil and of other liquids decreases with rise in temperature.

### The thermal conductivity of gases

A similar unexpected result followed from the application of the kinetic theory to the thermal conductivity of gases. In this case there is a temperature gradient, rather than a velocity gradient, and we are interested in the transfer of energy or heat, rather than of momentum by the molecules. By an argument similar to that for viscosity it can be shown that the rate of heat transfer is proportional to $n\bar{c}\lambda(d\theta/dx)$, where $d\theta/dx$ is the temperature gradient, and hence that the thermal conductivity is independent of the pressure; this also was confirmed by experiment. Belief in the general validity of the kinetic theory of gases was strongly reinforced by these successful predictions.

### The Brownian movement

A phenomenon which is now realised to be direct evidence of thermal molecular agitation, and to provide direct experimental proof of the principle of the equipartition of energy, is the Brownian movement. The botanist Brown discovered in 1827 that tiny grains of pollen, suspended in water, quivered with incessant, jigging motion. It was found that this occurs with all tiny particles (of diameter less than about $10^{-4}$ cm), and that the smaller the particle, or the higher the temperature, the more violent is the motion.

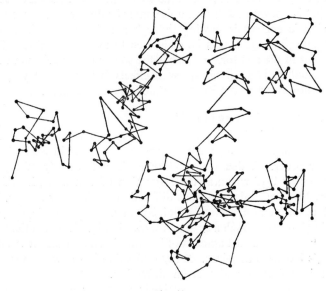

Fig. 41

The phenomenon can be demonstrated by viewing specks of indian ink in water with a high-power microscope; or cigarette smoke in a small black box, illuminated strongly from the side, with a low-power microscope.

Fig. 41 is a map made by Perrin showing the successive positions, every 2 min, of a tiny mastic grain suspended in water.

The cause of the Brownian movement is the unequal bombardment from different sides on a small particle by the molecules of the surrounding medium. By the principle of the equipartition of energy, the particle acquires the same kinetic energy as the molecules; as its mass is so much larger than theirs, its velocity is much smaller.

The distribution of the particles in a suspension obeys the same laws as the variation of the pressure of the atmosphere with height (p. 67). By counting the number of particles in different horizontal layers of a colloidal suspension, Perrin was able to confirm the theory (including equipartition) and also to deduce a value for Avogadro's number.

The Brownian movement sets a limit to the use of measuring instruments; the light, delicately suspended mirror of a very sensitive galvanometer, for example, trembles incessantly. Many modern measuring instruments operate close to their ultimate limit. Electronic amplifiers can now be made so sensitive that they are subject to what is known as Johnson noise, after its discoverer. Even when no electric current is flowing through a resistor there is a small fluctuating voltage across its ends, due to random motions of the electrons in the resistor, and this is the source of the Johnson noise.

The only way to minimise such effects is to work at very low temperatures, when the Brownian movement is reduced.

### The crystalline structure of solids

The geometrical shape of crystals suggests that the atoms or molecules of which they are composed are arranged in some kind of regular order. A decisive break-through in the study of crystals occurred in 1912 when, at the suggestion of von Laue, it was discovered that crystals behave as diffraction gratings for X-rays. The kind of diffraction pattern obtained on a photographic plate by passing X-rays through a crystal is shown in Fig. 42. From the study of such patterns a vast amount of information about the structure of crystals has been acquired. X-ray diffraction has now been supplemented by electron and neutron diffraction.

It has been found that practically all solids are crystalline in structure. If the surface of a metal is polished, etched with acid and examined under a microscope, it will be seen to consist of minute crystal grains, whose size depends on the previous treatment of the metal. A few apparently solid substances such as glass and plastics are not crystalline; they give no sharp diffraction pattern but only a broad hazy ring, showing that their molecules are not arranged in regular patterns. They may therefore be regarded, not as solids, but as supercooled liquids; from this point of view all solids are crystalline.

The constituents of a crystal may be atoms, molecules or ions (e.g. atoms which have lost or gained an electron) and they are arranged in what are known as *lattices*, which are repeated over and over again like the bricks forming a wall. The simplest type of lattice is the cubic structure in which the atoms are at the eight corners of a cube. A slightly more complicated type is the body-centred cubic structure (Fig. 43) in which there is an additional atom at the centre of the cube; this is a characteristic of sodium and the alkali metals, iron, etc. Another type is the face-centred cubic structure (Fig. 44)

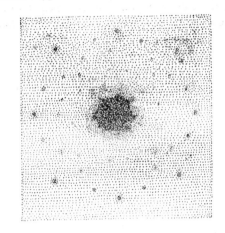

Fig. 42

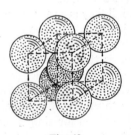

Fig. 43

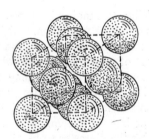

Fig. 44

in which there are additional atoms at the centres of the faces of the cube; this is characteristic of copper, silver, aluminium, etc. Many metals have a hexagonal lattice and not a cubic one.

A simple type of ionic crystal is rock salt (sodium chloride, NaCl); this contains no molecules as such but $Na^+$ ions and $Cl^-$ ions, in a face-centred cubic structure (Fig. 45).

The gravitational forces between the constituents of a crystal are negligible compared with the bonding forces which hold the crystal together. In ionic lattices the bonding forces are electrostatic, the attraction between the positive and negative charges: in atomic lattices the bonding forces are of a chemical nature, e.g. as a result of the sharing of electrons by covalent atoms; and in molecular lattices each molecule, although electrically neutral, behaves like an electric dipole (i.e. two, equal, point electric charges of opposite sign, separated by a small distance) because of the effect of neighbouring molecules in displacing the cloud of electrons surrounding the nucleus.

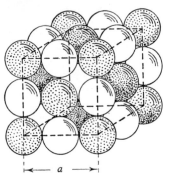

Fig. 45

When two molecules approach each other there is at first a force of attraction between them which is small until they are very close and then changes to a strong force of repulsion (Fig. 46). The distance apart of similar molecules, when the forces of attraction and repulsion annul each other, may be regarded as the diameter of each molecule. It is therefore possible to represent the molecules (or atoms or ions) of a crystal by spheres, which normally attract each other but resist being pushed too closely together. X-ray analysis shows the diameter to be of the order of $10^{-8}$ cm for simple molecules, the same value that we obtained in the approximate calculation on p. 78.

Two molecules in equilibrium at a distance apart equal to their diameter, if pulled farther apart, would oscillate about their positions of equilibrium. The constituents of a lattice execute vibrations about their mean positions, whose amplitude increases with temperature, eventually becoming so large that the lattice breaks up and the solid changes to a liquid.

The volume of a liquid is usually only a few per cent greater or less than that of the solid. Hence the molecules in a liquid are at about the same distance apart as in the solid but they are no longer arranged in a regular pattern and they can move about comparatively freely. This explains the two chief properties of a liquid, its small compressibility and its complete lack of rigidity.

### Explanation of macroscopic properties of solids and liquids

The elasticity of a solid below the elastic limit shows that the crystal lattices can be temporarily distorted by a stress and that they return to their original condition when the stress is removed. Permanent distortion of the solid (beyond the elastic limit) shows that slipping in the crystals can occur.

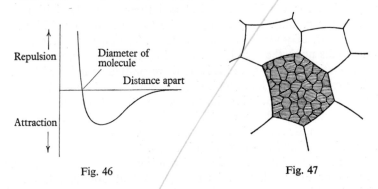

Fig. 46                    Fig. 47

Among the most elastic, and at the same time the most tough, materials are the metals. The metals owe their lack of brittleness to the ease with which their atoms can slip past each other. A single crystal of a metal is quite weak. A rod of cadmium, for example, treated so as to be in the form of a single crystal, can be stretched by the fingers up to five times its original length; it pulls out into a stepped flat strip, indicating that there has been slipping between a large number of parallel crystal planes.

A simple demonstration of the weakness of large metal crystals is to hold a thin copper wire horizontally and to run a bunsen flame along it, thereby annealing it into a number of quite perfect crystals. The wire is then so soft that it will bend if a small weight is hung on the far end. On being bent back it will support the weight and after being bent backwards and forwards several times it becomes quite stiff. The bending breaks up the crystals into a larger number of smaller crystals and this is responsible for the increased rigidity. Fig. 47 shows the fragmentation of a metal crystal by mechanical treatment, known as cold work.

M H

In a similar way the properties of other metals, particularly of iron and steel, can be considerably varied by different kinds of heat or mechanical treatment. They can also be varied by the addition of different kinds of atoms into the lattices, as in steel alloys. It is a general rule that the purer the metal the weaker it is.

Crystals are seldom perfect and they contain faults known as dislocations which may give rise to the breakage of a metal component in a machine, after being subjected to a long period of rapidly varying stress, a phenomenon known as metal fatigue.

In the atomic lattices of metals, the valency electrons can move readily from each atom to its neighbours. These free electrons are responsible for the high electrical and thermal conductivities of metals (see p. 142). They also give rise to the lustre, or ability to reflect light, of polished metallic surfaces. The energy of the light which falls upon the metal is absorbed by the electrons, setting up sympathetic vibrations, and it is partly re-emitted as reflected light.

The expansion of solids with rise in temperature is caused by the increase in the thermal vibrations of the constituents of a lattice and it is greatest for those solids in which the bonding forces are small—when the trough in Fig. 46 is shallow. In co-valent solids the trough is deep and the expansion is small.

The melting point of a solid also depends upon the bonding forces. Carbon or diamond, with its strong covalent bonding, has the highest melting point of all solids and, for the same reason, it is the hardest of all solids.

When a solid melts, work must be done to separate the molecules or atoms from their fixed positions in the lattice and this represents the latent heat of fusion. Similarly, when a liquid evaporates, the molecules escaping from the surface must have sufficient energy to overcome the attraction of the molecules in the boundary layers of the surface and this loss of energy by the liquid is the latent heat of vaporisation (see p. 119).

The subject-matter of the past few pages is an elementary part of a comparatively new and flourishing branch of physics known as Physics of the Solid State.

## QUESTIONS

1. Explain qualitatively, in terms of the simple kinetic theory:
    (a) why a gas exerts a pressure on the walls of its container;
    (b) why the pressure increases if the volume is reduced at constant temperature;

(c) why the pressure increases if the temperature is increased at constant volume;

(d) why the temperature of the gas rises if the gas is compressed in a container from which heat cannot escape.

2. State the differences in molecular properties of a perfect gas and of a real gas.

3. (a) Deduce the expression $p = \frac{1}{3}\rho\overline{c^2}$ for a perfect gas. What is the significance of $\overline{c^2}$ as compared with $c^2$?

(b) Given that 14 gm of nitrogen at s.t.p. occupy a volume of 22·4 l. calculate the root mean square velocity of the molecules. (Standard atmospheric pressure = $10^6$ dyne $cm^{-2}$.)

4. Use the expression $pv = \frac{1}{3}nm\overline{c^2}$ to explain quantitatively:
   (a) Boyle's law,
   (b) Graham's law of diffusion,
   (c) the significance of temperature.

5. A piston, compressing a gas in a cylinder, moves with velocity $v$. With what velocity will a molecule, striking the piston with a perpendicular velocity $c$, rebound? How does this explain the heating of a gas by compression?

6. Calculate the specific heat at constant volume of the following, given that $R/J = 2$ cal $mole^{-1}$ $deg^{-1}$ C, where $R$ is the gas constant and $J$ is the mechanical equivalent of heat:
   (a) The monatomic gas helium, of atomic weight 4.
   (b) The diatomic gas nitrogen of molecular weight 28.
Calculate also the specific heats at constant pressure, given that $\gamma$ for a monatomic gas is 1·67 and for a diatomic gas 1·40.

7. Why is the ratio of the specific heats at constant pressure and at constant volume different for diatomic gases and for monatomic gases?

8. Show that the experimental result that the thermal conductivity of a gas is independent of its pressure is strong confirmation of the postulates of the kinetic theory.

9. Explain what is meant by the Brownian movement.
What important theoretical conclusions can be established from its investigation and what are its practical implications for scientific measurements?

10. State the postulates on which the simple kinetic theory of gases is based and use the theory to derive an expression for the pressure of an ideal gas. What direct evidence is there for the kinetic theory of matter?
Calculate the temperature at which oxygen molecules have the same root-mean-square velocity as that of hydrogen molecules at $-100$ °C, given that the molecular weights of hydrogen and oxygen are 2 and 32 respectively and that both gases may be considered to be ideal. (N.)

11. Show that the perfect-gas equation may be deduced directly from the kinetic theory of gases. Deduce an expression for the density of a gas in terms of the pressure, temperature, and molecular weight.

Helium is stored in a cylinder at 200 atm pressure. The volume of the cylinder is 30 l. and its temperature 15 °C. How many atoms are there in the cylinder; what is their r.m.s. velocity; and what is the mass of gas stored?

(Gas constant $= 8.4 \times 10^7$ ergs per mole per °C. Avogadro's number $= 6.02 \times 10^{23}$ per mole. Atomic weight of helium $= 4$. Density of mercury $= 13.6$ gm/c.c.) (O. & C.)

12. Show how the kinetic theory explains qualitatively:
   (a) the pressure of a gas;
   (b) the viscosity of a gas;
   (c) the distinction between solids, liquids and gases (including an explanation of latent heat of vaporisation).

Assuming that the r.m.s. velocity of hydrogen molecules is $1.84 \times 10^5$ cm sec$^{-1}$ at 0 °C, calculate the r.m.s. velocity of oxygen molecules at 16 °C, given that the molecular weights of hydrogen and oxygen are 2 and 32 respectively and that both gases may be considered to be ideal. (N.)

13. How would you try to convince someone without scientific training that a gas consists of molecules?

What justification is there for Avogadro's hypothesis that equal volumes of gas measured at the same temperature and pressure contain equal numbers of molecules? How is Avogadro's number measured? (O.S.)

14. Using the simple kinetic theory of gases, derive an expression for the pressure exerted by an ideal gas and indicate how this is related to the kinetic energy of translation of the molecules contained in unit volume of the gas.

The temperature of a sample of gas, which may be assumed to behave ideally, is raised from 0 to 1 °C at constant volume. Using the data given below calculate what proportion of the total heat energy supplied to the gas takes the form of energy of translation of the molecules according to whether the gas is (a) argon, (b) oxygen.

Comment on the physical significance of your results.

| | Argon | Oxygen |
|---|---|---|
| Density at s.t.p. in gm per litre | 1·78 | 1·43 |
| Specific heat at constant volume in cal per gm per deg C | 0·075 | 0·156 |

(Standard atmospheric pressure $= 10^6$ dynes cm$^{-2}$; J $= 4.18 \times 10^7$ ergs cal$^{-1}$.) (N.)

15. Give a qualitative argument in terms of the kinetic theory to show that the number of molecules striking unit area of the containing vessel is proportional to the concentration of molecules and to their mean velocity.

Two vessels at different temperatures, containing the same gas at low pressure, are connected by a small aperture. By assuming that any molecule that falls upon the aperture passes from one vessel to the other, show that the gas is in equilibrium if the pressure in each vessel is proportional to the square root of the absolute temperature of the gas in that vessel.

What would be the ratio of the pressures in the two vessels if the aperture was large? (N.)

16. A specimen of nitrogen containing 10 % by weight of radon gas is sealed into a tube at a pressure of $10^6$ dyne $cm^{-2}$. The radon undergoes radioactive decay leaving only a solid deposit of negligible volume. Calculate the pressure of the gas when the radon has all decayed, if the temperature is unaltered.

(Mol.wt. of nitrogen = 28. Mol.wt. of radon = 222.) (C.S.)

17. Write a short essay on the kinetic theory of gases. A tank contains hydrogen at n.t.p. and has a small hole of area 1 mm² in it. Estimate the number of hydrogen molecules escaping from the tank per second. Make any critical remarks you can about the accuracy of your estimate.

(There are $6.0 \times 10^{23}$ molecules in 1 gm mol. The gas constant $R = 8.3 \times 10^7$ ergs/gm mol/°C.)

Hint. To a first approximation it can be assumed that $\frac{1}{6}$th of the molecules move towards the hole (see p. 73): hence number per unit area $= \frac{1}{6}n\bar{c}$. However, treating the problem more rigidly and allowing for the molecules reaching the hole from all directions, number per unit area $= \frac{1}{4}n\bar{c}$. (C.S.)

18. Describe any experiment which in your opinion shows in rather a direct way that matter is composed of discrete molecules.

Show how the r.m.s. velocity of the molecules of a gas may be calculated, and evaluate this quantity for helium at 0 °C. Use your result to estimate the temperature beyond which helium would not be retained in the atmosphere of the earth.

(Atomic weight of helium = 4·00; gram-molecular volume at n.t.p. = 22·4 litres; pressure of 1 atm = $1.014 \times 10^6$ dyn $cm^{-2}$; radius of earth = $6.38 \times 10^8$ cm; $g = 981$ cm $sec^{-2}$.)

Hint. Show that the velocity of escape from the earth is $\sqrt{(2gR)}$, where $R$ is the earth's radius. (C.S.)

19. Explain why the specific heat of a gas at constant pressure is not equal to its specific heat at constant volume. Show that the specific heat of an ideal diatomic gas at constant volume is $5R/2$ per mole.

An ideal gas is heated under such conditions that the product of pressure and absolute temperature is kept constant. What is the difference between the specific heat under these conditions and the specific heat at constant volume? (O.S.)

20. Show that for an adiabatic change in a perfect gas, $pV^\gamma = $ constant, where $\gamma = C_p/C_v$.

A mixture of 1 mole of argon ($\gamma = \frac{5}{3}$) and 1 mole of oxygen ($\gamma = \frac{7}{5}$) is initially at 300 °K and occupies a volume of 10 l. Find the effective value of $\gamma$ for the mixture. If the volume is adiabatically reduced to 5 l., calculate the final temperature. (C.S.)

21. The atoms in a crystal of a certain element are arranged in a cubic lattice (i.e. so that each atom is at the same distance from its nearest neighbours, which lie along each of three mutually perpendicular directions). If the spacing between neighbouring atoms is $3.0 \times 10^{-8}$ cm, the density of the crystal is $11.0$ gm cm$^{-3}$ and the atomic weight of the element is 180, calculate the value of Avogadro's number.　　　　　(C.S.)

CHAPTER 6

# DEVIATIONS FROM THE GAS LAWS AND LIQUEFACTION

The so-called permanent gases, such as hydrogen, oxygen and nitrogen, behave very like a perfect gas and obey Boyle's law quite accurately at normal laboratory pressures and temperatures. These gases were called permanent because no one could liquefy them until towards the end of the nineteenth century. The last gas to be liquefied was helium and its liquefaction was not achieved until 1908.

Other gases, such as sulphur dioxide, carbon dioxide, ammonia and chlorine, which are fairly easy to liquefy, exhibit marked deviations from Boyle's law under moderate pressures at room temperature. This suggests that deviations from Boyle's law and ease of liquefaction are closely related. A number of physicists and chemists in the nineteenth century devoted much effort to investigating both phenomena.

### Regnault's experiments

Prominent among the first investigators of deviations from Boyle's law was Regnault, whose earliest experiments were performed in 1847. In order that a measurable deviation should occur with a permanent gas, very considerable pressures are required. Regnault measured pressures of up to 14 atm by means of a column of mercury, about 30 ft high. One of the chief problems in experiments of this kind is that, as the pressure is increased, the volume becomes smaller and smaller (being reduced to about $\frac{1}{14}$th when the pressure is increased to 14 atm), with the result that the percentage accuracy in measuring the volume is continuously reduced. This is very serious when what is being sought consists, not of the volume itself, but of small deviations from the calculated volume for a perfect gas.

Regnault overcame the difficulty by pumping in more gas as the pressure was increased. His apparatus is indicated in Fig. 48. The gas was contained in a strong glass tube *ABC* and it was compressed by forcing in mercury by means of water from a force pump. The pressure was measured by the height of the mercury in the manometer tube *M*. The glass tube containing the gas had marks at *B* and *C* such that the volume *AB* was exactly half the volume *AC*. Surrounding the glass tube was a water bath to keep its temperature constant.

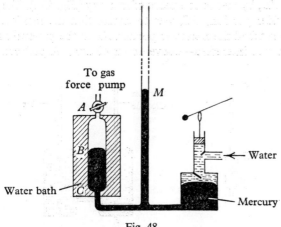

Fig. 48

Initially the gas had a volume *AC* and it was compressed until its volume was *AB*. More gas was then pumped in through the tap at *A* until the volume was again *AC*. The process was repeated as often as possible.

If Boyle's law were exactly obeyed, each time the volume of the gas was halved the pressure should have been doubled. Regnault found that at high pressures, for air and nitrogen, the pressure was not quite doubled. These gases became more compressible and the product *pv* decreased. Hydrogen, however, behaved in an anomalous manner, and became slightly less compressible at high pressures, the product *pv* increasing. This drew from Regnault the remark that hydrogen seemed to be a 'more than perfect gas'.

The deviations for the permanent gases were quite small. For air and nitrogen *pv* decreased by about 1 % at the highest pressure; for hydrogen it increased by about 1 %. On the other hand, the decrease for carbon dioxide was over 25 %.

### Andrews's experiments

In 1863 Andrews began his fundamental investigations on carbon dioxide. Since he was dealing with a gas whose deviations from Boyle's law were very considerable he had no need to adopt Regnault's device of increasing the mass of the gas as the pressure was increased. His experiments involved the liquefying of the gas and revealed important relations between the gaseous and liquid states.

The carbon dioxide was confined in a strong, thick-walled capillary tube $ABCD$, by means of a pellet of mercury (Fig. 49$a$). The purpose of the wider portion, $BC$, was to ensure that the meniscus of the mercury reached the narrower portion $AB$ at the pressures in which Andrews was interested—above about 40 atm. A preliminary cali-

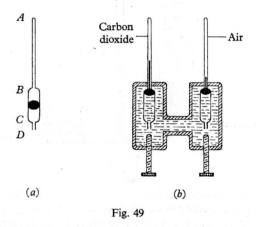

Fig. 49

bration of the bore of $AB$, by measuring the length of a thread of mercury in different parts of the tube, enabled the volumes of the carbon dioxide to be determined.

The tube was mounted, together with a similar tube containing air, in a strong metal vessel full of water (Fig. 49$b$). The pressure on the carbon dioxide and on the air was applied by forcing water into the tubes by means of screw plungers. The pressure was measured by observing the volume of the air, assuming that air obeys Boyle's law. The whole apparatus was enclosed in a water bath and a series of values of $p$ and $v$ at different temperatures was obtained.

Fig. 50 represents Andrews's results. Each continuous line is an isothermal, representing how the pressure and volume of a fixed mass of carbon dioxide vary at constant temperature. Considering the lowest isothermal at 13·1 °C, the portion *PQ* represents carbon-dioxide vapour; along the horizontal portion *QR* where the pressure remains constant and the volume decreases, the vapour is liquefying; at *R* the vapour is completely liquefied and *RS* is nearly vertical, the liquid being almost incompressible. We shall distinguish between a gas and a vapour shortly. Along *PQ* the vapour is said to be unsaturated and along *QR* it is saturated (p. 112).

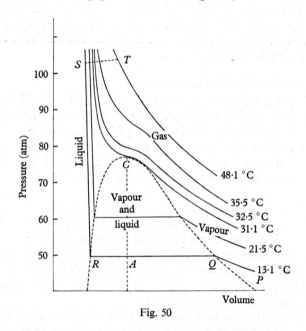

Fig. 50

The next isothermal, at 21·5 °C, has a shorter horizontal portion because the vapour has a higher density when it begins to liquefy (the volume being smaller at a higher pressure than at *Q*), and hence there is a smaller change of volume on liquefaction.

The isothermal at 31·1 °C is the first isothermal, as we proceed from lower to higher temperatures, without a horizontal portion. The vapour showed no signs of liquefying along this isothermal. The temperature above which a gas cannot be liquefied, whatever the applied pressure, is called the *critical temperature*. Andrews found that the critical temperature for carbon dioxide was 31·1 °C. He suggested that above the critical temperature the carbon dioxide should be called a gas, and below the critical temperature, when in the gaseous state, it should be called a vapour.

Thus in Fig. 50 all points above the critical isothermal at 31·1 °C represent gas; to the right of the dotted line $CQ$ and below the critical isothermal, vapour; within the dotted line $RCQ$, a mixture of liquid and vapour; to the left of the dotted line $RC$ and below the critical isothermal, liquid.

The chief importance of Andrews's experiments was their demonstration of the significance of the critical temperature, demonstrated earlier by Cagniard de la Tour, but not fully understood. It became clear why attempts to liquefy the permanent gases, employing pressures of over 2000 atm, had failed. The gases had not been cooled below their critical temperatures.

**Demonstration of critical temperature**

A simple demonstration of the behaviour of the liquid and the vapour at the critical temperature can be made with a strong glass tube (Fig. 51) about half-filled with a liquid such as carbon dioxide, sulphur dioxide or ether, all air having been expelled from the tube so that the liquid is in equilibrium with its vapour. As the tube is slowly warmed a little of the liquid evaporates and the meniscus descends slightly in the tube. At the critical temperature there is a curious flickering in the tube and the meniscus disappears. This is not a question of the liquid having all evaporated and the meniscus reaching the bottom of the tube. The states of the liquid and the gas have attained the same density at the critical temperature and they become indistinguishable; this is sometimes called the continuity of state.

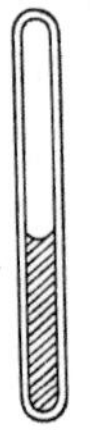

Fig. 51

The contents of the tube pass along the vertical line $AC$ in Fig. 50. With rise of temperature there is an increase of pressure at constant volume, both liquid and vapour being present, until the critical temperature is reached.

The critical pressure for carbon dioxide is 73 atm and the pressure inside the tube will exceed this above the critical temperature. It is therefore essential to protect the class and the demonstrator from a possible explosion. The best arrangement is to project an image of the tube and its contents on to a screen, and to erect round the tube an effective shield.

**Amagat's experiments**

From 1869 to 1893 Amagat carried out a series of classic experiments on the deviations of the permanent gases from Boyle's law. He measured pressures up to about 400 atm by means of a column of mercury 300 m high in a steel tube supported in a mine shaft, and pressures up to about 3000 atm with a new instrument, the principle of which is indicated in Fig. 52.

A double piston $AB$ 'floats' in equilibrium between the high pressure to be measured and a lower pressure which can be measured with a mercury manometer. Suppose that these two pressures are $p_1$ and $p_2$ and that the corresponding areas of cross-section of the piston are $a_1$ and $a_2$. Then $p_1 a_1 = p_2 a_2$, from which $p_1$ can be calculated if $a_1$, $a_2$ and $p_2$ are known. Amagat successfully surmounted the

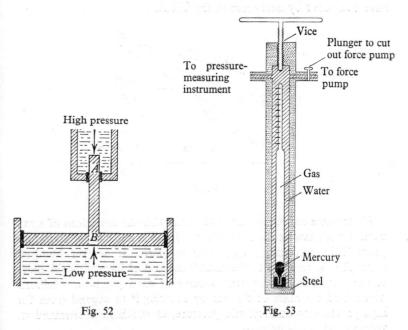

Fig. 52                    Fig. 53

chief technical difficulty of preventing leaks at the sides of the piston, making use of treacle for this purpose, and prevented the piston from sticking by keeping it rotating.

Above about 400 atm a glass tube will not withstand the pressure from the inside only and Amagat surrounded his glass tube with a strong steel cylinder in which an equal pressure was applied (Fig. 53). Since the glass tube was then invisible, Amagat measured the volume of the gas by sealing fine platinum wires through the walls, so that the mercury, as the gas was compressed, made electrical contacts at predetermined volumes. The complete electrical circuits are not indicated in Fig. 53 for the sake of clarity.

The gas was compressed at first by forcing in water with a force pump and then by means of the vice at the top. The glass tube was longer and narrower than indicated in Fig. 53; the volume of the gas was reduced to about $\frac{1}{3000}$th of its original volume. The temperature of the apparatus was kept constant by a bath in which water circulated.

The study of the properties of materials at high pressure, in which Amagat initiated several of the modern techniques, is now a well-established branch of physics, and pressures exceeding 100000 atm have been used by Bridgman in the U.S.A.

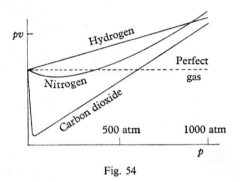

Fig. 54

We are here concerned, however, only with the deviations of a gas from Boyle's law at high pressures. Holborn and his collaborators (from 1915 onwards), who used pressures of several hundred atmospheres, reverted to Regnault's method of increasing the mass of the gas, using a constant volume at each pressure. Holborn determined the mass of the gas by allowing it to expand from the high pressure to atmospheric pressure, at which he determined its volume and hence its mass.

Deviations from Boyle's law are best shown by plotting $pv$ against $p$. If Boyle's law is accurately obeyed, $pv$ is constant and the graph is a straight line parallel to the pressure axis. Some of Amagat's results are shown in Fig. 54; the graphs refer to a constant temperature of 0 °C. It will be seen that $pv$ for hydrogen increases with $p$, as Regnault discovered. But for nitrogen and carbon dioxide, at higher pressures than Regnault could command, the decrease in $pv$ changes to an increase; the graphs descend to a minimum value and then rise at higher pressures.

We can explain the rise of the graphs as a result of the finite size of the molecules, which becomes more and more significant as the pressure of the gas increases and the volume decreases. If the pressure of the gas is doubled the number of collisions per second of the molecules on the walls of the containing vessel must be doubled and hence the space between the molecules must be halved. But the volume of the gas is less than halved because the volume of the molecules themselves remains constant. Hence $pv$ increases.

The initial drop of $pv$ in the graphs for nitrogen and carbon dioxide can be explained in terms of the mutual attractions of the molecules. These intermolecular attractions cause the molecules at the boundary of the gas to be drawn inwards and give rise to a slight shrinkage in the volume. Hence $pv$ decreases. We should expect the shrinkage to be greater at higher pressure because the gas is then more dense and the inward pull on the molecules at the boundary is greater. At the pressures of the minima in the curves for nitrogen and carbon dioxide in Fig. 54, the effect of the finite size of the molecules exactly counterbalances the effect of the intermolecular attractions. At higher pressures the effect of the intermolecular attractions is less than, and is masked by, the effect of the finite size of the molecules.

But why does hydrogen not show an initial decrease in $pv$? The intermolecular forces are not very effective unless the molecules remain near to each other for an appreciable time. Since hydrogen is the lightest known substance, its molecules travel more swiftly at a given temperature than those of any other gas. When the temperature is lowered the molecules move less swiftly and the effect of intermolecular attraction should increase. It is found that, at a sufficiently low temperature, hydrogen does show an initial decrease in $pv$ similar to that for nitrogen and carbon dioxide. This is clearly related to the fact that the critical temperature of hydrogen, below which it cannot be liquefied, is very low, $-240$ °C. The critical temperatures of nitrogen and carbon dioxide are $-146$ and $31 \cdot 1$ °C respectively.

To summarise, all gases under increasing pressure are at first more compressible, and then less compressible, than a perfect gas so long as their temperatures are sufficiently near to their liquefying points. There is no fundamental difference between the behaviour of the permanent gases and of those which are more easily liquefiable.

For every gas there is a characteristic temperature, known as the *Boyle temperature*, for which Boyle's law is quite closely obeyed, i.e. $pv$ is constant, over a wide range of pressures. At the Boyle temperature the effects due to the finite size of the molecules and to intermolecular attractions counterbalance.

### Van der Waals's equation

The equation of state for a perfect gas is $pV = RT$. The first, and in many ways the most useful, modification of this equation to apply to real gases was made by van der Waals in a doctoral dissertation at the University of Leyden in 1873.

Van der Waals introduced terms into the equation to represent the effect of the finite size of the molecules and of the intermolecular attractions. Because of the finite size of the molecules, the number of collisions between the molecules and the walls of the containing vessel is increased, and this is equivalent to a reduction in the volume of the gas. Hence van der Waals replaced the term $V$ by $(V-b)$, where $b$ is a small constant characteristic of the gas.

He assumed that the forces between the molecules were appreciable only over short distances. In the interior of the gas the average attractive force on a molecule is the same in all directions but molecules near the boundary of the gas are attracted inwards. The number of molecules on the boundary and the number attracting them inwards are both proportional to the density, $\rho$, of the gas. Hence the inward force is proportional to $\rho^2$, i.e. proportional to $1/V^2$. The pressure of the gas must therefore be replaced by $[p+(a/V^2)]$, where $a$ is a small constant characteristic of the gas. Van der Waals's equation is

$$[p+(a/V^2)]\,(V-b) = RT.$$

Thus a real gas of volume $V$ under a pressure $p$ may be regarded as equivalent to a perfect gas of volume $(V-b)$ under a pressure $[p+(a/V^2)]$.

The general form of the curves obtained by plotting $p$ against $V$ for different values of $T$ in this equation are shown in Fig. 55. They possess a marked resemblance to the experimental curves obtained by Andrews for carbon dioxide, except that the horizontal straight portions of Andrews's curves, where the vapour was liquefying, represented by $DH$ in Fig. 55, are replaced by wave-like portions, $DEFGH$.

The wave-like portions can be given a physical explanation. $DE$ represents a supersaturated vapour and $GH$ a supercooled liquid, both of which can be realised experimentally. $EFG$ cannot be realised experimentally; it represents an unstable condition.

Many other equations, alternative to that of van der Waals, have been put forward but none of them have achieved an equal simplicity, usefulness, or approximate validity for so many substances over so wide a range of temperatures and pressures.

**Joule's experiments to detect internal work when a gas expands**

In 1845 Joule carried out experiments to detect any internal work which might be done when a gas expands, as a result of the mutual attractions of its molecules. His determination of the mechanical equivalent of heat by compressing a gas involved equating the work done by the compressor on the gas to the heat gained by the gas. He realised that if the molecules, when they were pushed closer together

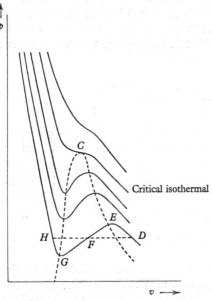

Fig. 55

by compression of the gas, attracted each other appreciably, their kinetic energy would increase, and this would vitiate his determination of the mechanical equivalent of heat.

The apparatus used in his first experiment is shown in Fig. 56. Two copper vessels, $A$ and $B$, connected by a pipe with a stopcock, were immersed in water in a calorimeter, so shaped that the mass of water was as small as possible. $A$ was filled with air at a pressure of 22 atm, and $B$ was evacuated. The stopcock was opened, and some of the air in $A$ rushed into $B$. No external work was done by the gas and any decrease in the heat content of the gas must have been the result of the using up of some of the kinetic energy of the molecules, to separate them against their mutual attractions. Joule found no change of temperature of the water in his calorimeter and hence no effect of intermolecular attractions.

In his second experiment Joule immersed vessels $A$ and $B$ in separate calorimeters. He found a slight fall in temperature in the calorimeter containing $A$ and a slight rise in that containing $B$. Work was done by the gas in $A$ in forcing some of itself into $B$ against the pressure of the gas which had already entered, while work was done *on* this gas already in $B$ by the later incoming gas. Joule found that the heat lost by $A$ was equal to that gained by $B$.

Although Joule measured his temperatures to $\frac{1}{200}$ °F his experiments were not very sensitive. He drew the conclusion, sometimes known as Joule's law for gases, that when a gas expands without

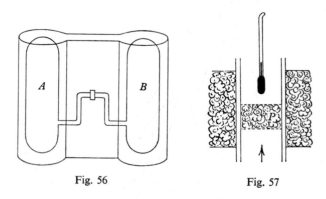

Fig. 56                    Fig. 57

doing external work and without taking in or giving out heat (i.e. adiabatically), its temperature remains unchanged. This may be expressed in the form that the internal energy of a gas depends upon its temperature only.

### The Joule–Kelvin porous-plug experiment

There was little doubt that some mutual attractions between the molecules of a gas must exist, and in 1852 William Thomson (later Lord Kelvin) suggested a sensitive experiment, which he and Joule performed jointly, known as the porous-plug experiment. A plug of cotton wool, $P$ (Fig. 57), was held in position by two perforated brass plates in a lagged boxwood tube (for thermal insulation). A gas at a known temperature and at a pressure of several atmospheres was forced slowly through $P$, the pressure on the other side of $P$ being atmospheric. A sensitive thermometer recorded the temperature of the gas after passing through $P$.

It was found that, in general, there was a slight fall in temperature of the gas, proportional to the difference in pressures on the two sides of the plug, and depending on the initial temperature of the gas. This is known as the Joule–Kelvin or Joule–Thomson effect. At room temperature the fall in temperature, for a difference in pressure of 1 atm, was about 0·2 °C for air and about 1·0 °C for carbon dioxide. But for hydrogen there was a *rise* in temperature of about 0·04 °C.

Once again hydrogen was behaving in an anomalous manner. An attraction between the molecules of a gas must result in a fall in temperature in the porous-plug experiment, because work must be done to separate the molecules, and it was clear that there was some other effect at work. This effect, as might be expected, is connected with the fact that hydrogen at room temperature deviates from Boyle's law differently from other gases.

The explanation of the effect, which we shall not give in detail, is that work must be done *on* the gas to push it through the plug and *by* the gas, at a lower pressure, to make room for itself on the far side. In the cases of air and carbon dioxide the latter is the greater, causing a cooling of the gas and augmenting the effect due to intermolecular attractions. In the case of hydrogen the former is the greater, causing a heating of the gas and masking the effect due to inter-molecular attractions.

At a temperature of − 80 °C hydrogen comes into line with other gases and exhibits a fall in temperature, instead of a rise, in the porous-plug experiment. Also it is found that all gases, on reaching a characteristic temperature known as the *inversion temperature* (dependent to some extent on the pressure), behave like hydrogen above − 80 °C, and exhibit a rise in temperature in the porous-plug experiment. The inversion temperature of air, for example, is 100 °C.

### The liquefaction of gases

Throughout the nineteenth century the fact that certain gases could not be liquefied was a constant challenge. The obvious method of liquefaction, to cool and compress the gas, left oxygen, nitrogen and hydrogen without sign of liquefaction, even under enormous pressures. The explanation was provided by Andrews's experiments: however high the pressure, a gas cannot be liquefied unless it is cooled below its critical temperature, and the earliest attempts to liquefy these gases were made at temperatures above the critical temperatures. Table 5 shows boiling points, critical temperatures and critical pressures. (The pressures required to liquefy the gases at temperatures below their critical temperatures are lower than the critical pressures.)

The table suggests the method, known as the *cascade process*, adopted by the earliest successful investigators. Gases were liquefied one by one in the order of difficulty, and the liquid of each was used to cool the next. Each liquid could be cooled well below its normal boiling point by boiling it under reduced pressure. Just as water can be made to boil at room temperature by placing it in the receiver of an air pump and pumping out the air, so any other liquid can be made to boil at a temperature lower than its normal boiling point, and to cool itself in giving up latent heat of vaporisation to the vapour formed.

Table 5

| Gas | Boiling point (°C) | Critical temperature (°C) | Critical pressure (atm) |
|---|---|---|---|
| Sulphur dioxide | −10·8 | 155·4 | 79 |
| Carbon dioxide | −78·2 | 31·1 | 73 |
| Ethylene | −103 | 10 | 52 |
| Oxygen | −183 | −118 | 50 |
| Nitrogen | −196 | −146 | 33 |
| Hydrogen | −253 | −240 | 12·8 |
| Helium | −269 | −268 | 2·26 |

Pictet of Geneva liquefied oxygen in 1877 by first liquefying sulphur dioxide, which he cooled to −70 °C by boiling under reduced pressure; he then liquefied carbon dioxide and, by boiling under reduced pressure, he attained a temperature of −130 °C, which is below the critical temperature of oxygen; at −130 °C oxygen could be liquefied by compressing it.

In 1883 Wroblewski and Olszewski in Poland employed the cascade process to liquefy oxygen and nitrogen. Ethylene, boiling under reduced pressure at a temperature of about −136 °C, was used to cool the oxygen, which was then liquefied by pressure. The liquid oxygen was used to cool the nitrogen below its critical temperature and this too was then liquefiable by pressure. Attempts to liquefy hydrogen by cooling it with liquid oxygen or nitrogen failed because the lowest temperature reached was well above the critical temperature of hydrogen. It was at this stage that the cascade process broke down.

The cooling of hydrogen and helium to below their critical temperatures required a new principle, and this was applied successfully by Dewar to liquefy hydrogen in 1898 and by Kamerlingh

Onnes to liquefy helium in 1908. The principle, represented in Fig. 58, was regenerative cooling by means of the Joule–Kelvin effect. The gas, cooled and under pressure, passed down the central tube and expanded through the small nozzle or valve at *A*, causing its temperature to fall (Joule–Kelvin effect). It then passed round the outside of the tube and cooled the succeeding flow of gas. In this way the gas was continuously cooled until liquefaction occurred; the process was cumulative or regenerative. Dewar and Onnes cooled the compressed gas to as low a temperature as possible before subjecting it to the Joule–Kelvin effect; Onnes, for example, cooled his compressed helium to 15 °K by means of hydrogen boiling under reduced pressure. The principle of regenerative cooling by the Joule–Kelvin effect was also employed by Linde in 1895 for the first commercial production of liquid air.

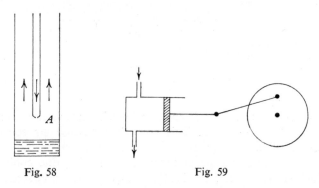

Fig. 58                    Fig. 59

In 1902 Claude modified the Linde process by an entirely different method of cooling, represented in Fig. 59. He cooled the air by causing it to do work adiabatically in driving the piston of a reciprocating engine. Suppose air at −25 °C and at a pressure of 150 atm expands adiabatically to a pressure of 6 atm. (These figures are taken from a modern commercial process.) The temperature of the air after expansion can be obtained from the equation,

$$\frac{T_1}{T_2} = \left(\frac{p_1}{p_2}\right)^{(\gamma-1)/\gamma},$$

derived on p. 64; its value is −176 °C. The cooling is very much greater than is obtained by the Joule–Kelvin effect.

The drawback of the Claude process was the difficulty of finding a lubricant suitable for use in an engine at temperatures of the order of −176 °C. For this reason it was not much used for nearly half a century. Modern plants, however, which may produce as much as 1000 tons of liquid oxygen per day, are based on the Claude process, although they utilise also the Joule–Kelvin effect.

Fig. 60 represents diagrammatically a modern plant for manufacturing liquid air. The air is first compressed to about 150 atm by means of the compressor. It is then freed of its water vapour and carbon-dioxide content by chemical means (not shown in Fig. 65), since ice and solid carbon dioxide would clog the pipes. It is cooled to $-25\,°C$ by a refrigerating plant (p. 181) and the greater part of it

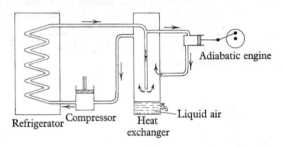

Fig. 60

passes through an adiabatic engine where it expands to 6 atm and cools to about $-160\,°C$. This cold, low-pressure air cools the remainder of the high-pressure air which passes down the central pipe of the heat exchanger and expands at a valve, thus cooling by the Joule–Kelvin effect. The heat exchanger contains, in fact, many thousands of copper pipes to facilitate an exchange of heat between the streams of gases.

Liquid air is manufactured primarily to produce liquid oxygen, for which there is a large industrial demand. The oxygen is separated from the nitrogen by fractional distillation, and the rare gas argon is also separated and recovered.

### Low-temperature physics

The persistent attempts by men like Onnes to approach and reach the absolute zero were regarded by many physicists as comparable with attempts to be first at the north and south poles, or, to take a present-day example, to be first on the moon. There was little realisation that a new and fascinating field of physical inquiry was being opened up.

Near the absolute zero some substances acquire extraordinary properties. At the absolute zero, contrary to the expectations of

classical physics, the internal energy of a substance does not completely disappear. The thermal energy vanishes but there is, within
the atoms, some motion not thermally excited, known as *zero-point
energy*. When the zero-point energy is comparable with the amount
of thermal energy, the laws of the quantum theory become dominant
and substances behave in an astonishing manner.

The necessity for the existence of zero-point energy follows from
Heisenberg's Uncertainty Principle, which shows that it is impossible
to determine simultaneously the position and momentum of an
atomic particle. An atom in a crystal lattice can never be at rest in
a particular place; it must move so that the product of the mean
uncertainty in its position and its momentum is proportional to the
elementary quantum of action, $h$ (see p. 164).

**Superconductivity**

Some metals, when cooled below a characteristic critical temperature, become perfect conductors of electricity. The phenomenon is
known as *superconductivity*. In one experiment a current of several
hundred amperes was induced in a lead ring and continued, without
measurable diminution, for over a year.

The phenomenon was discovered by Onnes in 1911 when investigating the electrical conductivity of mercury. Suddenly, below
4·1 °K, the electrical conductivity changed from a finite value to
zero. Superconductivity occurs in many metals but not in all—not,
for example, in copper, silver and gold, which are good electrical
conductors at normal temperatures.

Superconductivity can be temporarily destroyed by the application
of a magnetic field. This property may be utilised both for making or
breaking a circuit on receipt of a signal, or, with a slight elaboration,
as a memory device in computers. A superconductor, even though it
must be cooled with liquid helium, is superior for this purpose to
thermionic valves, since it can be very small and need not weigh more
than a few milligrams.

**The properties of liquid helium**

Liquid helium when cooled below 2·1 °K, known as the λ-point
(lambda-point), flows without viscosity, a phenomenon called *superfluidity*. It flows freely through the finest capillary tubes at a rate
which is independent of the pressure head and of the length of the
tube. On the other hand, if a solid disc is rotated in the liquid there is
a measurable resistance to the rotation. Liquid helium below the
λ-point, usually called helium II, is therefore believed to consist of

two fluids, a normal fluid with some viscosity and a superfluid with no viscosity.

Helium II is an enormously better thermal conductor than any other substance; its thermal conductivity is about 10000 times that of copper. The result is that it will not boil, because it is impossible to produce a temperature difference between the top and bottom of the liquid to allow the formation of a bubble of vapour.

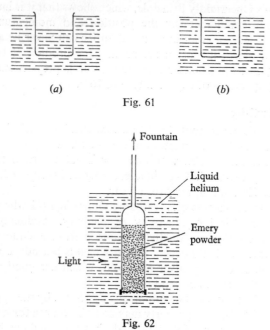

(a)                                              (b)

Fig. 61

Fig. 62

If a beaker is held in a larger vessel, both containing helium II at the same temperature, and the levels are different (Fig. 61a), the levels soon become the same (Fig. 61b). A very thin film spreads over the surface of the beaker, as a result of superfluidity, and is responsible for the transfer of the liquid.

Helium II tends to flow from a lower to a higher temperature, and this may be demonstrated by what is called the fountain effect (Fig. 62). A glass tube having a fine capillary nozzle is packed with emery powder, held in position with a gauze cap, and is immersed in helium II. A light is shone on the emery powder, causing a slight rise of temperature. The helium rushes up the temperature gradient with such force that it causes a jet or fountain to issue from the nozzle.

## The attainment of very low temperatures

The lowest pressure easily attained over liquid helium with mechanical pumps is about 0·2 mm of mercury and this produces a temperature of about 1 °K. For temperatures lower than this, special methods must be employed.

One method is to magnetise a paramagnetic salt isothermally at 1 °K, whereby heat is produced and removed, and then to demagnetise it adiabatically, causing cooling. Temperatures of $10^{-3}$ °K have been obtained in this way. An analogous process is the compression of a gas, the removal of the heat generated, and then the cooling of the gas by expansion.

We shall see in chapter 10 (p. 188) that, as a substance is cooled, there is an increase of internal order. At the absolute zero substances are in a state of perfect order.

### QUESTIONS

1. (a) Sketch the curves of volume against pressure obtained by Andrews for carbon dioxide at about 20 °C, at the critical temperature 31 °C, and at about 40 °C.

(b) From the curves elucidate the meaning of critical temperature and its bearing on the liquefaction of gases.

2. Some liquid ether is sealed in a thick-walled glass tube, leaving a space containing only the vapour. Describe what is observed as the temperature of the tube and its contents is raised above 197 °C, which is the critical temperature for ether.

(Assume that the vessel is strong enough to withstand the internal pressure.) (L.)

3. Describe the experiments you would perform to find how nearly sulphur dioxide obeys Boyle's law for pressures between ½ and 4 atm at the temperature of the laboratory. (O.)

4. Why do real gases not obey Boyle's law?

5. (a) Explain van der Waals's equation of state for a real gas.

(b) Show how the equation accounts for Andrews's isothermals for carbon dioxide.

6. A gas expands suddenly into a vacuum. Is there any change of temperature (a) if the gas is perfect, (b) if the gas is real? Explain.

7. (a) Describe the Joule–Kelvin porous-plug experiment and its interpretation.

(b) Why is it that with some gases cooling is observed and with others a rise in temperature?

(c) What bearing has the experiment on the liquefaction of gases?

8. (*a*) What are the conditions necessary for a gas to be liquefied?
(*b*) Explain the principles by which liquid air is manufactured.

9. Describe the researches which led to the knowledge of the conditions under which a gas can be liquefied.
What modifications have been made in the 'perfect' gas equation in order that it may represent more closely the results of these researches?
(N.)

10. Describe, with the help of a diagram, a method employed for the liquefaction of air. Explain how the cooling of the air is brought about and how, if at all, the method requires to be modified when applied to hydrogen.
(N.)

11. Some liquid nitrogen is contained at its normal boiling point of 77 °K in a thermos flask of negligible thermal capacity. The flask is connected to a pump and the vapour pumped off. What will be the temperature of the liquid when 10 % of it has boiled away?
(Latent heat of evaporation of nitrogen = 200 Joule gm⁻¹; specific heat of liquid nitrogen = 2 J gm⁻¹; log$_e$ 10 = 2·3.)
(C.S.)

CHAPTER 7

# VAPOUR PRESSURE

In this chapter we shall be concerned almost entirely with vapours and the pressures they exert—a vapour being defined as a gas below its critical temperature (p. 97). This will involve a consideration of evaporation, boiling, melting and the humidity of the atmosphere.

### Vapour pressure

A liquid in a closed space tends to evaporate until the space is saturated with the vapour. The pressure exerted by the vapour when it is in equilibrium with its liquid is called the *saturated vapour pressure*, often abbreviated to 'vapour pressure'.

To measure the saturated vapour pressures of comparatively volatile liquids at room temperature the apparatus in Fig. 63 may be used. A little of the liquid is introduced into the vacuum above the mercury in one of two barometer tubes by means of a bent pipette. Some of the liquid will evaporate and the depression of the mercury represents the saturated vapour pressure, due allowance being made for the pressure exerted by the thin layer of liquid on the mercury.

At 15 °C the values for water, methylated spirits and ether are 1·28, 7·2 and 35·8 cm of mercury respectively.

If the space above the mercury in the right-hand tube in Fig. 63 is increased by raising the tube slightly, more of the liquid resting on the mercury will evaporate, so that the saturated vapour pressure remains the same; similarly, if the space above the mercury is reduced by lowering the tube slightly, some of the vapour will condense.

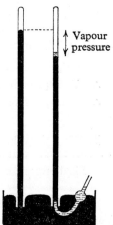

Vapour pressure

Mercury itself exerts a vapour pressure but at 15 °C this is negligible, compared with that of a volatile liquid.

## The behaviour of saturated and unsaturated vapours

The pressure of a saturated vapour at constant temperature is independent of the volume.

Fig. 63

It is not meaningful to say that the saturated vapour does not obey Boyle's law because the mass of the vapour changes when the volume changes. We shall see shortly that the graph of saturated vapour pressure and temperature is not a straight line. As before, it is not meaningful to say that the saturated vapour does not obey Charles's law because the mass of saturated vapour in a fixed volume increases with temperature.

Unsaturated vapours, on the other hand, do obey the gas laws approximately. We can use the equation $pV = RT$ to find roughly how the density of an unsaturated vapour varies with pressure and temperature. Since both air and unsaturated water vapour obey this equation approximately, the ratio of their densities remains constant at different pressures and temperatures; water vapour is $\frac{5}{8}$ as dense as air.

## Dalton's law of partial pressures

We have mentioned that when water evaporates into a vacuum at 15 °C the saturated vapour pressure is 1·28 cm of mercury. If the water evaporates into air at a pressure of 76·00 cm, it evaporates more slowly but the pressure of the water vapour ultimately reaches a maximum value of 1·28 cm. The total pressure exerted by the air and water vapour is $76·00 + 1·28 = 77·28$ cm.

This illustrates *Dalton's law of partial pressures: if two gases (or vapours) occupy a space, each exerts the same pressure that it would exert in that space if the other were absent.*

*Example. A sample of air at 14 °C and at a pressure of 76 cm of mercury contains just sufficient water vapour to saturate it. Calculate its pressure if the volume is (a) halved, (b) doubled, isothermally. (Saturation vapour pressure of water at 14 °C = 1·20 cm of mercury.)*

(*a*) When the volume is halved some of the vapour will condense, the saturation vapour pressure remaining constant.

$$\text{Original pressure of the air alone} \quad = 76 - 1\cdot2 = 74\cdot8 \text{ cm.}$$

$\therefore$ Final pressure of the air alone $\quad = 2 \times 74\cdot8 = 149\cdot6$ cm.

$\therefore$ Final pressure of air and water vapour $= 149\cdot6 + 1\cdot2$

$$= 150\cdot8 \text{ cm of mercury.}$$

(*b*) When the volume is doubled the vapour becomes unsaturated and we must assume that it obeys the gas laws, like air.

$$\text{Final pressure of air and water vapour} = \tfrac{1}{2} \times 76$$

$$= 38\cdot0 \text{ cm of mercury.}$$

### Variation of saturated vapour pressure with temperature

The way in which the saturated vapour pressure of a liquid such as water varies with temperature can be investigated by means of the apparatus shown in Fig. 64. Two barometer tubes are surrounded by a water bath and sufficient liquid is introduced into one of the tubes with a bent pipette so that there is always a thin layer of liquid on the surface of the mercury, to ensure that the vapour is saturated. The depression of the mercury in the tube containing the vapour is measured at different temperatures. The change in the density of the mercury with temperature introduces an error of less than 1 %.

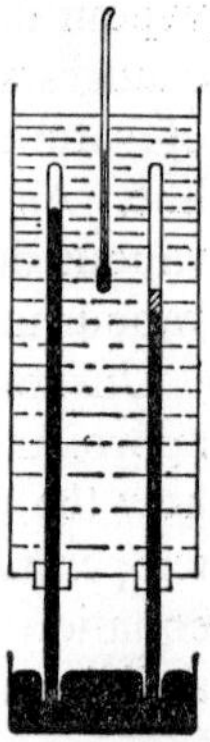

The method is called the static method, as opposed to the dynamic method which will be described shortly (p. 118). It is restricted to pressures from a few cm to about 60 cm or 70 cm of mercury.

Fig. 64

Values of the saturated vapour pressure of water at different temperatures are given in Table 6 and a graph in Fig. 65.

Note that the saturated vapour pressure increases fairly slowly with temperature at first, and then more rapidly as the boiling point is approached. The pressure at 100 °C is 76·00 cm of mercury and at 0 °C it is 0·46 cm.

The variation in saturated vapour pressure with temperature has been utilised for measuring temperatures. A vapour pressure thermometer consists of a bulb, partially filled with liquid, connected to a pressure gauge which can be calibrated to read temperature direct.

Such a thermometer is particularly sensitive in the region just below the boiling point of the liquid. The dash-board instrument indicating the temperature of the water in the radiator of a motor-car is often of this type. Helium vapour pressure thermometers are used to measure temperatures a few degrees above absolute zero.

## Table 6

| Temp. (°C) | 0 | 2 | 4 | 6 | 8 | 10 | 12 |
|---|---|---|---|---|---|---|---|
| s.v.p. (cmHg) | 0·46 | 0·53 | 0·61 | 0·70 | 0·80 | 0·92 | 1·05 |

| Temp. (°C) | 14 | 16 | 18 | 20 | 30 | 40 | 50 |
|---|---|---|---|---|---|---|---|
| s.v.p. (cmHg) | 1·20 | 1·36 | 1·55 | 1·75 | 3·17 | 5·51 | 9·23 |

| Temp. (°C) | 60 | 70 | 80 | 90 | 100 | 101 |
|---|---|---|---|---|---|---|
| s.v.p. (cmHg) | 14·92 | 23·35 | 35·51 | 52·58 | 76·00 | 78·75 |

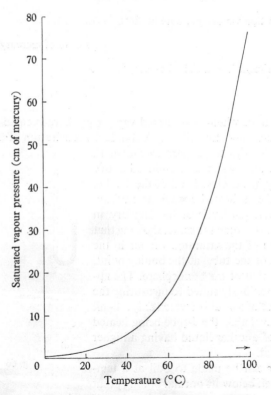

Fig. 65. Variation of the saturation vapour
pressure of water with temperature.

*Example. A uniform capillary tube, sealed at one end, contains air enclosed by a short thread of water, which keeps the air saturated with water vapour. The length of the air column is 15·6 cm at 20 °C, and 25·7 cm at 70 °C. Assuming that the pressure of saturated water vapour is 17 mm at 20 °C, calculate its value at 70 °C. (Height of mercury barometer = 760 mm.)* (O. & C.)

Pressure of the air in the column at 20 °C = $76 - 1·7 = 74·3$ cm.

Let pressure of the air in the column at 70 °C = $p_{70}$.

Applying the gas laws to the air (ignoring the water vapour),

$$\frac{pv}{T} = \text{constant.}$$

$$\therefore \quad \frac{p_{70} \times 25·7}{343} = \frac{74·3 \times 15·6}{293},$$

$$p_{70} = 52·8 \text{ cm of mercury.}$$

∴　Saturation vapour pressure at 70 °C = $76 - 52·8$

$$= 23·2 \text{ cm of mercury.}$$

This experiment is a useful laboratory exercise.

## Boiling

A liquid boils when its saturated vapour pressure is equal to that of the surrounding atmosphere. A simple demonstration of this fact can be made with the apparatus shown in Fig. 66. A little water is introduced above the mercury in the closed end of the J-tube. If the J-tube is heated in the steam from boiling water, the levels of the mercury in the two arms become the same, showing that the pressure of the saturated vapour in the closed arm of the tube, at the boiling point, is equal to that of the atmosphere. The apparatus is obviously suited to measuring the boiling point of a liquid of which only a small amount is available, the J-tube being heated in a bath of another liquid having a higher boiling point.

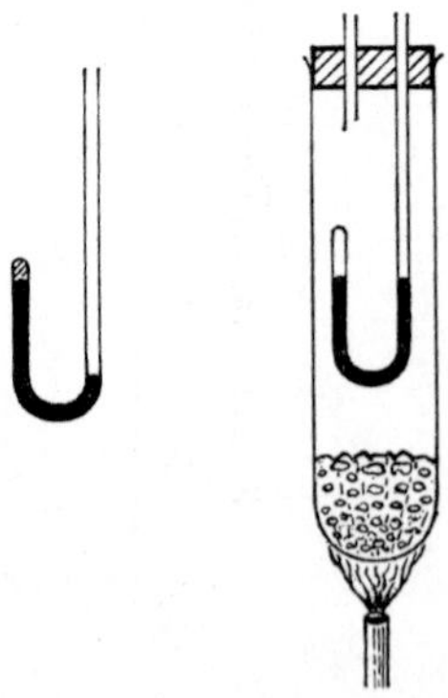

(a)　　　　(b)

Fig. 66

A liquid can be made to boil at a temperature well below its normal boiling point by reducing the pressure of the air above it. The atmospheric pressure at the top of a mountain, and hence the height of the mountain, can be estimated from the temperature at which water boils. Water boils on the summit of Everest (29000 ft) at about 74 °C. Similarly, when the pressure of the air or vapour above a liquid is increased, the boiling point is raised as, for example, in a pressure cooker.

The fundamental difference between evaporation and boiling is that, in the latter, vapour is formed throughout the bulk of the liquid as well as at the surface. Bubbles of vapour tend to form round tiny air bubbles, as nuclei, attached to the sides and bottom of the vessel. If water is freed from air by prolonged boiling it tends to superheat and boils explosively—a phenomenon known as bumping. Bumping can be minimised by placing small pieces of broken porous pot in the water; these provide tiny air bubbles on which the bubbles of vapour can form.

Surface tension tends to prevent bubbles from growing unless there is a nucleus of an air bubble to provide an initial radius at which the surface tension effect is small. If $r$ is the radius of the bubble and $\gamma$ the surface tension of the water, the pressure inside the bubble must exceed the external pressure by $2\gamma/r$. Taking the surface tension of water at 100 °C as about 53 dyn cm$^{-1}$, the excess pressure inside a bubble of radius $10^{-4}$ cm must be

$$\frac{2 \times 54}{10^{-4}} \simeq 10^6 \text{ dyn cm}^{-2} \simeq 1 \text{ atm.}$$

Hence the total pressure inside the bubble must be about 2 atm and the temperature of the water would have to rise to 120 °C for the vapour pressure to reach this value. Once formed, a bubble of vapour is unstable. A slight increase in its radius reduces the surface-tension effect and hence the radius increases further at an increasing rate.

In view of the possibility of a liquid superheating when boiling, it is desirable to place a thermometer to measure its boiling point in the vapour or steam rather than in the liquid itself. In Fig. 66 the J-tube is placed in the steam.

In the bubble chamber, invented by Glaser in 1953 for recording the tracks of atomic particles, a liquid is heated under pressure and then the pressure is reduced suddenly, leaving the liquid superheated. A high-energy particle passing through the liquid causes ebullition and leaves a track of small vapour bubbles. One liquid which has been used is liquid hydrogen and this is particularly useful for studying proton collisions because hydrogen nuclei are protons.

## Dynamic method of measuring the variation of saturated vapour pressure with temperature

The fact that the saturated vapour pressure of a boiling liquid is equal to the pressure of the surrounding atmosphere provides a method of finding how the saturated vapour pressure varies with temperature. Fig. 67 represents suitable apparatus for use with water. The water is contained in a flask $F$ and is made to boil at room temperature by reducing the pressure over it by means of an air pump. This pressure, which is equal to the saturated vapour pressure of the water at the temperature recorded by the thermometer, is measured by the mercury manometer $M$, and is equal to $H-h$, where $H$ is the height of the mercury barometer.

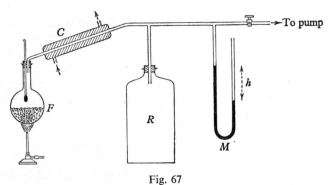

Fig. 67

The pressure in the apparatus is then slightly increased and the water is made to boil again by heating it slightly. In this way a series of values of temperature and saturated vapour pressure can be obtained. The condenser $C$ causes the steam to condense and return to the flask. The reservoir $R$ prevents large fluctuations of pressure.

By using a compression pump, such as a bicycle pump, instead of an exhaust pump, the water can be made to boil at temperatures above 100 °C.

## Latent heat of vaporisation

When a liquid evaporates it tends to cool because its latent heat of vaporisation is extracted from itself and also from the surroundings. This cooling is particularly noticeable, for example, if a volatile liquid like ether or petrol is spilt on the hands.

The latent heat can be subdivided into two components: the 'internal' latent heat required to separate the molecules against their mutual attraction and the 'external' latent heat required to provide the work needed to push away the surrounding atmosphere to make way for the vapour as it is formed.

Consider water boiling at 100 °C under standard atmospheric pressure, which is about $10^6$ dyn cm$^{-2}$. One gram of boiling water has a volume of approximately 1 c.c. and it changes to about 1670 c.c. of steam at 100 °C and standard atmospheric pressure. The change of volume is (1670−1) c.c. which is approximately 1670 c.c. The work done in displacing the atmosphere is the product of the (constant) pressure, and the increase in volume (p. 55), i.e. $10^6 \times 1670$ ergs.

$$\therefore \text{ External latent heat} = \frac{1 \cdot 67 \times 10^9}{4 \cdot 18 \times 10^7} = 40 \text{ cal gm}^{-1}.$$

Hence the internal latent heat is $539-40 \simeq 500$ cal gm$^{-1}$.

## The kinetic theory and vaporisation

We saw in chapter 5 that a gas may be regarded as consisting of molecules in constant motion and sufficiently far apart for their mutual attractions to be negligible. On condensation from the gaseous to the liquid state there is usually a large diminution of volume, indicating that the molecules have approached each other much more closely. The mutual attractions of the molecules are now sufficiently great to keep them together so that the liquid, unlike the gas, does not expand to fill its containing vessel and it is almost incompressible. Nevertheless, the fact that two liquids can diffuse one into the other shows that the molecules have some freedom of movement. As in the case of a gas, the velocities of the molecules in a liquid are not all the same; at a particular instant some molecules are moving more quickly than the average and some more slowly.

Evaporation consists of the escape from the surface of the liquid of molecules having a higher velocity than the average. In order to escape from the surface a molecule must overcome the force of attraction of the remainder of the molecules in or near the surface and this explains why only the swifter molecules can break free. Since only the swifter molecules escape, the average velocity of the remainder of the molecules is lowered and the liquid is cooled. Energy must be supplied to keep the temperature of the liquid constant and this is the internal latent heat of vaporisation.

A molecule of the vapour coming within the attractive force of the surface may be captured and return to the liquid. When the vapour reaches its saturated vapour pressure as many molecules return to the liquid as escape and there is a condition known as *dynamic equilibrium.* The presence above the liquid of another gas, such as air, impedes the escaping molecules and retards evaporation. A draught of air removes vapour molecules from the vicinity of the surface, thereby reducing the number of those returning to the liquid and increasing the rate of evaporation.

A rise in temperature of the liquid causes the molecules to move more quickly and, as indicated by the expansion of the liquid, the molecules are farther apart and attract each other less. Hence more molecules can escape and the saturated vapour pressure increases.

### Vapour pressure over curved surfaces

The vapour pressure above a convex liquid surface is greater than above a plane surface, and the vapour pressure above a plane surface is greater than that above a concave surface. The effect is so small as to be negligible at ordinary curvatures, but it is of decisive importance at the great curvatures of minute drops which are just in process of formation.

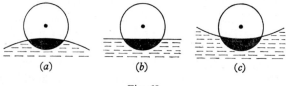

(a)          (b)          (c)

Fig. 68

Fig. 68 represents a molecule above the three types of surface. The circle round each molecule represents the sphere of molecular attraction, greatly exaggerated for the sake of clearness, beyond which the attractive force of the molecule is negligible. The dark-shaded portions represent those parts of the liquid within the sphere of molecular attraction and it can be seen that the molecule is least strongly attracted to the liquid in (a) and most strongly attracted in (c). Hence the vapour pressure is greatest in (a) and least in (c).

It can be shown that the vapour pressure over a drop of radius $10^{-7}$ cm is double that over a plane surface. Hence, unless the air is supersaturated to this extent, such a drop must immediately evaporate.

### The cloud chamber

Air can be supersaturated with water vapour without condensation occurring if it contains no dust particles to serve as nuclei; nuclei start drops forming at a radius for which the vapour pressure is not too high. Drops form readily on charged molecules, i.e. ions, and this is the principle of the cloud chamber used for recording the tracks of high-energy particles such as α-particles from a radioactive substance. The cloud chamber consists of a cylinder with a glass plate at one end and a piston at the other, containing air saturated with water vapour. An adiabatic expansion is caused by a sudden movement of the piston, causing cooling and supersaturation of the air. A high-energy particle passing through the chamber will ionise molecules in its path by collision and tiny droplets of water condense on these ions, making the track of the particle visible (Fig. 69).

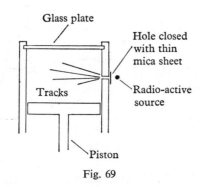

Fig. 69

## Melting

If a liquid like naphthalene is cooled and its temperature is recorded every minute a graph similar to that in Fig. 70 may be obtained. In the horizontal portion of the graph the liquid is solidifying. The temperature remains constant because the latent heat of fusion is given out at a rate which exactly compensates for the loss of heat to the surroundings. This temperature is the *melting point*, which may be defined as *the temperature at which the solid and the liquid are in equilibrium*.

Mixtures and non-crystalline substances do not have a sharp melting point. In their cases the cooling curve never becomes horizontal (Fig. 71).

A liquid like naphthalene may supercool, i.e. its temperature may fall below the melting point without solidification taking place (Fig. 72). Solidification can be started by dropping in a tiny crystal of naphthalene or even by a slight mechanical shock.

Most substances contract on solidifying; the surface of naphthalene solidified in a test tube, for example, is concave since it first solidifies at the circumference and then the middle of its surface sinks. Iron is an exception among the metals in expanding on solidification; hence it makes good castings, whereas aluminium, which contracts by 11 % on solidifying, does not. Similarly, type metal, an alloy of lead, antimony and tin, is used for making sharp type because it expands on solidification.

Increase of pressure raises the melting point of substances like ice which contract on melting; it lowers the melting point of substances which expand on melting. Thus ice tends to melt when pressure is applied; its reduction of volume on melting tends to relieve the pressure. This is an example of a more general principle known as

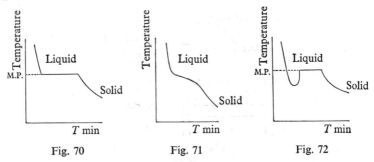

Fig. 70      Fig. 71      Fig. 72

*Le Chatelier's principle*: if one of the factors of any system in equilibrium is changed, thus disturbing the equilibrium, the effect produced tends to restore that factor to its original value. An increase of pressure of 1 atm causes the melting point of ice to be depressed by 0·0075 °C. The effect of pressure on the melting point is far less than its effect on the boiling point.

### Sublimation

Some solids exert appreciable vapour pressures and can pass direct from the solid to the vapour state, a process known as *sublimation*. The fact that solid camphor or naphthalene produces a smell which rapidly fills a room shows that the solid is giving off vapour. Naphthalene moth balls exposed to the air gradually disappear—over the course of months or years—but if kept in a stoppered vessel they last indefinitely.

The saturated vapour pressure of ice at 0° C is 4–6 mm of mercury, and this decreases as the temperature of the ice is lowered.

### The triple point

Fig. 73 shows three graphs: (1) the *steam line* representing the variation of the saturated vapour pressure of water with temperature;

(2) the *hoar-frost line* representing the variation of the saturated vapour pressure of ice with temperature; (3) the ice-line representing the variation of the melting point of ice with pressure.

The steam line is the same curve as Fig. 65. All points below it represent vapour and all points above it represent liquid. Consider a point on the steam line and let the pressure be reduced by increasing the volume, at constant temperature, until a point below the steam line is reached. This second point must represent unsaturated vapour. Now suppose that we go above the steam line by increasing the pressure at a constant temperature; at this pressure all the vapour

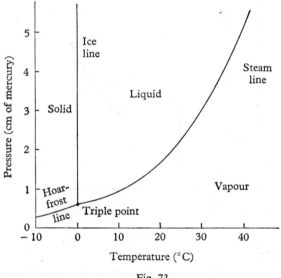

Fig. 73

must be condensed to liquid. Similarly, points to the left of the ice line represent the solid state. The three graphs must meet in a point because, if they did not do so and enclosed a space, we could show by arguments similar to the above that the space must represent solely liquid, solely vapour and solely solid, which is absurd.

The point at which the graphs meet is called the *triple point* and its co-ordinates are 0·46 cm of mercury and 0·01 °C. Only at this pressure and temperature can water, water vapour and ice exist together in equilibrium. If the temperature or pressure is slightly changed, one of the phases, solid or liquid or vapour, must disappear. The triple point of water is used as a fixed point in thermometry (p. 8).

The peculiar behaviour of solid carbon dioxide in changing direct to vapour without passing through the liquid phase is readily explained from Fig. 74. Note that the line corresponding to the ice line slopes the other way—since carbon dioxide expands on melting. The co-ordinates of the triple point are 388 cm of mercury and $-56 \cdot 6\ ^{\circ}C$. At atmospheric pressure, i.e. about 76 cm of mercury, a rise in temperature of the solid carbon dioxide, which is at a temperature of $-78 \cdot 5\ ^{\circ}C$, causes the carbon dioxide to pass from solid to vapour. Only at pressures above 388 cm does a rise in temperature cause solid carbon dioxide to change to the liquid state.

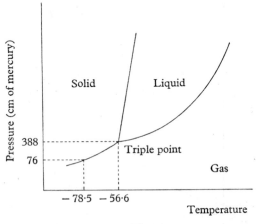

Fig. 74

### Relative humidity

The study of the humidity of the atmosphere, known as *hygrometry*, is important in meteorology, in some industrial processes and in the storage of such things as food and tobacco. Although we speak of the humidity of the atmosphere we can treat the water vapour quite independently of the air; by Dalton's law of partial pressures the pressure exerted by the water vapour is the same as if the air were absent. What we normally require to know is how near the water vapour is to saturation. If it is nearly saturated the atmosphere feels 'muggy', our sense of discomfort is caused by the fact that the body's perspiration cannot evaporate sufficiently quickly.

The *relative humidity* (R.H.) of the atmosphere may be defined as follows:

$$\text{R.H.} = \frac{\text{Pressure of the vapour present in the atmosphere}}{\text{Saturation vapour pressure at the same temperature}}.$$

### Dew-point hygrometers

If a polished metal surface is slowly cooled there appears upon it eventually a mist of minute water droplets known as dew. The *dew-point* is defined as the mean of the temperatures at which the dew appears and disappears (when the surface is slowly warmed). The relative humidity can be calculated from a knowledge of the dew-point by means of the relation

$$\text{R.H.} = \frac{\text{Saturated vapour pressure at the dew-point}}{\text{Saturated vapour pressure at the original temperature}}.$$

Suppose that the temperature of the air is 17·3 °C, that the dew appears at 8·6 °C and disappears at 9·4 °C, so that the dew-point is $\frac{1}{2}(8\cdot6+9\cdot4) = 9\cdot0$ °C. From tables:

Saturated vapour pressure at 17·3 °C =  8·6 mm.

Saturated vapour pressure at  9·0 °C = 14·8 mm.

$$\therefore \text{Relative humidity} = \frac{8\cdot6}{14\cdot8} = 0\cdot58 \text{ or } 58\%.$$

The method is based on Regnault's principle, enunciated in 1845, that when moist air is slowly cooled, the pressure of the vapour content remains constant until saturation is reached and dew is deposited.

Several hygrometers are based on this principle, Regnault's own instrument being shown in Fig. 75. The glass tube on the left has a silver thimble at its lower end and contains ether, through which air is slowly bubbled. The ether is cooled by evaporation and its temperature is observed when the dew appears; it is then allowed to warm up and the temperature observed at which the dew disappears. The silver thimble of the other glass tube provides a comparison surface to facilitate the observation of the onset of dew. Care must be taken to ensure that the observer's breath does not modify the humidity in the vicinity of the instrument.

There is bound to be a slight lag between the temperature recorded by the thermometer in the ether and the temperature of the surface; this can be avoided by measuring the temperature of the surface by means of a thermocouple attached to the surface. It is difficult to decide the exact instant at which dew appears; the personal element can be eliminated by the use of a photocell. Light falling on the surface is scattered when dew appears and this can be made to modify the light falling upon, and hence the electric current through, the photocell.

### Wet- and dry-bulb hygrometer

By far the most popular hygrometer in industry and meteorology is the wet- and dry-bulb hygrometer. It is not very accurate or sensitive and it is almost entirely empirical, i.e. it has no satisfactory theoretical basis. Its merit is its simplicity. It consists simply of two thermometers, one of which has its bulb kept moist by a wick consisting of a piece of muslin dipping in water (Fig. 76). The wet-bulb thermometer reads lower than the dry-bulb thermometer (unless the relative humidity is 100 %); the difference in the two readings depends on the rate of evaporation from the wet bulb and hence on the dryness of the atmosphere. The relative humidity can be obtained from tables.

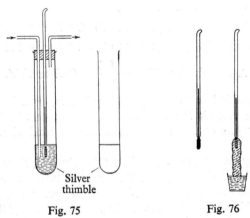

Silver
thimble

Fig. 75                              Fig. 76

The depression of the wet-bulb thermometer depends on the ventilation. Normally the instrument is protected from draughts; for meteorological observations, it is kept in a wooden box with louvered sides, called a Stevenson screen. But there is another type, known as the ventilated wet- and dry-bulb hygrometer or psychrometer, in which a current of air is made to stream past the thermometers either by means of a clockwork fan or by whirling the instrument. This requires a table for determining relative humidities slightly different from the above.

### Humidity control

Air conditioning or humidity control is normally performed by cooling the air, saturating it at this temperature by a water spray, and then warming it; its relative humidity will depend on its final temperature and the temperature at which it was saturated. Comfortable conditions for sedentary work are a temperature of 70 °F and a relative humidity of 55 %.

Example. *Calculate the mass of water vapour present in* 1 $m^3$ *of air when the temperature is* 20 °C *and the relative humidity is* 55 % (S.V.P. *at* 20 °C = 1·75 *cm of mercury; the density of water vapour is* ⅝ *that of air under the same conditions of temperature and pressure; the density of dry air at s.t.p. is* 1·30 *gm/l.*)

Pressure of the water vapour at 20 °C = $1·75 \times \dfrac{55}{100}$ cm of mercury.

Assume that water vapour obeys the gas laws, $pv/T$ = constant.
Volume of 1 $m^3$ of water vapour at 20 °C when reduced to s.t.p.

$$= \frac{273}{293} \frac{1·75 \times 0·55}{76} = 0·0118 \text{ m}^3.$$

Density of water vapour at s.t.p. = $1·30 \times ⅝$ gm l.$^{-1}$.

∴   Mass of water vapour required = $1·30 \times ⅝ \times 11·8$

$$= 9·6 \text{ gm.}$$

## QUESTIONS

1. (a) Explain what is meant by (i) a saturated vapour, (ii) an unsaturated vapour.

   (b) What will happen to each if temperature is decreased at constant volume?

2. A mass of unsaturated vapour is gradually compressed at constant temperature. Draw a rough graph to show how the volume changes with the pressure.

3. How would you measure the saturated vapour pressure of water at (a) room temperature, (b) 105 °C?

4. A small quantity of (a) water, (b) dry air is introduced into the space above the mercury in a barometer. How is the accuracy of the barometer affected in each case?

5. (a) State Dalton's law of partial pressures.

   (b) How may it be verified for a mixture of air and ether vapour?

6. Air is contained in a closed vessel containing a quantity of water. If the pressure in the vessel is 76·0 cm of mercury at 6 °C what will be the pressure when the temperature is 20 °C? (See Table 6 on p. 115.)

7. Hydrogen at 16·0 °C and a pressure of 75·0 cm of mercury collected over water has a volume of 50·0 c.c. Calculate the volume of dry hydrogen at s.t.p. (see Table 6 on p. 115).

8. A small quantity of hot tea is poured into a vacuum flask; the cork is replaced and the flask is shaken. The cork blows out. Explain this and point out how it illustrates Dalton's law of partial pressures. (C.)

9. A narrow tube of uniform bore, closed at one end, has some air entrapped by a small quantity of water. If the pressure of the atmosphere is 76 cm of mercury, the equilibrium vapour pressure of water at 12 °C and at 35 °C is 10·5 mm of mercury and 42·0 mm of mercury respectively, and the length of the air column at 12 °C is 10 cm, calculate its length at 35 °C. (L.)

10. (a) Why is it possible to estimate the height of a mountain from the boiling point of a pure liquid at its summit?

(b) How could you use a thermometer to test whether a boiling liquid is pure?

(c) Explain bumping in boiling.

11. Air is forced, by means of a bicycle pump, into a large bottle containing a little water and fitted with a bung through which passes a tube attached to a bicycle valve. The air is allowed to cool down and then the bung is removed from the bottle. Explain what may be observed in the bottle and why.

12. (a) Sketch a curve showing how the vapour pressure of a liquid varies with temperature.

(b) Explain whether the vapour pressure is influenced: (i) by the presence of impurities dissolved in the liquid, (ii) the curvature of the free surface of the liquid, (iii) the pressure on the surface.

13. At what depth in water, boiling under a pressure of 76 cm of mercury, is the temperature 101 °C? (See Table 6 on p. 115; density of mercury = 13·6 gm cm⁻³.)

14. The apparatus in Fig. 77, known as Wollaston's cryophorus, contains water and water vapour only. Explain why, when the bulb $A$ is surrounded by a mixture of ice and salt, the water in $B$ is eventually frozen.

15. Why will a small drop of water evaporate in a space in which water vapour is in equilibrium with a plane water surface?

16. Explain, in terms of the kinetic theory:

(a) the fall in temperature of a liquid when it evaporates;

(b) the increase in saturated vapour pressure with temperature;

(c) the lowering of the saturated vapour pressure of water when salt is dissolved in the water.

17. When a small crystal of a substance is dropped into 150 gm of the liquefied substance, which is at 72 °C, some solid separates out and the temperature rises to 79 °C. Account for this and estimate the mass of the solid formed, assuming that the specific heat of the liquid is 1·34 J gm⁻¹ deg⁻¹ C and the latent heat of fusion is 146 J gm⁻¹.

18. It is often stated that burning a gas-fire in a room makes the air 'dry'. How do you interpret this statement, and how would you test its truth experimentally?

19. The curve in Fig. 78 represents the variation of the saturated vapour pressure of water with temperature. When the condition of the water vapour in the atmosphere is represented by the point *A*, what is the dew-point and what is the relative humidity?

20. What would be the hygrometric state of the atmosphere if (*a*) the temperature of the wet-bulb thermometer equalled that of the dry-bulb thermometer, (*b*) the temperature of the wet-bulb thermometer approached the dew-point?

21. Find the relative humidity of an atmosphere whose temperature is 16·0 °C, if the dew-point is 12·0 °C. (Use Table 6 on p. 115.)

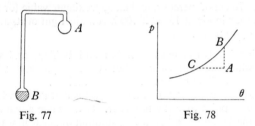

Fig. 77                    Fig. 78

22. An air-conditioning plant saturates air at 10·0 °C and then raises its temperature to 20·0 °C. What is the relative humidity? (See Table 6 on p. 115.)

23. (*a*) What is meant by the triple point?

(*b*) Suggest why the triple point of water is now preferred to the melting point of pure ice as a thermometric fixed point.

24. What is a saturated vapour? Describe and explain an experiment to determine the saturation pressure of water vapour at temperatures in the range 60 to 95 °C.

The shorter (closed) limb of a uniform vertical J-tube contains air and a small quantity of alcohol sufficient to keep the space saturated. The air and the alcohol are trapped by mercury introduced at the open end of the tube. When the temperature of the short limb is 20 °C the length of the air–alcohol column is 5·0 cm and the mercury levels are the same in both tubes. On raising the temperature of the short limb to 40 °C the mercury level in that tube falls 1·8 cm. Calculate the saturation pressure of the alcohol vapour at 40 °C, assuming that its value at 20 °C is 9·0 cm of mercury and that the barometric pressure is 76 cm of mercury.    (N.)

25. A mixture of gas and a saturated vapour is contained in a closed space. Assuming that the vapour remains saturated throughout the experiments describe how the pressure of the mixture will vary (*a*) when the

volume is changed at constant temperature, (b) the temperature is changed at constant volume.

An open flask containing air and a little water to ensure saturation is heated to 70 °C and is then securely corked at that temperature. It is opened mouth downwards under water at 17 °C and it is found that the air remaining in the flask occupies $\frac{2}{3}$ of the total volume when its pressure is atmospheric. Assuming that the vapour pressure of water at 17 °C is 13 mm and the atmospheric pressure 753 mm throughout the experiment, calculate the vapour pressure of water at 70 °C. (C.)

26. What is meant by saying that a vapour is saturated?

Some ether vapour is confined in a tube in such a way that its volume and temperature can be changed. Discuss, giving sketch graphs, how the pressure in the tube alters (a) if the volume is changed at constant temperature, (b) if the temperature is changed at constant volume.

Given that 1 gm of water becomes 1600 cm³ of steam at 100 °C and a pressure of 76 cm of mercury, find an approximate value for the pressure of water vapour in air at 15 °C if 100 l. contain 1 gm of it, and state any assumptions you make. (C.)

27. Distinguish between evaporation and boiling, and describe an experiment which shows that a liquid boils when the pressure of its saturated vapour is equal to the pressure of the surroundings.

Give an explanatory diagram of the apparatus that is used when checking the upper fixed point of a thermometer. Is the same apparatus suitable for finding the boiling point of a 5 % solution of sugar in water? If not, state what apparatus you would use, giving your reasons.

A quantity of water at 20 °C is raised to 100 °C and boiled away. An equal mass is allowed to evaporate at 20 °C. Discuss qualitatively whether the quantity of heat that must be supplied is the same in each case. (C.)

28. If the latent heat of liquid oxygen is 51 cal/gm at its boiling point, determine the fraction of this energy required to overcome the atmospheric pressure of 76 cm of mercury. You may assume that the temperature of the liquid oxygen is − 183 °C and that its density is 1·1 gm/c.c. The density of oxygen at s.t.p. is 1·43 gm/l., that of mercury 13·6 gm/c.c. and the mechanical equivalent of heat is 4·18 × 10⁷ ergs/cal. (N.)

29. Define *dew-point* and describe an experiment to determine its value. What further information would you require to determine the relative humidity?

A sample of moist air at 20 °C has a dew-point of 11 °C. Calculate the mass of dry air contained in one cubic metre of the moist air if the barometric height is 760·0 mm of mercury. Assume that the saturation vapour pressure of water at 11 °C is 9·8 mm of mercury and that the density of dry air is 1·293 gm l.⁻¹ at s.t.p. (N.)

CHAPTER 8

# THERMAL CONDUCTION

There are three modes of heat transfer: *conduction, convection* and *radiation.*

When one end of a poker is placed in a fire heat is conducted along the bar. Conduction is the transfer of heat through a material medium as a result of a difference of temperature, with no apparent movement of the medium, the intervening layers of the medium being warmed to intermediate temperatures.

Convection occurs, for example, when the bottom of a vessel containing a liquid is heated. The liquid near the bottom expands, becomes less dense and hence is displaced by the cooler, denser liquid above it. Convection is the transfer of heat by the relative motion of parts of a fluid as a result of a difference of density and an Archimedean upthrust.

Conduction is concerned mainly with solids while convection, impossible in solids, is normally far more important than conduction in liquids and gases.

Radiation is the form in which energy reaches us from the sun. It requires no material medium for its transmission, and it travels with the velocity of light.

## Flow of heat and temperature gradient

Fig. 79 represents a copper bar of uniform cross-section heated electrically at one end, by means of a current-carrying coil wrapped round it, and cooled at the other end by a spiral copper tube carrying a steady flow of cold water. The whole bar is lagged with cotton wool, to minimise loss of heat from the sides, and thermometers are inserted at intervals in holes in the bar. Heat will pass along the bar and, at first, some of the heat will be used to raise the temperature of the bar. Eventually, when a *steady state* is reached, as indicated by steady readings of the thermometers, as much heat will be extracted per second from the cold end of the bar as is supplied to the hot end. The fall in temperature per unit distance along the bar, known as the *temperature gradient,* will be found to be uniform (Fig 79b).

Suppose now that the power supplied to the heater and hence the rate of flow of heat through the bar is doubled. It will be found that the temperature gradient is doubled also. The temperature at the cold end of the bar will rise only slightly, since the mean temperature of the cooling water will not be raised very much, but the temperature of the hot end of the bar will rise to about twice its former value.

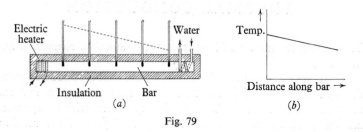

Fig. 79

## Definition of thermal conductivity

From experiments similar to the above it can be shown that *the rate of flow of heat through a bar is proportional to the temperature gradient*. It is also reasonable to assume that the rate of heat flow is proportional to the area of cross-section of the bar. A bar with twice the area of cross-section of another bar of the same material will conduct twice as much heat per unit time for a given temperature gradient. We are thus led to the following equation which defines the *thermal conductivity*, $k$, of a substance (Fig. 80):

$$Q = k \frac{\theta_1 - \theta_2}{x} At,$$

where $Q$ is the quantity of heat flowing in time $t$ at right angles to an area $A$, and $\theta_1$ and $\theta_2$ are the temperatures at points a distance $x$ apart, so that $(\theta_1 - \theta_2)/x$ is the temperature gradient, assumed to be uniform.

If $Q$ is measured in calories, $\theta_1$ and $\theta_2$ in °C, $x$ in cm, $A$ in cm², and $t$ in sec, the units of $k$ are cal cm$^{-1}$ sec$^{-1}$ deg$^{-1}$ C. If $Q$ is measured in joules, the units of $k$ are watts cm$^{-1}$ deg$^{-1}$ C.

As is the case with most of the fundamental equations of physics, the validity of the equation defining $k$ does not depend on direct experimental verification—of the kind we have outlined—but upon the many verifiable quantitative deductions which can be made from it.

We can define thermal conductivity in words as *the rate of flow of heat per unit area per unit temperature gradient*.

## Range of thermal conductivities

Table 7 shows the thermal conductivities of a number of substances (at about 20 °C).

The best conductors are the metals. Alloys in general have a lower thermal conductivity than pure metals although, in Table 7, constantan is seen to be a better conductor than bismuth. Non-metallic solids such as glass have a lower thermal conductivity than the metals; and most liquids, such as water, have a still lower thermal conductivity. The good thermal insulating properties of substances like asbestos, cork and cotton wool are due to the tiny pockets of air which they contain.

### Table 7

| Substance | $k$ (cal cm$^{-1}$ sec$^{-1}$ deg$^{-1}$ C) | Substance | $k$ (cal cm$^{-1}$ sec$^{-1}$ deg$^{-1}$ C) |
|---|---|---|---|
| Silver | 0·97 | Glass | 0·002 |
| Copper | 0·918 | Water | 0·0015 |
| Gold | 0·70 | Rubber | 0·00045 |
| Aluminium | 0·50 | Asbestos | 0·0003 |
| Iron | 0·176 | Cork | 0·00010 |
| Constantan | 0·054 | Cotton wool | 0·00006 |
| Bismuth | 0·019 | Air | 0·000058 |

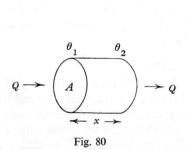

Fig. 80

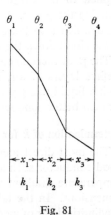

Fig. 81

No thermal insulator can match the best electrical insulators. There is no leakage of electricity from insulated wires but there is always some leakage of heat from lagged hot-water pipes.

### Flow through a series of plates

Suppose that there is a steady perpendicular flow of heat through a series of parallel-sided slabs of different materials in contact (Fig. 81). Let the thermal conductivities of the materials be $k_1$, $k_2$, $k_3$, the thicknesses of the slabs $x_1$, $x_2$, $x_3$, and the temperatures of the faces

$\theta_1$, $\theta_2$, $\theta_3$, $\theta_4$. The quantity of heat, $Q$, flowing in time $t$ through a cross-section, $A$, of each slab is the same. Hence

$$\frac{Q}{At} = k_1 \frac{\theta_1 - \theta_2}{x_1} = k_2 \frac{\theta_2 - \theta_3}{x_2} = k_3 \frac{\theta_3 - \theta_4}{x_3}.$$

The temperature gradient is largest in the poorest conductor. In Fig. 88 the sloping lines represent the temperature gradients and hence the middle slab is the poorest conductor; $k_2$ is the least thermal conductivity and $(\theta_2 - \theta_3)/x_2$ is the greatest temperature gradient.

A surface film of gas, about $\frac{1}{40}$ in. thick, forms between the steel plate of a boiler and the furnace and the temperature drop across this gas film is very much greater than that across the steel. Suppose that the steel is $\frac{1}{4}$ in. thick—ten times the thickness of the gas film. Since the conductivity of steel is about 10000 times that of the gas, the temperature drop across the steel is only about $\frac{1}{1000}$th that across the gas. The existence of the surface film can be demonstrated by sticking a sheet of paper to the underside of a kettle of water; a flame applied to the bottom of the kettle will boil the water without charring the paper. Inside a kettle or boiler there is often a film of scale which also takes part of the available temperature drop and hence slows down the flow of heat.

The poor thermal contact between solid conductors, caused by the surface layers of air, may be improved by smearing the surfaces with a liquid like glycerine. The liquid is a poor conductor but it is a much better conductor than air.

### Determination of $k$ for a good conductor

The most direct method of finding the thermal conductivity of a good conductor such as a metal is to measure the heat flow and the temperature gradient under steady conditions in a bar of known dimensions. In the laboratory method devised by Searle (Fig. 82) a cylindrical bar of metal, about 20–30 cm long and 4–5 cm diameter, is heated at one end by steam and cooled at the other end by water circulating in a copper tube wrapped round the bar. A steady flow of water is ensured by means of a constant-head apparatus and the volume passing through in a known time is measured with a measuring cylinder; the temperatures at inflow and outflow are read by thermometers. The temperature gradient in the bar is obtained by means of two thermometers inserted in holes in the bar at a measured distance apart. The bar is lagged with felt or cotton wool and the readings of the thermometers are taken only after they have become steady.

Some of the early investigators, using a similar method, did not insert thermometers in the bar to find the temperature gradient and made the mistake of assuming that the end of the bar in the steam bath was 100 °C, with the result that they obtained values for thermal conductivities which were far too low. The temperature of the end of the bar in the steam bath may differ very considerably from 100 °C because it is covered with a film of moisture which, being a poor conductor, takes up a considerable part of the available temperature drop.

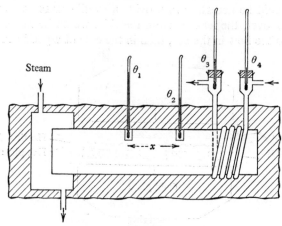

Fig. 82

The diameter of the bar is measured with callipers and the area of cross-section, $A$ cm², is calculated. Suppose that the readings of the thermometers are $\theta_1$, $\theta_2$, $\theta_3$ and $\theta_4$ °C as shown in Fig. 82, and that the distance apart of the two thermometers inserted in the bar is $x$ cm. Let the flow of water be $m$ gm per sec.

Substituting in the equation

$$Q = kA\frac{\theta_1-\theta_2}{x}t \quad \text{(p. 132),}$$

we have

$$m(\theta_3-\theta_4) = kA\frac{\theta_1-\theta_2}{x},$$

from which $k$ can be calculated.

The method may be improved by replacing the steam heating with electrical heating. It is then possible to calculate the heat supplied to the bar at the hot end, as well as the heat extracted from the bar at the cold end, and hence to find how much heat is leaking away through the lagging. Again, the holes drilled in the bar to take the thermometers disturb the linear flow of heat; hence it is better to replace the thermometers by thermocouples, which may be soldered to the surface of the bar and do not necessitate holes.

### Determination of $k$ for a poor conductor

To determine the thermal conductivity of a poor conductor it is necessary to use a thin plate rather than a long bar since a very high temperature difference between the ends of a long bar of a poor conductor would be necessary to provide a readily measurable flow of heat; moreover, the leakage from the sides would be much higher, relative to the flow in the bar, than in the case of a good conductor.

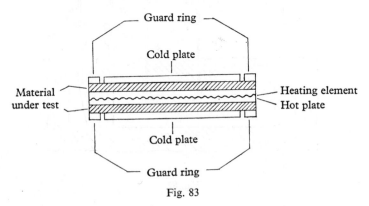

Fig. 83

A typical arrangement is shown in Fig. 83. Two thin plates of the material under test are placed between a hot plate, consisting of a copper plate in which is embedded an electric heating element insulated by mica, and two cold plates, each consisting of a hollow copper plate in which water circulates. Each cold plate is surrounded by a small air gap and an annular guard ring with a separate cooling system, whose function we shall explain. The temperatures of the faces of the hot and cold plates in contact with the material, and of the guard rings, are measured by means of thermocouples (not shown in Fig. 83) when the apparatus has reached a steady state, which may take hours or days.

The purpose of each guard ring is to eliminate the error due to leakage of heat from the sides of the specimen, which results in the direction of the flow of heat through the specimen near its sides not being perpendicular to the faces. This is represented in Fig. 84, $H$ and $C$ being the faces of the hot and a cold plate in contact with the specimen respectively, while *GG* represents the guard ring. The heat passing perpendicularly through the central part of the specimen in contact with the cold plate is measured. The guard ring is maintained at the same temperature as the cold plate but the heat passing to it is not required.

The rate of flow of heat through each slab of the material is $m\theta$, where $m$ is the mass of water flowing through a cold plate per second, and $\theta$ is its rise in temperature. This should be equal to about half the heat generated in the hot plate per second (some heat going to the guard ring). If $\theta_1$ and $\theta_2$ are the temperatures of the faces of the

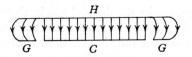

Fig. 84

material, $x$ is the thickness of the material, and $A$ is the area of cross-section of the cold plate, then the thermal conductivity of the material is given by

$$m\theta = kA \frac{\theta_1 - \theta_2}{x}.$$

## Use of a guard ring with good conductors

Thermal conductivity is one of the most difficult physical quantities to measure accurately, particularly in the case of good conductors. The modern tendency is to use direct, steady-state methods similar to the ones we have already described.

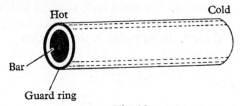

Fig. 85

In the most accurate determinations for good conductors by the bar method a guard ring is substituted for the lagging. A guard ring consists of a hollow cylinder of the same material as the bar, supported coaxially with the bar and separated from it by a small air gap (Fig. 85). Its ends are maintained at the same temperatures as the bar.

The temperature gradients in the bar and guard ring are made the same, so that the bar is everywhere along its length surrounded by a part of the guard ring at the same temperature and hence does not lose heat through its sides. The temperature gradient in an unlagged guard ring, heated at one end and cooled at the other, is similar to Fig. 88b because of heat loss along its length. It is therefore necessary to have separate electric heaters along the length of the guard ring to ensure that its temperature gradient (measured by thermocouples) is linear.

### Determination of $k$ for rubber in the form of a tube

As a laboratory exercise the thermal conductivity of a poor conductor such as rubber in the form of a tube may be determined by passing steam through the tube immersed in a calorimeter of water (Fig. 86). The method is essentially the same as those just described.

The water in the calorimeter is cooled to about 5 °C below room temperature; its temperature is taken at half-minute intervals while steam is passed through the tube until the temperature is about 5 °C above that of the room. By plotting temperature against time and drawing a tangent to the curve at room temperature, $\theta$ °C, the rate of rise of temperature of the calorimeter and water, $\Delta\theta$ °C per sec, can be obtained. When the calorimeter and water are at room temperature they are not gaining or losing heat from the room. If the mass of the water is $m$ gm and the water equivalent of the calorimeter is $w$ gm, the heat conducted through the rubber tube is $(m+w)\Delta\theta$ cal sec$^{-1}$.

The length, $l$ cm, of the rubber tube immersed in the water must be found; also the internal and external radii, $r_1$ and $r_2$ cm, preferably by a travelling microscope. The mean area, through which the heat is conducted, is $2\pi.\frac{1}{2}(r_1+r_2)\,l$ cm$^2$. The mean temperature gradient is $(100-\theta)/(r_2-r_1)$ °C cm$^{-1}$. Substituting in the equation

$$Q = kA\frac{\theta_1-\theta_2}{x}t,$$

$$(m+w)\Delta\theta = k\pi(r_1+r_2)\,l\frac{100-\theta}{r_2-r_1},$$

from which $k$ can be calculated.

A source of inaccuracy in this method is that the temperatures of the rubber surfaces are not equal to the temperatures of the steam and of the water respectively because of surface films.

### More accurate calculation of radial heat flow through a cylindrical tube

When heat flows radially through a cylindrical tube the temperature gradient in the tube is not uniform. We were obliged to approximate in the above calculation for the rubber tubing (without, in fact, introducing a serious error) because our defining equation for $k$,

$$Q = kA\frac{\theta_1 - \theta_2}{x}t,$$

applies only to cases in which the temperature gradient is uniform.

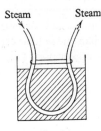

Fig. 86

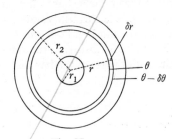

Fig. 87

To generalise this equation to include non-uniform temperature gradients, consider two planes in a conductor at right angles to the flow of heat and at distances $x$ and $x + \delta x$ from some suitable origin. Let the temperatures at these two planes be $\theta$ and $\theta - \delta\theta$ respectively. The temperature gradient at distance $x$ is

$$\lim_{\delta x \to 0} -\frac{\delta\theta}{\delta x} = -\frac{d\theta}{dx}.$$

Hence our defining equation for $k$ becomes

$$Q = -kA\frac{d\theta}{dx}t.$$

The negative sign indicates that the heat flows down, i.e. in the negative direction of, the temperature gradient.

Now consider a thin cylindrical shell of the rubber tube (Fig. 87), of internal and external radii $r$ and $r + \delta r$, and suppose that the temperatures are $\theta$ and $\theta - \delta\theta$ respectively. The temperature gradient at radius $r$ will be $-d\theta/dr$. Let the length of the tube be $l$, the thermal conductivity $k$, and the flow of heat in time $t$, $Q$.

$$Q = -k2\pi r l\frac{d\theta}{dr}t.$$

Let the temperatures of the internal and external surfaces of the tube, of radii $r_1$ and $r_2$, be $\theta_1$ and $\theta_2$ respectively,

$$Q \int_{r_1}^{r_2} \frac{dr}{r} = -2\pi klt \int_{\theta_1}^{\theta_2} d\theta,$$

$$Q \log_e \frac{r_2}{r_1} = 2\pi klt(\theta_1 - \theta_2),$$

$$k = \frac{Q \log_e(r_2/r_1)}{2\pi lt(\theta_1 - \theta_2)}.$$

### Unlagged bar heated at one end

Suppose that a metal bar is heated at one end and exposed to the air (Fig. 88 a). When a steady state is reached its temperature gradient will be as shown in Fig. 88 b. Heat is being conducted along the bar but it is also being lost from the sides of the bar, more heat escaping from the hotter parts of the bar than from the cooler parts (Fig. 89 b).

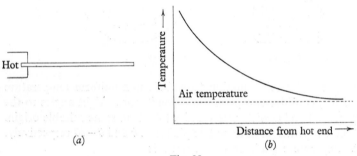

(a)

(b)

Fig. 88

The heat conducted through any cross-section of the bar must escape from the surface between there and the cold end of the bar; hence the heat conducted becomes less and less towards the cold end of the bar, and the temperature gradient becomes smaller and smaller, as can be seen from the change in slope of the curve in Fig. 88 b. The temperature of the cold end of the bar will never quite reach the air temperature, unless the bar is infinitely long.

### Ingenhausz's method of comparing thermal conductivities

Ingenhausz devised a method of comparing the thermal conductivities of metals which is not particularly accurate but is an interesting example of the use of unlagged bars.

Bars of the metals to be compared, having the same cross-section and the same surface finish, e.g. lacquering or silver plating, are coated with wax and heated at one end in a bath of boiling water (Fig. 90). When a steady state is reached, let the wax have melted along lengths $l_1$, $l_2$, $l_3$ and $l_4$ of the bars, whose thermal conductivities are $k_1$, $k_2$, $k_3$ and $k_4$, respectively. Then $k_1:k_2:k_3:k_4 = l_1^2:l_2^2:l_3^2:l_4^2$.

To indicate in a general way why the thermal conductivities are proportional to the squares of the lengths of the wax melted, suppose that the wax has melted twice as far along bar $A$ as along bar $B$. The temperature gradient in $A$ is only half that in $B$ and its rate of loss of

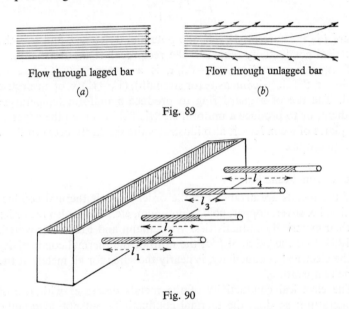

Flow through lagged bar       Flow through unlagged bar

(a)                 (b)

Fig. 89

Fig. 90

heat is double because the surface area along which the wax has melted is double. Since twice the flow of heat is obtained in $A$ by means of a temperature gradient half that of $B$, the thermal conductivity of $A$ is four times that of $B$.

The rate at which heat is conducted along a bar depends only upon the thermal conductivity; the rate at which the wax melts, however, which is the rate of travel of the temperature, depends also upon thermal capacity per unit volume, i.e. upon the product of the specific heat and density. Wax melts more rapidly along a bismuth bar than along an iron bar but it does not melt so far. The thermal conductivities of iron and bismuth are 0·176 and 0·019 cal cm$^{-1}$ sec$^{-1}$ deg$^{-1}$ C; their thermal capacities per unit volume are 0·79 and 0·29 cal deg$^{-1}$ C cm$^{-3}$ respectively.

### Analogy between the flow of heat and the flow of electricity

The equation defining $k$ can be written in the form

$$\frac{Q}{t} = \frac{\theta_1 - \theta_2}{x/kA}, \quad \text{(p. 132)}$$

and this is exactly analogous to Ohm's law for the flow of an electric current,

$$i = \frac{V_1 - V_2}{x/\sigma A},$$

where $i$ is the current, $V_1 - V_2$ the potential difference, and $\sigma$ is the electrical conductivity (equal to the reciprocal of the resistivity).

Temperature gradient, $(\theta_1 - \theta_2)/x$, is a vector quantity like its analogue, the electric intensity (or strength), $(V_1 - V_2)/x$, of an electric field. The use of a guard ring to produce a uniform temperature gradient, or to produce a uniform electric field between the edges of the plates of a condenser, also illustrates the similarity between these two quantities.

### Wiedemann–Franz law

If the metals are arranged in the order of their thermal conductivities, i.e. silver, copper, gold, aluminium, etc., this is also the order of their electrical conductivities. Wiedemann and Franz discovered, in 1854, that the value of $k/\sigma$, the ratio of the thermal conductivity to the electrical conductivity, is nearly the same for all metals at the same temperature.

The electrical conductivity of the metals decreases with rise of temperature; so does the thermal conductivity but not so rapidly. In 1872 Lorenz found that $(k/\sigma) \propto T$, where $T$ is the absolute temperature. This is very nearly true for all pure metals except at very low temperatures.

### The mechanism of thermal conduction in solids

The quantitative relationship between the thermal and electrical conductivities of metals suggests that both phenomena have the same basic mechanism. Metals are excellent conductors of electricity because they contain free electrons which move under the action of a potential difference, and constitute an electric current. Similarly, these free electrons move from a region of higher temperature to one of lower temperature, carrying thermal energy with them, and they are the chief agents of thermal conductivity in metals.

There is another mechanism which is of relatively small importance in metals but which becomes more important in substances of lower thermal conductivity until in the cases of substances which have no free electrons (electrical insulators) it is all-important. This is the passing on of thermal vibrations between adjacent fixed particles of the substance.

## Determination of the thermal conductivity of fluids

The determination of the thermal conductivity of liquids and gases is difficult for two main reasons: (1) the need to prevent convection, (2) the liability of serious error being introduced by any slight transfer of heat by convection or radiation because of the low thermal conductivity, particularly in the case of gases.

Methods similar to that for poor solid conductors, described on p. 136, are perhaps the most satisfactory; to eliminate convection the layer of liquid or gas is made very thin and it is heated at the top.

Another method, comparable with that for the thermal conductivity of rubber in the form of a tube, has been perfected for gases. The gas is contained in a narrow glass tube down the centre of which passes a fine platinum wire, through which an electric current is passed. The heat generated in the wire can be calculated from the current and potential difference across the wire. The heat flows radially through the gas to the glass walls of the tube, which are kept at a constant temperature by a water bath.

The space between the wire and the inside surface of the glass can be regarded as a cylindrical tube of gas; hence the equation derived on p. 140,

$$k = \frac{Q\log_e(r_2/r_1)}{2\pi lt(\theta_1 - \theta_2)},$$

may be applied, $Q$ being the heat generated in the wire in time $t$, $r_1$ and $r_2$ the radius of the wire and the internal radius of the glass tube respectively, $l$ the length of the wire, and $\theta_1$ and $\theta_2$ the temperatures of the wire and of the glass tube respectively.

The temperature of the wire is obtained from its resistance while the current is flowing. Convection is small because the tube is narrow (of the order of 1 mm in diameter); its effects may be estimated by using the tube in both horizontal and vertical positions, and also by varying the pressure of the gas. The thermal conductivity of a gas is independent of the pressure, as may be proved by the kinetic theory (p. 84).

Errors known as end effects are caused by the conduction of heat from the ends of the platinum wire through the leads and also by a non-radial flow of heat near the ends of the wire. These can be eliminated by using two similar wires in similar tubes of different lengths (Fig. 91), for which the end effects will be the same. Let $Q_1$ and $Q_2$ be the heats generated in the wires, of lengths $l_1$ and $l_2$. By substituting $Q_1 - Q_2$ for $Q$, and $l_1 - l_2$ for $l$, in the above equation for $k$, the end effects are eliminated.

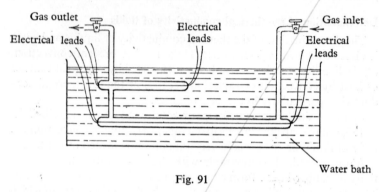

Fig. 91

Example 1. *The walls of a hot-water tank are 0·80 cm thick and are made of material of thermal conductivity 0·12 cal cm⁻¹ sec⁻¹ deg⁻¹ C. The tank is protected by lagging of thickness 2·0 cm and thermal conductivity 0·0096 cal cm⁻¹ sec⁻¹ deg⁻¹ C. When conditions are steady the temperature of the water in the tank is 70 °C and the temperature of the outer surface of the lagging is 40 °C. Find (a) the temperature of the interface between the tank and the lagging, (b) the loss of heat per square metre per second.*

(O. & C.)

Let $\theta$ °C = temperature of interface, $Q$ cal = heat loss per square metre per second. The heat passing through the walls of the tank is the same as that passing through the lagging.

Substituting in the equation

$$Q = kA \frac{\theta_1 - \theta_2}{x} t,$$

$$Q = 0·12 . 100^2 . \frac{70 - \theta}{0·80} = 0·0096 . 100^2 . \frac{\theta - 40}{2·0},$$

whence $\theta = 69·1$ °C and $Q = 1395$ cal.

Example 2. *Water passes through a glass tube 30 cm long at the rate of 165 c.c. per min. It enters the tube at 20 °C and leaves at 40 °C, the outside of the tube being maintained at 100 °C. If the internal and external radii of the tube are 6 and 8 mm respectively, determine the thermal conductivity of the glass.*

*Draw a diagram of the arrangement of the apparatus required for the performance of the experiment indicated in this problem.* (L.)

*Approximate method*

Average temperature gradient $= \dfrac{100 - \frac{1}{2}(20+40)}{0.8 - 0.6} = 350$ deg C cm$^{-1}$.

Average area through which heat is conducted

$$= 2\pi\left(\frac{0.8 + 0.6}{2}\right).30 = 42\pi \text{ cm}^2.$$

Heat conducted per minute $= 165(40-20) = 3300$ cal.
Substituting in the equation

$$Q = kA\frac{\theta_1 - \theta_2}{x}t,$$

$$3300 = k.42\pi.350.60,$$

$$k = 1.19 \times 10^{-3} \text{ cal cm}^{-1} \text{ sec}^{-1} \text{ deg}^{-1} \text{ C}.$$

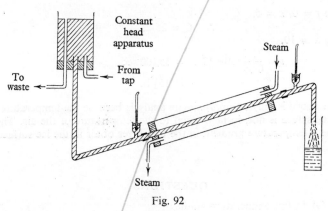

Fig. 92

*Exact method*

Substituting in the equation

$$k = \frac{Q\log_e(r_2/r_1)}{2\pi l t(\theta_1 - \theta_2)} \quad \text{(p. 140)}.$$

$$k = \frac{3300\log_e(0.8/0.6)}{2\pi.30.60(100 - \frac{1}{2}(20+40))}$$

$$= 1.20 \times 10^{-3} \text{ cal cm}^{-1} \text{ sec}^{-1} \text{ deg}^{-1} \text{ C}.$$

Fig. 92 is a diagram of apparatus suitable for the experiment indicated in the problem.

Example 3. *The thickness of the ice on a pond is 5 cm and the temperature of the air is* $-10$ °C. *How long will it take for the thickness of the ice to be doubled?*

(*Thermal conductivity of ice* $= 0.005$ *cal cm*$^{-1}$ *sec*$^{-1}$ *deg*$^{-1}$ *C. Density of ice* $= 0.92$ *gm cm*$^3$. *Latent heat of fusion of ice* $= 80$ *cal gm*$^{-1}$.

When the ice is $x$ cm thick let $\delta Q$ be conducted through an area of 1 cm² in $\delta t$ sec. From the defining equation for $k$

$$\delta Q = 0.005 \frac{10}{x} \delta t.$$

Suppose that in the time $\delta t$ sec, the thickness of the ice increases by $\delta x$ cm.

$$\delta Q = 80 \times 0.92 \, \delta x,$$

$$\therefore \quad \frac{0.05}{x} \delta t = 73.6 \, \delta x,$$

$$x \, \delta x = \frac{0.05}{73.6} \delta t.$$

Integrating, $\qquad \frac{1}{2}x^2 = \frac{0.05}{73.6} t + C.$

When $t = 0$, $x = 5$,

$$\therefore \quad C = 25/2.$$

When $x = 10$,

$$t = \frac{73.6}{0.05}(50 - 12.5) = 55\,100 \text{ sec}$$

$$= 15\tfrac{1}{3} \text{ h.}$$

The above is only an approximate analysis because the temperature of the ice surface is not, in fact, equal to the temperature of the air. There will be a temperature gradient in the thin layer of air at the ice surface.

## QUESTIONS

1. (a) Define temperature gradient.

(b) Two lagged bars of equal lengths and equal cross-sections are joined end to end in good thermal contact. If the ratio of their thermal conductivities is 2:1 and the free ends are at 100 and 0 °C, what is the temperature of the interface in the steady state?

2. Copper and iron bars of identical dimensions and efficiently lagged are each heated at one end with an electric heater and cooled at the other end by water circulating in a spiral copper tube wrapped round the bar. If the electric heaters generate the same power compare (a) the rates of flow of heat, (b) the temperature gradients, in the bars.

The electric heaters are now replaced by steam baths. Assuming that the temperatures of the ends of the bars in the steam baths are the same, again compare (a) the rates of flow of heat, (b) the temperature gradients, in the bars.

Why will the temperatures of the ends of the bars in the steam baths not, in fact, be the same?

(The thermal conductivity of copper is five times that of iron.)

3. (a) Define thermal conductivity.

(b) The thermal conductivity of copper is 0·918 cal/cm²/sec/deg C/cm. Find its value in Btu/sq.ft/h/deg F/in.

(30·5 cm = 1 ft; 454 gm = 1 lb.)

4. An aluminium saucepan which has a base of area 16 cm² and of thickness 4 mm contains boiling water and rests on an electric hotplate. The water boils away at the rate of 12 gm/min. What is the temperature of the underside of the saucepan, assuming it to be uniformly heated and neglecting heat losses from the side?

(Latent heat of vaporisation of water = 2260 J cal gm⁻¹. Thermal conductivity of aluminium = 2·1W cm⁻¹ deg⁻¹ C.)

5. An iron boiler is made of metal 4 mm thick and has become coated with a layer of scale 1·5 mm thick. Compare the rate of flow of heat through the coated walls with that obtained when the walls are clean, assuming in each case the same temperature difference between the outer wall of the boiler and the water inside.

(Thermal conductivities of iron 0·14, and of scale 0·005 cal sec⁻¹ C deg⁻¹ cm⁻¹.) (O.)

6. In order to maintain a temperature difference of 10 °C between the faces of a sheet of cardboard 1·0 mm thick, it is necessary to expend 0·20 W/cm² of surface, all the energy passing through the cardboard. What is the thermal conductivity of cardboard? (N.)

7. An ice box is built of wood 1·75 cm thick lined with cork 3·0 cm thick. If the temperature of the inner surface of the cork is 0 °C, and that of the outer surface of the wood 12 °C, what is the temperature of the interface?

(The conductivity of the wood is 0·00060 and of cork 0·00012 cal cm⁻¹ sec⁻¹ deg⁻¹ C.) (N.)

8. What are the differences in the design of apparatus for measuring the thermal conductivity of a poor conductor from that for a good conductor?

9. One end of a copper rod, immersed in boiling water, does not reach the temperature of the water because of a surface air film. Would the end of a glass rod, also immersed in the water, more nearly reach the temperature of the water, assuming it to be covered with an air film of the same thickness?

10. (a) Why is lightly crushed aluminium foil an effective heat insulator?

(b) Why is it possible, by putting poor lagging on a pipe of small diameter, to increase rather than to reduce the heat loss?

(c) A test tube filled with water is held in a beaker of boiling water. Will the water in the tube boil or not? Explain.

(d) A piece of ice is sunk in a test tube of water by tying it to a metal sinker. The water is boiled at its surface by a flame applied to the top of the test tube. Will the ice melt? Explain.

11. A steady stream of water flows at 1000 gm/min through a glass tube 14 cm long, with internal and external diameters 0·9 and 1·0 cm

respectively. The outside of the tube is surrounded by steam at 100 °C and the water entering at 15 °C is found to leave at 25 °C. Find an approximate value for the thermal conductivity of glass.    (O.)

12. Draw rough graphs to show the variation in temperature along a uniform bar of metal: (a) when the ends of the bar are kept at constant but different temperatures and the bar is lagged by heat-insulating material, (b) when the bar is heated at one end and the rest is exposed to the air. Discuss the factors which affect the loss of heat of a portion of the bar in the latter case.    (C.)

13. Discuss the parts played by conduction, convection and radiation in warming a room which is (a) centrally heated, (b) heated by an open fire. Discuss the relative merits of these two methods of space heating.

Describe a simple experiment for the determination of the thermal conductivity of a good conductor.    (N.)

14. Define *thermal conductivity*.

Heat is supplied to a slab of compressed cork, 5 cm thick and of effective area 2 m², by a heating coil spread over its surface. When the current in the coil is 1·18 A and the potential difference across its ends 20 V, the steady temperatures of the faces of the slab are 12·5 and 0 °C. Assuming that the whole of the heat developed in the coil is conducted through the slab, calculate the thermal conductivity of the cork.

Draw a diagram showing how you would propose to carry out the experiment suggested in this example.    (N.)

15. Describe a method of measuring the coefficient of thermal conductivity of a material which is a poor conductor of heat. Outline the experimental difficulties of the method.

A cubical copper box of 1000 l. capacity, suspended in air, is to be kept at a temperature of 60 °C by means of an internal electric heater. What saving of electric power would be achieved if the box were covered with a layer of asbestos 1 cm thick? The room temperature is 15 °C.

(You may assume that in both cases the outer surfaces lose heat to their surroundings at the rate of $10^{-3}$ W from each square centimetre of surface for each degree temperature difference from their surroundings. The coefficient of thermal conductivity of asbestos is $1·26 \times 10^{-3}$ W cm$^{-1}$ deg$^{-1}$.)
    (O. & C.)

16. A portion of a rubber pipe through which steam, at 100 °C, is passing is immersed in a calorimeter of cold water, and the initial rise of temperature observed. Calculate approximately the thermal conductivity of rubber from the following data.

| | |
|---|---|
| Length of pipe immersed | = 20 cm |
| External radius of pipe | = 0·5 cm |
| Internal radius of pipe | = 0·3 cm |
| Mass of water in calorimeter | = 300 gm |
| Water equivalent of calorimeter | = 15 gm |
| Initial temperature of water | = 16 °C |
| Initial rate of rise of temperature | = 2 °C per min.    (N.) |

17. Estimate the daily loss of heat by conduction through the windows of the average house. (Conductivity of glass = 0·0025 cal cm$^{-1}$ °C$^{-1}$ sec$^{-1}$.) Make reasonable estimates of the values of the quantities involved.

(C.S.)

18. Show that the rate of increase of thickness of ice on a pond is given by

$$\frac{dx}{dt} = \frac{k\theta}{\rho L x},$$

where $x$ is the thickness at time $t$; $k$, $\rho$ and $L$ are the thermal conductivity, density, and latent heat of ice respectively, and $\theta$ is the temperature of the air.

19. If the air temperature remains constant at $-10$ °C find the increase in thickness of the ice on a pond between 7 p.m. and 7 a.m. if the initial thickness was 10 cm.

(Conductivity of ice = 0·005 cal/cm²/unit C temp gradient/sec. Density of ice = 0·917 gm/c.c. Latent heat of ice = 80 cal/gm.) (C.S.)

20. Describe a method suitable for the determination of the thermal conductivity of a liquid. Give the relevant theory.

An insulated wire, whose specific resistance is $5 \times 10^{-5}$ Ω cm, and diameter 1 mm, carries a current of 5 A. The insulation is 1 mm thick and has a thermal conductivity of $5 \times 10^{-4}$ c.g.s. centigrade units. Find the temperature difference between the inner and outer surfaces of the insulating material.

($J = 4·2$ J/cal; $\log_e 3 = 1·098$.)

21. Define thermal conductivity and describe an experiment for determining its value for copper.

Steam at 100 °C is passed continuously through a hollow rubber sphere of diameter 40 cm and water is found to accumulate inside the sphere at the rate of 25 gm/min when the temperature of the outer surface of the sphere is constant at 60 °C. If the thickness of the rubber is 0·40 cm find its thermal conductivity. Assume that the latent heat of steam at 100 °C is 540 cal gm$^{-1}$. (N.)

22. Describe how you would attempt to measure the thermal conductivity of window glass.

The glass of the window of a room is 5 mm thick and has an area of 4 m². If heat can escape only through the window calculate the electrical power required to keep the room at a uniform temperature 20 °C above the external temperature. Repeat the calculation for a double window of the same area which consists of two sheets of glass 5 mm thick separated by a layer of air 2·5 mm thick. Assume that there is no convection of the air between the sheets of glass.

Comment briefly on the answers you obtain in the two cases.

(Thermal conductivities in cal cm$^{-1}$ s$^{-1}$ °C$^{-1}$: glass $2·5 \times 10^{-3}$, air $5·0 \times 10^{-5}$.) (C.S.)

$K_{air} = 24 \times 10^{-3}$

$K: glass = 7 \times 10^{-4}$

CHAPTER 9

# THERMAL RADIATION

In 1800 Sir William Herschel investigated the heating effect of the different parts of the solar spectrum by means of a sensitive mercury thermometer and found that the heating effect extended beyond the red into what is now known as the infra-red. He showed that the infra-red radiation could be reflected and refracted and spoke of it as 'invisible light', but this view of the nature of radiation was not generally accepted for 50 years.

The invisible radiation given off by a hot body is usually called *thermal radiation* (or radiant heat) because its origin is the thermal agitation of the particles of the body. We shall sometimes use the alternative term *infra-red radiation* when we wish to relate the radiation to the rest of the spectrum.

The history of the study of thermal radiation can be divided into four main phases. During the first phase it was conclusively demonstrated that the heating effect of thermal radiation is caused, not by a flow of caloric through space, but by the energy of invisible waves similar to light. This was in the first half of the nineteenth century when both the wave theory of light and the kinetic theory of heat were being established.

During the second phase, which overlapped with the first, physicists were interested in the relative powers of different surfaces to emit and to absorb thermal radiation, and in the absorption of thermal radiation during its transmission through solids, liquids and gases. This was an almost wholly experimental phase, when many useful facts were discovered, but no new or exciting vistas were opened.

The third phase proved to be of profound significance for the whole of physics. It began, as we shall see, with the concept of black-body radiation, which is independent of the nature of the body emitting it and is determined only by the temperature. This stimulated, on the one hand, precise experimental measurements of the distribution of the energy among the different wavelengths in black-body radiation and, on the other, the formulation of mathematical theories to account for the experimental results, culminating in the quantum theory of Max Planck.

In the fourth and present phase the improvement of measuring instruments has enabled the vast and intricate field of infra-red spectral bands and lines to be explored and this has yielded information about the structure of molecules, since infra-red radiation is emitted as a result of changes in the vibrational and rotational states of molecules, caused by thermal agitation.

This chapter will be concerned mainly with the third phase. Some reference will be made to the other phases but not necessarily in chronological order.

## Measuring instruments

There are two types of instrument used for detecting and measuring thermal radiation: (a) thermal detectors, (b) photo-detectors. We shall consider in detail only thermal detectors, because they were the type used in the investigation of black-body radiation.

The simplest thermal detector is, of course, the human skin, which experiences a sensation of warmth when thermal radiation falls upon it. The earliest investigators used thermometers; we have already mentioned Sir William Herschel's use of the mercury thermometer. John Leslie (1766–1832) devised a sensitive differential air thermometer (Fig. 97, p. 156). Two blackened glass bulbs containing air are connected by a glass U-tube containing a liquid; if the radiation falling on one of the bulbs is greater than on the other, the expansion of the air will cause the liquid to move.

The two chief thermal detectors used today are the thermopile and the bolometer. The thermopile was first employed by Nobili in 1830 and then by Melloni and others for half a century. In 1880 Langley invented the bolometer and it was far more sensitive than contemporary thermopiles, enabling wavelengths of infra-red radiation to be measured with gratings for the first time. Today there is little to choose between the thermopile and the bolometer, except that, as we shall see, superconducting bolometers at the temperature of solid hydrogen are the most sensitive of all thermal detectors.

## The thermopile

An old type of thermopile still used for demonstration purposes is represented diagrammatically in Fig. 93. Thermocouples consisting of tiny rods of antimony and bismuth, which give a large thermo-e.m.f., are connected in series, and they are arranged so that the radiation falls on one set of junctions, causing a rise in temperature, while the other set of junctions remains cold. The current through the galvanometer is a measure of the intensity of the radiation. In

Fig. 93 only two thermocouples are shown but, in practice, there may be twenty-five, arranged to form a solid cube, the rods being insulated from each other by thin sheets of mica. The 'hot' junctions are blackened, so as to absorb as much of the radiation as possible, and they are screened by means of a conical metal hood. Only radiation contained within the solid angle of the conical hood reaches the 'hot' junctions and hence the galvanometer reading is independent of the distance of the thermopile from the radiating surface (so long as the surface subtends an angle at the thermopile no smaller than the angle of the conical hood).

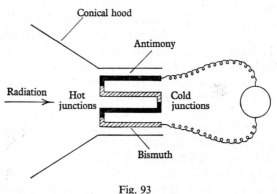

Fig. 93

An equally sensitive thermopile,† made of copper–constantan thermocouples, may be constructed in the laboratory. Constantan strip, 0·3 mm broad and $\frac{1}{100}$ mm thick, rolled from No. 44 s.w.g. constantan wire, is mounted on a brass frame, of the shape shown in Fig. 94, and coated with shellac varnish, so that half of the winding lies flat against the back of the frame and the other half is stretched between the two ridges. A coating of copper is deposited on half of the winding by electrolysis, using a copper sulphate solution. Copper is so much better an electrical conductor than constantan that the resulting winding is equivalent to a set of copper–constantan thermocouples. The whole unit may be mounted, with a hood similar to that in Fig. 93; the radiation should fall on the free junctions between the ridges of the frame.

One of the early problems in the use of thermopiles was that the existing galvanometers had too high a resistance. Boys overcame this difficulty in his radio-micrometer by incorporating a single thermo-couple of antimony and bismuth in series with a low resistance

† See *Science Masters' Book. Part I. Physics, Series I.* London: John Murray.

moving-coil of a mirror galvanometer. His instrument was a great advance at the time but is not now used.

In modern practice, galvanometers are replaced by thermionic amplifiers and only a single thermocouple is used. There may be another thermocouple, connected in opposition and not exposed to the radiation, in order to reduce the effects of ambient temperatures, i.e. changes in temperature not caused by the radiation.

Since its sensitivity depends upon the rise in temperature of the 'hot' junction, a thermocouple should have as low a thermal capacity as possible. Modern thermocouples often take the form of thin evaporated or sputtered films of, say, antimony-bismuth or tellurium-bismuth or some thin insulating backing. Attached to the 'hot' junction there is usually a thin, blackened metal foil to act as the receiver of the radiation.

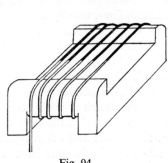

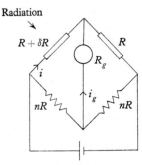

Radiation

Fig. 94                    Fig. 95

## The bolometer

Langley's bolometer consisted of two very thin blackened strips of platinum forming two arms of a balanced Wheatstone bridge (Fig. 95). The radiation to be measured was allowed to fall on one of the strips, thereby raising its temperature and hence increasing its electrical resistance from $R$ to $R+\delta R$. The Wheatstone bridge became unbalanced and the out-of-balance current, $i_g$, was measured with a sensitive galvanometer.

The student should prove that

$$i_g = \frac{i\delta R}{2R_g+(n+1)R}.$$

From this equation the change in the resistance, $\delta R$, of the bolometer can be obtained. It is then possible to calculate the rise in temperature of the bolometer, knowing the temperature coefficient of resistance of platinum, and the heat energy of the radiation, knowing the thermal capacity of the bolometer.

Modern bolometers are often made of semiconductors, which have a much higher (negative) temperature coefficient of resistance than platinum; instead of direct current and a galvanometer, alternating current and thermionic amplifiers are employed.

The superconducting bolometer utilises a thin ribbon of niobium nitride, cooled by means of solid hydrogen to 14 °K, at which temperature it is in the intermediate zone between its normal and its superconducting state (see p. 109). A change of temperature of 1 °C results in a change of resistance of about 10 $\Omega$, enabling a pulse of radiation of $10^{-6}$ erg to be detected.

### Photo-detectors

Thermal detectors respond to all wavelengths but a photo-detector has a well-defined long wavelength limit, usually within the near infra-red (i.e. just beyond the red end of the spectrum). Photo-detectors are based on either the photo-electric effect, which is the emission of electrons from certain surfaces when radiation falls upon them, or photo-conductivity, which is a kind of internal photo-electric effect, the electrons being emitted in the interior of the sub-stance and giving rise to an increase in electrical conductivity. During the Second World War, using photo-detectors, the Germans developed a type of infra-red television. Aircraft and other objects were floodlit at night by a searchlight radiating in the near infra-red and an image was formed on a phosphorescent screen.

### The nature of infra-red radiation

That infra-red radiation (or thermal radiation) travels with the same velocity as light is evident from the fact that the heat is cut off at the same moment as the light when the sun is obscured by clouds or at an eclipse. It is evident too that infra-red radiation can travel through a vacuum.

Infra-red radiation obeys the same laws of reflection as light and can be focused by concave parabolic mirrors as in Fig. 96. If a hot source such as a metal ball at a temperature just below red heat is placed at $S$, a thermopile placed at $T$ will be strongly affected even though the mirrors may be many metres apart. Again, infra-red radiation is obviously refracted like light because it may be dispersed into an extension of the visible spectrum by a prism. The controversy about the nature of infra-red radiation was settled in 1847, when Fizeau and Foucault showed that it exhibited interference.

The wavelength is usually expressed in microns, denoted by $\mu$; $1\,\mu$ is a millionth of a metre or $10^{-4}$ cm. The visible spectrum lies between $0\cdot4\,\mu$ (violet) and $0\cdot75\,\mu$ (red). There was another controversy about the extension of the infra-red spectrum, and for a long time the spectrum was thought not to extend beyond $1\,\mu$. The improvement of detectors, however, enabled longer and longer wavelengths to be measured and the gap between infra-red and very short radio waves has now not only been closed but overlapped. An arbitrary limit to infra-red radiation is put at $1000\,\mu$ or 1 mm, and the infra-red spectrum is subdivided according to the techniques of measurement, as follows:

| | |
|---|---|
| $0\cdot75$–$1\cdot5\,\mu$ | Near infra-red |
| $1\cdot5$–$10\,\mu$ | Intermediate infra-red |
| $10$–$1000\,\mu$ | Far infra-red. |

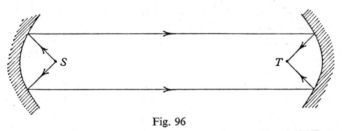

Fig. 96

## Prévost's Theory of Exchanges

We must now turn back to the end of the eighteenth century to consider the genesis of one of the basic ideas in the theory of radiation.

If a thermopile is placed in front of a block of ice the deflection of the galvanometer is opposite to the normal direction as though the ice were radiating 'cold' instead of heat. To account for phenomena of this kind Prévost, in 1792, put forward his *theory of exchanges*. He assumed that bodies at all temperatures are emitting thermal radiation but that bodies at lower temperatures emit less thermal radiation in a given time than similar bodies at higher temperatures. Thus ice emits less thermal radiation than a thermopile at room temperature. The thermopile receives less than it emits, losing on the exchange, and its temperature falls. A body which remains at constant temperature absorbs thermal radiation from its surroundings at the same rate as it emits. Prévost's valuable contribution to physics was this concept of *dynamic equilibrium*.

An unlikely alternative would be that a body, once it reaches the temperature of its surroundings, ceases to radiate. Kirchhoff stated clearly the unacceptability of this hypothesis: 'A luminous body in space sends out light rays that are independent of the bodies on which they fall; similarly all heat rays which a body sends out are independent of the bodies which form its environment.'

## Absorptivity and emissivity

One of the fundamental facts about thermal radiation is that it is absorbed and emitted to a different extent by different kinds of surfaces. A black surface is a good absorber and a good emitter whereas a polished surface is a poor absorber (because a good reflector) and a poor emitter.

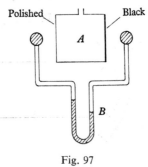

The phenomena were investigated by Leslie at the beginning of the nineteenth century using the apparatus in Fig. 97. *A* is a hollow metal box containing hot water, known as Leslie's cube, and *B* is Leslie's differential air thermometer. The four vertical faces of the cube were prepared in different ways, one being coated with lamp-black and the opposite one brightly polished. The black surface emitted more radiation than the polished surface, as shown by the movement of the liquid in Fig. 97. By using a differential air thermometer having one bulb blackened and the other polished, Leslie showed that a black surface is a better absorber, as well as a better emitter, than a polished surface.

Fig. 97

It follows from Prévost's theory of exchanges that good absorbers must be good emitters. The temperature of a good absorber, which was a poor emitter instead of a good one, would spontaneously rise above that of its surroundings and this would be contrary to experience.

If a piece of porcelain, having a dark pattern on a white ground, is raised to white heat, the pattern appears to be reversed; the dark parts are brighter than the white parts, since the better absorbers are the better emitters.

A body which absorbs all the radiation falling upon it is called a *black body*. No perfect black body exists in nature although lamp-black (i.e. soot) absorbs about 0·95 of incident radiation in the visible, near infra-red and intermediate infra-red. The ratio of the energy absorbed to the energy falling upon a surface is known as the *absorptivity* of the surface. It varies from 0 for a perfect reflector or transmitter to 1 for a black body.

Because a black body is a perfect absorber it must also be a perfect emitter. The radiation it emits is known as *black-body radiation*. The ratio of the energy emitted by a surface to that emitted at the same temperature by a black body of the same area in the same time is known as the *emissivity*† of the surface. Emissivity, like absorptivity, varies from 0 to 1.

### Kirchhoff's law

Suppose that a body is placed in an enclosure, evacuated of air to eliminate convection and conduction, and kept at a constant temperature—known as a *constant-temperature enclosure*. The radiation in the enclosure is black-body radiation, as we shall show shortly.

Let the intensity of the radiation in the enclosure be $I$ and the absorptivity and emissivity of the body be $a$ and $e$ respectively. When the body has attained the steady temperature of the enclosure it will be emitting radiation at the same rate as it absorbs it:

$$eI = aI,$$
$$\therefore \quad e = a.$$

Thus *the emissivity of a surface is equal to its absorptivity*. This is the substance of *Kirchhoff's law*, although not as Kirchhoff himself expressed it.

A perfectly transparent body, since it has zero absorptivity, must have zero emissivity. Glass, when strongly heated, glows only slightly—a hazard for the glass blower. The fact that it glows at all shows that it is not perfectly transparent at the high temperature concerned. A perfect reflector, likewise, has zero absorptivity, and so must have zero emissivity.

A small hole in a constant-temperature enclosure has unit absorptivity since it admits and absorbs all radiation. Hence it must have unit emissivity, i.e. it behaves as a black body. As this argument may not seem completely convincing we will discuss the conclusion more fully.

### Black-body radiation in a constant-temperature enclosure

When two bodies which emit radiation of different wavelengths are placed in a constant-temperature enclosure and attain the same

† The term emissivity is also used to denote a quite different quantity, namely the heat lost per unit time from unit area per degree difference in temperature with the surroundings.

temperature it is not easy to see why their radiations should balance. The key to the problem is the fundamental conception that the radiation inside a constant-temperature enclosure is black-body or full radiation, being independent of the nature and shape of the walls and depending only upon the temperature. This is of such far-reaching theoretical importance that we will consider it in a little detail.

Suppose that we put a body coated with lamp-black, which is a nearly perfect black body, in a constant-temperature enclosure with polished walls. The black body acquires the same temperature as the enclosure and the radiation inside the enclosure must be black-body radiation, otherwise the temperature of the black body would fall. If we put other bodies, with emissivities less than 1, in the enclosure they will absorb some of the black-body radiation, and reflect the rest. But what will happen if we remove the black body from the polished enclosure and leave the latter empty? The walls of the enclosure do not absorb and emit much radiation, but they reflect well and, as a result of innumerable reflections, a state of equilibrium will be attained in which the enclosure contains black-body radiation.

To prove that this must be so, suppose that two enclosures at the same temperature, one with lamp-blacked walls and one with polished walls, are put into communication by making a small hole in each. If the energy density of the radiation in the black enclosure is higher than that in the polished enclosure, there will be a net transfer of radiation from the black to the polished enclosure. This will be absorbed by the polished enclosure, since the equilibrium conditions will be disturbed, and the temperature of the polished enclosure will rise. Similarly, the temperature of the black enclosure will fall. The phenomenon could be adapted to run a perpetual-motion machine and hence we must conclude, from the principle of the conservation of energy, that the energy densities of the radiation in the two enclosures are the same.

A constant-temperature enclosure, with a hole small enough not to upset the equilibrium of the radiation inside it, is used as a source of black-body radiation (Fig. 98). If the enclosure is red- or white-hot, the glow one sees on looking into the hole gives no indication of the nature of the walls. The brightness of $F$ in Fig. 98 is the brightness one would see if there were no reflections, plus the brightness of $E$ once reflected, plus the brightness of $D$ twice reflected, and so on *ad infinitum*.

Cavities in a very hot coal fire, which approximate to constant-temperature enclosures, are indistinct in outline and it is often difficult to distinguish the boundaries of the separate pieces of coal.

## Stefan's law

In 1879 Stefan discovered empirically the law that the total radiation from a body is proportional to the fourth power of the absolute temperature of the body, and in 1884 Boltzmann showed theoretically that this is true only for a black body. The law, which is sometimes known as *Stefan's law* and sometimes as the Stefan–Boltzmann law, may be stated as follows: *the total radiation from a black body is proportional to the fourth power of the absolute temperature of the body.*

The law may be expressed mathematically in the form $E = \sigma T^4$, where $E$ is the energy radiated in ergs per cm² per sec by a black body, $\sigma$ is a constant known as Stefan's constant, and $T$ is the

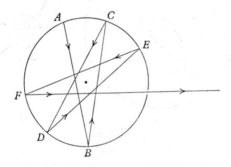

Fig. 98

absolute temperature of the body. The net loss of energy per cm² per sec from the body is $\sigma(T^4 - T_0^4)$, where $T_0$ is the absolute temperature of the surroundings.

The law was accurately verified in 1897 by Lummer and Pringsheim for the range of temperatures 100 to 1300 °C. Their black body was a cavity with a small opening and their measuring instrument was a bolometer. The value of Stefan's constant, $\sigma$, is $5 \cdot 75 \times 10^{-5}$ erg cm⁻² sec⁻¹ deg⁻⁴ C.

If a surface has the same emissivity, $e$, for all wavelengths it is said to be *grey*; it appears uncoloured, since it reflects all visible wavelengths to the eye. Its net loss of energy per cm² per sec is $e\sigma\,(T^4 - T_0^4)$, using the same symbols as before.

## The temperature of the sun

An impressive application of Stefan's law is to calculate the temperature of the surface of the sun, regarding the sun and the earth as black bodies. It is assumed that the earth has reached a condition of equilibrium in which the radiation received from the sun counterbalances the radiation emitted by the earth into space. The only data required are the mean temperature of the surface of the earth, 17 °C, and the angle subtended at the earth by the diameter of the sun, 32 min.

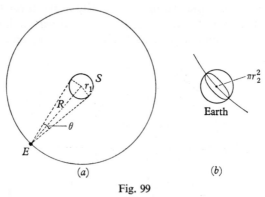

(a)                    (b)

Fig. 99

In Fig. 99(a) let E represent the earth, and S the sun. The radius of the earth's orbit and of the sun are $R$ and $r_1$ respectively and $\theta$ is the angle subtended by the sun at the earth.

$$\frac{r_1}{R} = \frac{\theta}{2}.$$

Let $T$ °K = temperature of surface of sun

$\quad r_2$ = radius of earth.

Applying Stefan's law:

Energy radiated by sun $\quad = 4\pi r_1^2 \sigma T^4$.

Energy radiated by earth $= 4\pi r_2^2 \sigma\, 290^4$.

The fraction of the sun's energy received by the earth is the ratio of the area of the earth's diametral plane, $\pi r_2^2$ (Fig. 99b), to the area of the sphere of radius $R$ surrounding the sun, $4\pi R^2$.

∴ Fraction of sun's energy received by earth $= \pi r_2^2 / 4\pi R^2$.

$$\therefore \frac{\pi r_2^2}{4\pi R^2} \cdot 4\pi r_1^2 \sigma T^4 = 4\pi r_2^2 \sigma 290^4.$$

$$T^4 = 290^4 \frac{4R^2}{r_1^2}$$

$$= 290^4 \frac{16}{\theta^2}$$

$$= \frac{290^4 \times 16}{\left(\dfrac{32 \times \pi}{180 \times 60}\right)^2}.$$

$$T = 6010 \,°\text{K.}$$

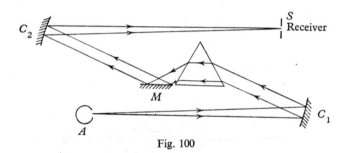

Fig. 100

### The distribution of energy in the spectrum of black-body radiation

The principle of a modern instrument, known as a spectro-radiometer, for investigating the distribution of energy in the spectrum of black-body radiation, is indicated in Fig. 100. A uniformly heated cavity $A$ with a small aperture is the source; the prism is of rock salt or fluorite (since glass absorbs infra-red radiation) and the beams are focused by concave mirrors, $C_1$ and $C_2$, which have the advantage over lenses, apart from non-absorption, of possessing the same focal length for visible as for invisible radiation, and hence of easy adjustment. A receiver, such as a linear bolometer or thermopile, is placed behind the slit $S$ and is fixed in position while the spectrum is made to traverse the slit by rotating the prism. The function of the mirror $M$ is to annul the deviation caused by the prism and hence to ensure that the whole spectrum is scanned at $S$ in the minimum deviation position.

The readings of the receiver give the intensities, $E_\lambda$, of the radiation for different wavelengths, $\lambda$. Fig. 101 shows the variation of $E_\lambda$

with $\lambda$ for different temperatures. It will be seen that there is a position of maximum energy at each temperature and that this maximum is displaced towards the shorter wavelengths as the temperature of the source increases.

The total radiation emitted by the source at each temperature is $\int_0^\infty E_\lambda \, d\lambda$, which is represented by the area under the curve. These areas are found to be proportional to the fourth power of the

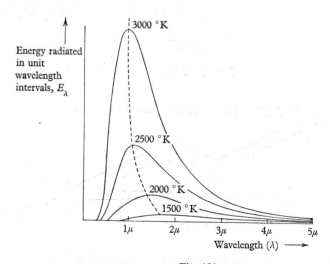

Fig. 101

absolute temperature, in accordance with Stefan's law. Note how considerably they increase with rise of temperature, particularly above 2000 °K.

If we wish to increase the radiative heating, as opposed to the convective heating, of an electric fire we can do so by raising the temperature of its heating element. This will greatly increase the energy radiated, while affecting very little the heat distributed by convection currents in the air.

The temperature of the filament of the ordinary electric light bulb must be as high as possible in order to produce the maximum of energy in the visible region. The filament of the gas-filled tungsten lamp has a temperature of about 3000 °C; that for special photographic bulbs is about 3500 °C.

## Wien's displacement law

In 1896 Wien deduced, by thermodynamical reasoning, that the wavelength of maximum intensity, $\lambda_{max.}$, is related to the absolute temperature, $T$, of the source by the simple equation

$$\lambda_{max}. T = \text{constant}.$$

This was verified by the experiments of Lummer and Pringsheim, three years later. The constant in Wien's equation is 0·29 cm deg C.

Wien's displacement law provides another method of determining the temperature of the surface of the sun, and indeed of the stars. The wavelength of maximum energy in the solar spectrum is $4·9 \times 10^{-5}$ cm. If $T$ is the absolute temperature of the sun,

$$4·9 \times 10^{-5}T = 0·29,$$

$$T = 5920 \text{ °K}.$$

## The quantum theory

Several attempts were made to deduce mathematically equations representing the curves in Fig. 101. Wien obtained a radiation law, but it contained an unknown function which could not be deduced by the thermodynamical methods he employed.

Lord Rayleigh proved, from the principles of Newtonian dynamics, that the energy should be concentrated in the short-wavelength region—a result which has been called the ultraviolet catastrophe and which is in complete disagreement with the experimental results.

Planck, starting from Wien's radiation law, found by trial and error an expression† which fitted the experimental facts. He then attempted to deduce the expression from first principles.

According to classical theory, electromagnetic waves are radiated as a result of the non-uniform motion of an electric charge; for example, high-frequency alternating currents radiate electromagnetic waves. Planck imagined the walls of a constant-temperature enclosure to contain electric oscillators, say vibrating electrons, of all possible frequencies, emitting and receiving thermal radiation. By the principle of the equipartition of energy, the mean energies of the oscillators

† Planck's radiation law may be expressed as follows:

$$E_\lambda d\lambda = \frac{8\pi ch}{\lambda^5} \frac{1}{e^{ch/k\lambda T}-1} d\lambda.$$

$E_\lambda$ is the emissive power of a black body for wavelength $\lambda$, so that $E_\lambda d\lambda$ represents the energy radiated in the narrow wavelength interval $d\lambda$. $T$ is the absolute temperature, $c$ is the velocity of light, $h$ is Planck's constant, $k$ is Boltzmann's constant and $e$ is the base of natural logarithms (2·7183).

should be the same. The possible number of frequencies is infinite and there will be far more oscillators of high frequency than of medium or low frequency. Hence nearly all the energy should be of high frequency, i.e. of short wavelength—the result obtained by Rayleigh.

Planck could find no way of surmounting this difficulty except by assuming that the energy of his vibrating oscillators could exist only in discrete amounts, called quanta. Each quantum has an energy $hv$, where $h$ is a universal constant now known as Planck's constant, and $v$ is the frequency of the vibration. Thus the quanta of high frequency represent a larger amount of energy than the quanta of low frequency.

Now thermal radiation is radiation due to temperature and the energy of the oscillators is derived from thermal motions. The quanta of high-frequency oscillators above a certain limiting frequency will be greater than the thermal energy available and the energy will therefore be distributed among the oscillators with a lower frequency than this limiting frequency.

In this way Planck was able to deduce his radiation law, but only at the expense of producing a revolution in physics. His conception that energy is not continuous but atomic, and can exist only in discrete quantities, has been called by Professor William Wilson 'perhaps the greatest of all scientific discoveries which have ever been made'.

Planck published his theory in 1900 and at first it was not taken seriously. When, however, it was applied by Einstein to explain the photo-electric effect (1905) and the variation of specific heat with temperature (1907), and by Bohr to explain the radiation from Rutherford's nuclear atom (1913), it became universally accepted. It now dominates atomic physics.

### Radiation pyrometers

Above about 1000 °C the best method of determining the temperature of a body is to measure the radiation it emits. Instruments used for this purpose are termed radiation pyrometers and they are of two types: (a) total radiation pyrometers which respond to both invisible and visible radiation; (b) optical pyrometers which respond only to visible radiation.

### Total radiation pyrometer

An example of the first type is the instrument designed by Féry, which is essentially a reflecting telescope having a thermocouple at the focus of the objective (Fig. 102). The radiation from the hot body falls upon a gold-plated concave mirror and is focused on a small piece of blackened metal foil attached to a junction of a thermocouple. The mirror is pierced at its centre to allow observation through an eyepiece to ensure that the foil is correctly placed at the position where the radiation is focused. The foil is heated by the radiation and reaches an equilibrium temperature when it is losing heat as fast as it is receiving it. This equilibrium temperature is measured by the deflection of a millivoltmeter connected to the thermocouple. The temperature of the surroundings must remain approximately constant while the instrument is in use.

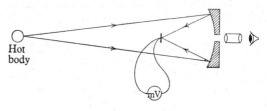

Fig. 102

The instrument may be calibrated at 1063·0 °C by sighting it on molten gold at its freezing point and then Stefan's law may be applied to determine other temperatures. If $T$ is the temperature of the hot body and $T_0$ that of the foil on which the radiation falls,

Deflection of millivoltmeter $= k(T^4 - T_0^4)$

$$\simeq kT^4 \quad (T_0^4 \text{ is small compared with } T^4).$$

The constant, $k$, is determined by the deflection at the gold point.

It is usual, however, not to apply Stefan's law, but to calibrate the instrument at a number of known temperatures because, for various minor reasons, the deflection of the millivoltmeter is not strictly proportional to the net energy absorbed by the foil.

The readings of the instrument give not the actual temperature of the body but what is known as its *black-body temperature*, i.e. the temperature of the black body emitting the same intensity of radiation as the body. To calculate the body's actual temperature its emissivity must be known. In the case of the metals this may be less than 0·5. A common industrial use of the instrument, however, is to find the temperature of a furnace, and an aperture in a furnace approximates to a black body.

### Optical pyrometer

A typical optical pyrometer is the disappearing-filament pyrometer and this consists of a refracting telescope having a tungsten lamp filament at the focus of its objective (Fig. 103). The eye observes, through the eyepiece and a red filter, the filament against a background formed by the image of a small area of the hot body. If the image of the hot body is brighter than the filament, the filament appears dark on a bright ground and vice versa. The current through the lamp is adjusted until the filament disappears.

The optical pyrometer has been used to establish the International Temperature Scale in the range between the gold point and 2000 °C by determining subsidiary fixed points such as the freezing point of

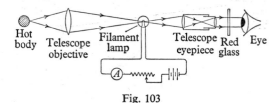

Fig. 103

palladium (1552 °C) and of rhodium (1960 °C). The instrument is calibrated at the gold point. It is then sighted, say on molten palladium, and the filament is made to disappear by rotating in front of the instrument a disc from which a sector has been cut. If the sector cut away has an angle $\theta$ radians, the fraction of the radiation transmitted is $\theta/2\pi$. Hence, if the current through the filament is unchanged from that at the gold point (actually a minor adjustment may be necessary) the radiation from the palladium has an intensity $2\pi/\theta$ that at the gold point. The temperature of the palladium may then be found by applying Planck's radiation law connecting the intensity of the radiation of the particular narrow range of wavelengths employed and the temperature.

The optical pyrometer is simpler and more accurate than the total radiation pyrometer. The latter has the advantage, however, that the radiation received is strong enough to actuate automatic recording or controlling devices.

### Diathermancy and athermancy

Substances which transmit thermal radiation are said to be *diathermanous* and those which absorb thermal radiation are said to be *athermanous*; the corresponding terms for light are transparent and opaque respectively. A dark solution of iodine in carbon disulphide is diathermanous but opaque; glass, on the other hand, is athermanous (beyond about 2·5 $\mu$) but transparent.

Since glass is athermanous, it should not be used for the prisms and lenses in apparatus designed for dispersing thermal radiation into a spectrum. A rock salt or fluorite prism may be employed.

Water too is transparent but athermanous and hence can be used as a filter in a projection lantern, to protect delicate transparencies from the thermal radiation emitted by a powerful projection lamp.

### The greenhouse

Glass is athermanous and yet it is used for greenhouses. The explanation is that glass transmits up to about 2·5 $\mu$ and hence admits into the greenhouse most of the energy of sunlight, whose

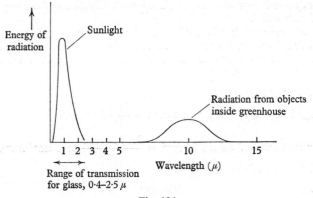

Fig. 104

maximum is at about 0·5 $\mu$ (Fig. 104). Plants and flowerpots absorb this radiation but emit thermal radiation of much longer wavelength, in the neighbourhood of 10 $\mu$, all of which is absorbed by the glass and re-radiated part into and part outside the greenhouse.

### Atmospheric transmission of thermal radiation

About 40 % of the sun's radiation is lost by molecular scattering and reflection but, of the rest, only about 6 % is absorbed by the atmosphere. Of the energy radiated by the earth, however, even on a clear night about 70 % is absorbed by the atmosphere. The explanation is similar to that given above for the greenhouse. The sun has a temperature of 6000 °K and the maximum energy of its radiation is at about 0·5 $\mu$, whereas the corresponding figures for the earth are

290 °K and 10 $\mu$. Water vapour, carbon dioxide and other compound gases in the atmosphere transmit visible radiation but absorb infra-red radiation.

The atmosphere has several well-defined bands of transmission for infra-red radiation, known as atmospheric windows. Modern study of its selective absorption has shown that it contains, in small quantities, such substances as HDO (heavy water vapour), CO, $CH_4$ and $N_2O$.

The energy that the earth would receive from the sun per unit area per unit time in the absence of the atmosphere is known as the *solar constant*. Its value is about 2 cal cm$^{-2}$ min$^{-1}$, which is sufficient to melt a layer of ice 1·6 cm thick every hour.

Example. *Find the temperature of the surface of the sun, given that the solar constant, which is the energy that the earth receives from the sun per unit area per unit time, allowing for the absorption by the earth's atmosphere, is 2 cal cm$^{-2}$ min$^{-1}$.*

(*Stefan's constant is* 5·7 × 10$^{-5}$ *erg cm*$^{-2}$ *sec*$^{-1}$ *deg*$^{-4}$ *C, and the radii of the earth's orbit and of the sun are* 9·3 × 10$^7$ *and* 4·3 × 10$^5$ *miles respectively.*)

Taking $S$ as the solar constant, $R$ the radius of the earth's orbit and $r$ the radius of the sun,

Total energy radiated by sun $= 4\pi R^2 S$.

Energy radiated by sun per unit area $= \dfrac{4\pi R^2 S}{4\pi r^2} = \dfrac{R^2}{r^2} S.$

Solar constant $= 2$ cal cm$^{-2}$ min$^{-1} = \dfrac{2 \times 4\cdot18 \times 10^7}{60}$ ergs cm$^{-2}$ sec$^{-1}$.

Applying Stefan's law to the sun,

$$E = \sigma T^4,$$

$$\left(\frac{9\cdot3 \times 10^7}{4\cdot3 \times 10^5}\right)^2 \left(\frac{2 \times 4\cdot18 \times 10^7}{60}\right) = 5\cdot7 \times 10^{-5} T^4,$$

$$\therefore \quad T = 5820 \ °K.$$

## QUESTIONS

1. Name four instruments which may be used to indicate or measure thermal radiation. What is the principle of each?

2. How would you show that thermal radiation:
   (a) can be reflected like light;
   (b) has a longer wavelength than red light?

3. The reading of a thermopile with a conical hood is independent of the distance of the thermopile from a large radiating surface. Show that this indicates that thermal radiation obeys the inverse square law.

4. A thermos flask consists of a glass vessel with thin double-walls, the space between the walls being evacuated and the surfaces of the walls, facing each other across the vacuum, being silvered (Fig. 105). Explain why it can be used for storing hot tea or liquid air.

5. In Fig. 106 A is a Leslie cube, with one face blackened and the opposite face polished. The bulbs B and C of the differential air thermometer are made of the same metal as the Leslie cube, B having a blackened face opposite A, and C a polished face opposite A. What happens to the liquid in the thermometer?

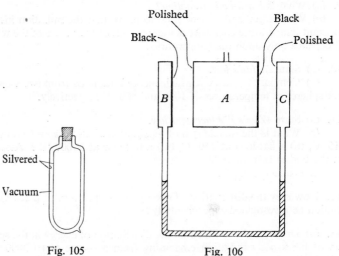

Fig. 105          Fig. 106

The Leslie cube is turned through 180°, so that two black faces adjoin and similarly two polished faces adjoin. What happens now to the liquid in the thermometer?

What deductions can be drawn from this experiment (first performed by Ritchie in 1833)?

6. A piece of ice is placed at the focus of a concave mirror. Facing this mirror and some distance from it is a second concave mirror at the focus of which is the bulb of a thermometer. Explain the reading of the thermometer.

7. State Prévost's theory of exchanges. Show that the emissivity of a body is equal to its absorptivity.

8. Explain the following with reference to the physical principles involved.

(a) When an atomic bomb was dropped on Japan, blue dots on a white dress, at some distance from the centre of the explosion, were burnt out but not the white dress.

(b) All bodies in a furnace at a uniform high temperature appear to have the same colour.

(c) A thermometer with a bulb coated with lamp-black reads higher in the sunshine than one uncoated.

(d) The dross on the surface of strongly heated molten lead glows red but when the dross is swept aside the surface looks black.

(e) Iron glows more brightly than glass in the same flame.

(f) A white chalk mark on an iron plate looks dark when the plate is strongly heated.

9. (a) What is *black-body radiation*?

(b) What arguments can be used to prove that the radiation inside a constant-temperature enclosure is independent of the nature of the walls and depends only upon the temperature?

10. (a) State *Stefan's law*.

(b) Compare the rates at which energy is radiated from two similar black spheres at temperatures of 1000 and 500 °K respectively.

11. (a) State *Wien's displacement law*.

(b) What is the wavelength of maximum radiation from (i) a body at 15 °C, (ii) a flat-iron at 150 °C, (iii) a hot star at 50000 °K? Assume that the bodies behave as black bodies and take the constant in Wien's equation as 0·29 cm deg C.

12. How may the distribution of energy in the spectrum of black-body radiation be investigated experimentally?

13. (a) Draw graphs to illustrate the distribution of energy in the spectrum of black-body radiation emanating from a source at (i) 3000 °K, (ii) 1000 °K. Comment on any special features the graphs exhibit.

(b) In electric light bulbs as much as possible of the energy expended is converted into visible radiation. How is this accomplished?

14. (a) What is the fundamental postulate of the quantum theory?

(b) Planck's constant $h$ is $6·56 \times 10^{-34}$ joule-sec. Calculate the energy of the following quanta: ultraviolet radiation of wavelength $3 \times 10^{-6}$ cm; yellow light of wavelength $6 \times 10^{-5}$ cm; infra-red radiation of wavelength $3 \times 10^{-3}$ cm.

(The velocity of light is $3 \times 10^{10}$ cm sec$^{-1}$.)

15. Stefan used the experimental result of Tyndall that the radiation from a platinum wire at 1200 °C is 11·7 times that at 525 °C. Show how far this verifies Stefan's law, assuming the temperature of the surroundings to be 20 °C. Why is Stefan's law not strictly obeyed?

16. State *Stefan's radiation law*. Under what conditions is it applicable? How has the law been applied to determine furnace temperatures?

A hot 'black body' of mass 64 gm, surface area 16 cm$^2$, and specific heat 0·10 cal/gm/deg C is allowed to cool inside an evacuated enclosure surrounded by melting ice. It is found that at 300 °C the body cools at the rate of 21 °C/min. Calculate Stefan's constant.

(1 cal = $4 \cdot 18 \times 10^7$ ergs.) (N.)

17. How can the existence of radiation from a hot but not luminous body be demonstrated, and the laws of transmission, reflection and refraction of such radiation investigated? Compare its behaviour in these respects with that of light. What reasons are there to conclude that the radiation is of the same type as light but of longer wavelength?

(O. & C.)

18. A solid copper sphere cools at the rate of 2·8 °C/min when its temperature is 127 °C. At what rate will a solid copper sphere of twice the radius cool when its temperature is 227 °C if, in both cases, the surroundings are maintained at 27 °C, and the conditions are such that Stefan's law may be applied? (N.)

19. Explain what is meant by a perfectly black body. How does the radiation from a black body depend upon its temperature? How is it possible to obtain in practice a close approximation to a black body?

Assuming that the human body has an effective surface area of 2 m², and that it radiates as a black body at 35 °C, find in watts the net rate of loss of energy by radiation when the surroundings are at 15 °C.

(Take Stefan's constant to be $5 \cdot 7 \times 10^{-5}$ erg cm$^{-2}$ sec$^{-1}$ °C$^{-4}$.) (O.)

20. What is meant by a *black body*? What is the nearest approach to a black body that we can construct in the laboratory?

The mean temperature of the filament of a 40 W electric light bulb is 2500 °C; its length is 10 cm and its diameter 0·1 mm. Assuming that all the heat is lost by radiation, what is the emissivity of the filament ('emissivity' is the ratio of the energy radiated by an actual body to that radiated by a similar black body at the same temperature)?

(Stefan's constant is $5 \cdot 67 \times 10^{-5}$ c.g.s. units.) (O. & C.)

21. Describe an instrument for the measurement of radiant energy, and explain how to use it to find how the energy emitted in this form varies with the temperature of the emitter. What result would you expect to obtain for a black body?

The element of an electric fire attains a steady temperature of 727 °C when joined to its normal supply. What will its temperature become if the power supplied to it is increased by 20 %? Assume that the element is a black body, that all heat is lost in the form of radiation, and that the radiation received from the surroundings is negligible. (C.)

22. By considering a domestic fire obtain an approximate value for Stefan's radiation constant.

(Make reasonable estimates of the values of the quantities involved.)

(C.S.)

23. Explain Prévost's theory of exchanges, giving illustrative examples. Develop the conception of black body or full radiation, and explain how it can be produced experimentally. How does the energy of the radiation vary with the temperature?

The mean temperature of the surface of the earth is 17 °C. Assuming that the earth's surface receives no heat except from the sun and that both sun and earth radiate as black bodies, calculate the temperature of the sun's surface, given that the radius of the sun is $4\cdot3 \times 10^5$ miles, and that of the earth's orbit $9\cdot3 \times 10^7$ miles. (O. & C.)

24. If the mean temperature at the equator is 80 °F, estimate the mean temperature of places at latitude 60°. (C.S.)

25. Explain what is meant by *black-body radiation*.

How can a close approximation to a black body be obtained in practice? Give a short account of the distribution of energy in the spectrum of the radiations emitted by a black body.

It has been found that the energy received by the earth from the sun is equal to $1\cdot4 \times 10^6$ ergs/cm$^2$/sec. Assuming that the sun emits black-body radiation, and that the ratio of the radius of the earth's orbit to the sun's radius is 216, calculate the surface temperature of the sun.

(Stefan's constant $= 5\cdot7 \times 10^{-5}$ erg cm$^{-2}$ sec$^{-1}$ deg$^{-4}$.) (O. & C.)

26. Discuss the methods employed for measuring temperatures higher than 600 °C and describe one in detail.

Assuming that the earth as a whole absorbs and radiates like an ideal black body in space at 0° abs. obtain a value for the average temperature of its surface. Assume that the intensity of solar radiation at the surface of the earth is 2 cal/cm$^2$/min and that the value of Stefan's constant is $5\cdot7 \times 10^{-5}$ erg cm$^{-2}$ sec$^{-1}$ deg$^{-4}$ C. (N.)

27. Explain how the radiation laws are utilised to establish temperatures above about 1000 °C. Describe one form of radiation pyrometer.

28. The distance of Venus, Earth and Mars from the sun are approximately in the ratio 0·72:1·00:1·52 respectively. Assuming that all radiate as black bodies, calculate approximate values for the mean temperatures, due to solar radiation, of Venus and Mars, taking that of Earth to be 15 °C.

Discuss why the actual temperatures may be very different from those indicated by your calculation. (N.)

29. Discuss the various mechanisms whereby heat may be transferred from one region to another.

Consider, in particular, the rise of temperature of the lower atmosphere during a sunny day and the maintenance of the high temperature inside a greenhouse when the sun is shining. (C.S.)

CHAPTER 10

# THERMODYNAMICS

Two generalisations sprang from the study of heat which are of such wide application in the whole of natural science that they are among the four or five most fundamental laws of nature. One is the first law of thermodynamics, or the principle of the conservation of energy; the other is the second law of thermodynamics, or the principle of the degradation of energy.

We discussed the first law of thermodynamics in chapter 3 and saw that a given quantity of work can be completely converted into heat in accordance with a fixed rate of exchange. The second law of thermodynamics arose from a consideration of the inverse process— the conversion of heat into work. Even under ideal conditions, as we shall see, a given quantity of heat cannot be converted completely into work. There is still the same fixed rate of exchange but some of the heat remains heat and cannot be changed into work.

In the steam engine, for example, a great deal of the heat derived from the coal is lost in the exhaust steam from the cylinders or turbines by being puffed into the atmosphere or by being given up to the cooling water in the condenser. This wasted heat falls from a higher temperature to the lower temperature of the atmosphere and hence ceases to be available for conversion into work; its energy is said to be dissipated or degraded.

## Carnot's ideal heat engine

A machine for converting heat into work is known as a *heat engine*. The theory of its working originated from the study of the steam engine by the French engineer Sadi Carnot (1796–1832). When Carnot was a young man the steam engine was spreading throughout Europe as the prime mover in the industrial expansion of the early nineteenth century.

Carnot considered what fundamentally determines the efficiency of a steam engine. By efficiency is meant the ratio of the work done by the engine to the heat supplied to the engine, both quantities being measured in the same units; thus, if all the heat supplied were converted into work, the efficiency would be 1. Carnot asked how the efficiency could be made a maximum. Would a different working substance be more efficient than steam? Would a different type of engine—for example a turbine rather than a piston engine—be more efficient? What would be the effect of raising the temperature of the steam before it entered the engine?

In any conceivable type of heat engine heat must fall from a higher to a lower temperature. Carnot, guided by the analogy of a water mill in which the work done is proportional to the vertical height through which the water falls, realised that the bigger the difference in temperature through which a heat engine works the greater the efficiency. He thought of heat as caloric, indestructible like water, and hence believed that exactly the same quantity of heat is rejected by an engine at the lower temperature as is taken in at the higher temperature (ignoring heat losses due to faulty insulation, etc.). We now know, from the principle of the conservation of energy, that less heat is rejected by a heat engine than is taken in and that the difference in these two quantities is equivalent to the work done by the engine. Carnot's mistake, however, did not invalidate his fertile concepts and arguments.

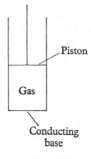

The steam engine is somewhat complicated, since water must be boiled to produce the steam and the steam is eventually condensed back to water. Carnot therefore imagined an ideal heat engine, with a gas such as air as its working substance, consisting of a frictionless piston in a perfectly thermally insulated cylinder, the base of the cylinder being a perfect conductor (Fig. 107). The engine is operated by alternately heating and cooling the gas through the base of the cylinder, which causes the gas to expand and contract and hence to move the piston up and down. Carnot asked: What are the conditions that such an engine should have its maximum efficiency?

Fig. 107

It is an experimental fact that when a gas expands, doing work, it is cooled; similarly, when a gas is compressed, having work done upon it, it is heated. Carnot argued that, since the engine produces work by heat falling through a difference of temperature, and since the work is actually performed by the expansion and contraction of the gas, the maximum efficiency will be attained when there is no change of temperature of the gas except that caused by a change of volume. He wrote: 'All change of temperature which is not due to a change of volume of the bodies can be only a useless re-establishment of equilibrium in the caloric.'

The way we should put it today is that, for maximum efficiency, there must be no exchange of heat between bodies at *different* temperatures because this is wasting the temperature difference. The working substance must be always in thermal equilibrium with the source of heat, or with the sink to which the heat is rejected.

## The Carnot cycle

How then must Carnot's ideal engine operate if it is to fulfil these conditions? Fig. 108 represents what is known as a Carnot cycle.

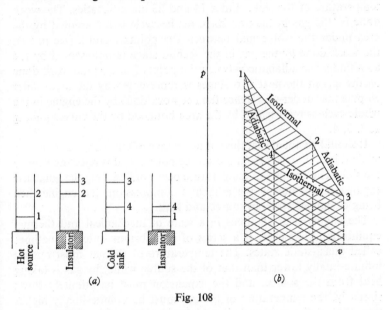

Fig. 108

The cylinder is first placed on a source of heat and a suitable load is placed on the piston causing it to take up position 1. The load is gradually reduced so that the gas expands isothermally, taking heat from the source to keep its temperature constant, until the piston arrives at position 2. The cylinder is then placed on an insulator and the gas is allowed to expand adiabatically (i.e. without receiving or giving out heat), again by reducing the load on the piston, until the temperature of the gas has fallen to that of the sink, the piston reaching position 3. The cylinder is next placed on the sink and the gas is compressed isothermally by gradually increasing the load on the piston, heat being given up to the sink and the piston reaching position 4. The cylinder is finally placed on an insulator and compressed adiabatically until the temperature has risen to that of the source. The piston will now be back in position 1 and the gas will be in exactly the same state as when the cycle started. The internal energy of the gas at the end will be identical with that at the beginning and there is no question of any heat or work disappearing as internal energy.

The changes in the pressure and volume of the gas during the cycle are shown in Fig. 108(*b*). The lines 12 and 43 are isothermals, the former being at the temperature of the source and the latter at the temperature of the sink. Lines 14 and 23 are adiabatics. The work done *by* the gas in the first stage of the cycle is represented by the area under the isothermal between the points 1 and 2 (see p. 59); the work done *by* the gas in the second stage is represented by the area under the adiabatic between the points 2 and 3; the work done *on* the gas in the next two stages is represented by the area under 34 plus that under 41. Hence the net work done by the engine in the whole cycle is represented by the area bounded by the curves joining 1, 2, 3, 4.

It should be noted that there is no change of temperature of the gas while it is taking heat from the source nor while it is rejecting heat to the sink. The changes of temperature occur only during the adiabatic expansion and during the adiabatic compression, the engine then being disconnected from source and sink.

The engine is at all times in a state of mechanical and thermal equilibrium. The cycle is a series of equilibrium states, sometimes called quasi-static states. The temperature of the gas must remain infinitesimally lower than that of the source while the gas is taking heat from the source, and the expansion must be infinitely slow; similarly, the temperature of the gas must be infinitesimally higher than that of the sink while it is giving up heat to the sink, and the compression must be infinitely slow. The adiabatic expansion and contraction must likewise be infinitely slow, so that there is at all times mechanical equilibrium; otherwise eddies will be set up in the gas causing a transfer of internal energy of the gas to mechanical energy of the gas and back again to internal energy—entailing a fall and rise of temperature not complying with Carnot's condition that the change of temperature must be due solely to a change of volume.

## Reversibility

When Carnot's engine is made to pass through the cycle in the reverse direction, the engine has net work done upon it, instead of doing work, and it gives out heat at the higher temperature of the source and takes in heat at the lower temperature of the sink. In fact, it behaves as a refrigerator or as a heat pump (p. 182).

Carnot realised that his engine was reversible, in the sense that, if it did work $W$ by taking in heat $Q_1$ from the source and rejecting heat $Q_2$ to the sink, then, operating in the reverse direction, it would give out heat $Q_1$ to the source and absorb heat $Q_2$ from the sink if the same amount of work $W$ were done upon it.

## Arguments from reversibility

Carnot proved that no engine can be more efficient than a reversible engine, the proof being based on the impossibility of perpetual motion. Imagine an engine that is more efficient than a reversible engine and let it drive the reversible engine backwards.

Suppose that the non-reversible engine takes heat $Q_1$ from the source and rejects heat $Q_2$ to the sink. For simplicity, suppose that the reversible engine takes heat $Q_2$ from the sink; let it reject heat $Q_1'$ to the source. Since the non-reversible engine is more efficient than the reversible engine, $Q_1 - Q_2 < Q_1' - Q_2$, i.e. $Q_1 < Q_1'$. Hence the non-reversible engine takes less heat from the source than the reversible engine delivers to the source. In this way an excess of heat, $Q_1' - Q_1$, can be transferred during each cycle from the sink to the source without requiring any work from an external agency. The continuous supply of heat to the source can be used to run another engine as a perpetual-motion machine—a state of affairs that is contrary to experience.

Carnot drew the following remarkable and fundamentally important conclusions:

(1) No engine can be more efficient than a reversible engine.

(2) All reversible engines working through the same difference of temperature have the same efficiency, whatever their working substance or whatever their design and mode of operation.

(3) The efficiency of a reversible engine depends only upon the temperatures of the source and sink.

(4) Heat cannot be converted completely and continuously into work.

Applying these conclusions to the steam engine, the maximum possible efficiency of the engine can be increased only by increasing the difference between the temperatures of the steam when it enters and leaves the engine, e.g. by superheating the steam. Any change in the design of the engine or in the nature of the working substance will not increase the maximum possible efficiency unless it results in the engine working through a greater difference of temperature.

## Calculation of the efficiency of a reversible engine

We will now calculate the efficiency of Carnot's reversible engine, assuming it to contain $n$ moles of perfect gas as the working substance. Let the engine traverse the cycle $ABCD$ in Fig. 109. Suppose that the

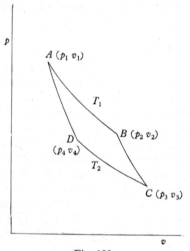

Fig. 109

temperatures, on the perfect gas scale, of the source and sink are $T_1$ and $T_2$ respectively and the pressure and volume at $A$, $B$, $C$ and $D$ are $p_1v_1$, $p_2v_2$, $p_3v_3$ and $p_4v_4$ respectively.

The heat $Q_1$ absorbed by the engine from the source at temperature $T_1$ is equal to the work done by the gas in the isothermal expansion from $A$ to $B$.

$$\therefore Q_1 = \frac{nRT_1}{J} \log_e \frac{v_2}{v_1} \quad \text{(p. 60).}$$

Similarly, the heat $Q_2$ rejected to the sink at temperature $T_2$ is equal to the work done on the gas in the isothermal compression from $C$ to $D$.

$$\therefore Q_2 = \frac{nRT_2}{J} \log_e \frac{v_3}{v_4}.$$

The work done by the engine, according to the principle of the conservation of energy, is equivalent to the heat destroyed, $Q_1 - Q_2$, and hence

$$\text{Efficiency} = \frac{Q_1 - Q_2}{Q_1}$$

*or* $H_1 - H_2$
$H_1$

$$= \frac{\dfrac{nRT_1}{J} \log_e \dfrac{v_2}{v_1} - \dfrac{nRT_2}{J} \log_e \dfrac{v_3}{v_4}}{\dfrac{nRT_1}{J} \log_e \dfrac{v_2}{v_1}}.$$

Since $AB$ and $DC$ are isothermals,

$$p_1 v_1 = p_2 v_2 \quad \text{and} \quad p_3 v_3 = p_4 v_4.$$

Since $AD$ and $BC$ are adiabatics,

$$p_1 v_1^\gamma = p_4 v_4^\gamma \quad \text{and} \quad p_2 v_2^\gamma = p_3 v_3^\gamma.$$

Whence

$$\frac{v_2}{v_1} = \frac{v_3}{v_4}.$$

$$\therefore \text{Efficiency} = \frac{T_1 - T_2}{T_1}.$$

This represents the efficiency of an ideal engine working between temperatures $T_1$ and $T_2$ and hence is the maximum possible efficiency of a practical engine, whatever the working substance. The efficiency could be 1 only if $T_2 = 0$, i.e. if the lower temperature were the absolute zero.

Summarising,

$$\text{Efficiency} = \frac{Q_1 - Q_2}{Q_1} = \frac{T_1 - T_2}{T_1},$$

i.e. $\dfrac{Q_1}{T_1} = \dfrac{Q_2}{T_2}.$

## Efficiency of a steam engine

We will calculate the efficiency of a steam locomotive, in which the steam is superheated to 200 °C before entering the cylinder and exhausts at 100 °C into the atmosphere, assuming the engine to operate as a Carnot engine (although it can never do this, for obvious reasons).

$$\text{Efficiency} = \frac{T_1 - T_2}{T_2} = \frac{473 - 373}{373} = 0 \cdot 27.$$

The actual efficiency of a steam locomotive is about $0 \cdot 15$.

## The Otto cycle

A Carnot cycle cannot be operated in a practical engine because the motion would be infinitely slow. It is a typical idealisation of physics; its purpose is to enable us to calculate the maximum possible efficiency for an engine working between two temperatures. We will now consider a practical cycle, that of the normal motor-car engine, known as the Otto cycle, and shown in its idealised form in Fig. 110.

The cycle includes one working stroke for every four strokes of the piston. $AB$ represents the inlet stroke when a mixture of air and petrol vapour is drawn into the cylinder; $BC$ represents the compression stroke when the mixture is compressed adiabatically; $CD$ represents the explosion of the mixture by means of an electric spark

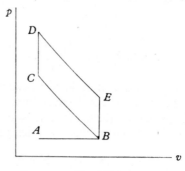

Fig. 110

and $DE$ the working stroke, which is an adiabatic expansion. At $E$ a valve opens and the pressure falls to that of the atmosphere, represented by $EB$; $BA$ is the exhaust stroke, when the spent gases are swept out of the cylinder by the piston.

Since the working substance is almost entirely air, the function of the petrol vapour being merely to heat the air, we can imagine that the same air stays in the cylinder and continually repeats the cycle $BCDEB$. The obvious difference between this and the Carnot cycle is that the heat is not taken in isothermally. The temperature of the air, while it is taking in heat, rises from $T_C$ at $C$ to $T_D$ at $D$.

The work done per cycle is represented by the area of $BCDE$, which is proportional to $(v_B - v_C)$. The engine can be made more efficient by increasing $(v_B - v_C)$, and this is done in high-compression engines by increasing the adiabatic compression $BC$. The compression ratio, $v_B/v_C$, cannot be increased too much, however, because if the temperature becomes too high, the petrol will ignite before the spark occurs; the compression ratio is also limited by the strength of the cylinder.

For an engine of given strength and weight we can choose between high efficiency with low power and lower efficiency with higher power. The more nearly equal are the temperatures, and hence the pressures, at $C$ and $D$, the more efficient will the engine be, because the more nearly does the cycle then correspond to the Carnot cycle, but the lower the power developed; the higher the temperature at $D$, as compared with that at $C$, the lower the efficiency, but the higher the power developed.

## The refrigerator

The principle of the refrigerator is the exertion of a cooling effect by the absorption of latent heat when a liquid evaporates. The liquid

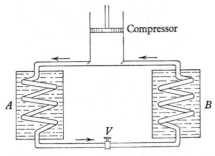

Fig. 111

is used over and over again by re-liquefying its vapour by pressure and hence the critical temperature of the vapour must be above normal atmospheric temperatures. Also the latent heat of evaporation of the liquid should be reasonably large and the pressure required for liquefaction should not be too high. Suitable substances are ammonia, carbon dioxide and sulphur dioxide.

In Fig. 111 the liquid evaporates in the pipes on the right, surrounded by the brine bath $B$. The latent heat necessary for the evaporation is supplied by the brine, which is therefore cooled and can then be used for refrigerating purposes. The compressor, on its upstroke, draws in vapour from the right, on its downstroke the vapour is compressed and forced into the pipes on the left where it is cooled by a cold-water condenser $A$ and liquefied. The cold water absorbs the latent heat given out when the vapour liquefies. The liquid then passes through the throttle valve $V$ into the pipes on the right and once more evaporates as the pressure is reduced by the upstroke of the compressor.

For Fig. 111 to represent a domestic refrigerator the pipes on the right should not be surrounded by brine and the condenser on the left should be air-cooled rather than water-cooled.

The ideal refrigerator may be regarded as a Carnot engine worked backwards and we may apply the formula on p. 179,

$$\frac{Q_1}{T_1} = \frac{Q_2}{T_2},$$

where $Q_1$ is the heat rejected to the condenser at temperature $T_1$ and $Q_2$ is the heat extracted from the brine or refrigerated chamber at temperature $T_2$. The work done by the motor is $Q_1 - Q_2$. The coefficient of performance (C.P.) of the refrigerator is defined as the ratio of the heat extracted to the work done.

$$\text{C.P.} = \frac{Q_2}{Q_1 - Q_2}$$

$$= \frac{T_2}{T_1 - T_2}.$$

The coefficient of performance increases as $T_1 - T_2$ becomes less. Hence a domestic refrigerator uses less power on a cold day than on a hot day.

## The heat pump

The heat pump is essentially the same as a refrigerator. If the primary purpose of the machine is to deliver heat to a higher temperature it is called a heat pump; if it is to extract heat from a lower temperature it is called a refrigerator.

A heat pump may be used to extract heat from a lake in winter and deliver it at a higher temperature to warm a building. Most existing installations use the same machine both as a heat pump and as a refrigerator, to heat the building in winter and to cool it in summer. The use of a machine as a heat pump only is uneconomic because the cost of the electric power to work the machine is too high compared with the cost of solid or liquid heating fuel.

The coefficient of performance of a heat pump is defined as follows:

$$\text{C.P.} = \frac{Q_1}{\text{Work}} = \frac{Q_1}{Q_1 - Q_2} = \frac{T_1}{T_1 - T_2}.$$

It is clear that the coefficient of performance is greater than unity, i.e. the heat delivered is greater than the work done.

## Kelvin's thermodynamic scale of temperature

Lord Kelvin realised that, since the efficiency of a reversible engine is a function of the temperature only, it provides a means of defining a scale of temperature which is independent of the properties of any substance.

Suppose that a reversible engine absorbs heat $Q_1$ and rejects heat $Q_2$ at the two temperatures between which it is working. Then these temperatures, $\theta_1$ and $\theta_2$ on Kelvin's thermodynamic scale, are defined by the equation

$$\frac{Q_1}{Q_2} = \frac{\theta_1}{\theta_2}.$$

We have seen that, if $T_1$ and $T_2$ are the temperatures on the perfect gas scale,

$$\frac{Q_1}{Q_2} = \frac{T_1}{T_2} \quad \text{(p. 179)}.$$

Hence the thermodynamic scale and the perfect gas scale are identical, so long as we arrange that the numerical values on the two scales for at least one temperature are the same; the numerical values for all other temperatures will then be the same. Lord Kelvin made the numerical values on the two scales the same for the ice point and also for the steam point. Today the numerical values on both scales are fixed by assigning 273·16 to the temperature of pure ice, water and water vapour in equilibrium at the triple point.

It may be asked what is the value of the thermodynamic scale if it is merely the same as the perfect-gas scale. First, a scale which is independent of the properties of any substance, even of an ideal substance, is intellectually satisfying. Secondly, it enables us to give a significance to temperatures beyond the range of a gas thermometer, and to calibrate, for example, the scales of radiation pyrometers from thermodynamic reasoning.

To make the meaning of the thermodynamic scale a little clearer imagine a set of reversible engines coupled in series; let the first engine absorb heat $Q_1$ at temperature $\theta_1$ and reject heat $Q_2$ at temperature $\theta_2$; let the second engine absorb the heat which the first engine rejects, namely $Q_2$ at $\theta_2$, and reject $Q_3$ at $\theta_3$; and so on. If we arrange the temperatures so that each engine does the same amount of work, then the temperature differences, $\theta_1 - \theta_2$, $\theta_2 - \theta_3$, etc., are equal.

The proof is as follows. Since the engines do equal work,

$$Q_1 - Q_2 = Q_2 - Q_3, \text{ etc.}$$

But $\qquad \dfrac{Q_1}{\theta_1} = \dfrac{Q_2}{\theta_2} = \dfrac{Q_3}{\theta_3}$.  (Definition of $\theta_1$, $\theta_2$ and $\theta_3$.)

Substituting for $Q_2$ and $Q_3$ from the second equations in the first equation,

$$Q_1 - Q_1\frac{\theta_2}{\theta_1} = Q_1\frac{\theta_2}{\theta_1} - Q_1\frac{\theta_3}{\theta_1},$$

i.e. $\qquad\qquad\qquad\qquad \theta_1 - \theta_2 = \theta_2 - \theta_3$.

In Fig. 112 two adiabatics are shown and four isothermals, $\theta_1$, $\theta_2$, $\theta_3$ and $\theta_4$. The temperature intervals between the isothermals are equal if the shaded areas, representing the work done by each engine, are equal.

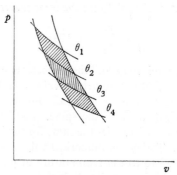

Fig. 112

The heat rejected by each successive engine becomes successively less, i.e. $Q_2 > Q_3 > Q_4$, etc. The final engine will reject zero heat and the sink will be at the absolute zero.

Although each of the engines does the same amount of work they become progressively more efficient, the final engine having an efficiency of 1 since it rejects zero heat and converts all the heat it absorbs into work.

### The second law of thermodynamics

The most fundamental idea in Carnot's work was the concept of reversibility. Only in a reversible process can the maximum possible work be obtained from heat. A reversible process is an ideal which can never be realised in practice because all natural processes involving a transfer of heat are irreversible. Whenever heat has flowed because of a difference of temperature it can never go back, any more than water can flow uphill, unless some external agency is employed. Also, as we have already explained, in a reversible process there must be at all times mechanical as well as thermal equilibrium; otherwise heat will be generated, and it will flow irreversibly through a difference of temperature.

Carnot, when he wrote his book *La Puissance motrice du feu* ('The Motive Power of Heat'), had not grasped the principle of the conservation of energy although it is believed that he did so before the end of his short life. Hence it was necessary for his ideas to be reconciled with the principle of the conservation of energy, and this was done by Clausius and, shortly afterwards, by Lord Kelvin, on the lines of our discussion in this chapter.

Clausius and Kelvin endeavoured to express Carnot's underlying principle, as a basis for the logical development of thermodynamics, in what is known as the *second law of thermodynamics*. Clausius expressed the law in the abbreviated form: heat cannot of itself pass from a lower to a higher temperature.

That this is not completely satisfactory can be seen from the following example. Suppose that a gas at high pressure and low temperature is separated by a movable piston from a gas at low pressure and high temperature. The piston will move from the high-pressure to the low-pressure side, causing the gas at high temperature to become compressed and hence hotter. Heat has been transferred from the cold to the hot gas. Clausius therefore elaborated the statement of the law: *it is impossible for any machine, working continuously in cycles, and not aided by an external agency, to convey heat from a lower to a higher temperature.* The second law of thermodynamics refers to a cyclic process, i.e. one in which the working substance returns to its original state.

Kelvin stated the law in the form that *it is impossible continuously to transform heat into work by cooling a body below the temperature of its surroundings.* This can be shown to be equivalent to Clausius's statement as follows. To cool a body below the temperature of the surroundings we require a refrigerator, which must be supplied with work, $W$, from an external agency. If Kelvin's law is untrue, we can obtain more work, $W'$, from an engine working through the temperature difference created than was required to operate the refrigerator. This excess work, $W' - W$, not derived from an external agency, can be used to operate another refrigerator and convey heat from a lower to a higher temperature. Hence the law of Clausius can be violated if that of Kelvin is untrue.

An engine which violates the second law of thermodynamics, although conforming with the principle of the conservation of

MH

energy, is called a perpetual-motion machine of the second kind, to distinguish it from the first kind in which energy is not conserved. An example of a perpetual-motion machine of the second kind is one designed to drive a ship by heat extracted from the sea.

The first law of thermodynamics states that in all heat processes energy is conserved; the second law of thermodynamics states, in effect, that all actual heat processes are irreversible and hence that they result in the dissipation or degradation of energy.

### Entropy

The essence of thermodynamics is embodied in the equation

$$\frac{Q_1}{T_1} = \frac{Q_2}{T_2} \quad \text{(p. 179),}$$

where $Q_1$ is the heat absorbed by the working substance in a reversible engine from a source at absolute temperature $T_1$, and $Q_2$ is the heat rejected to a sink at absolute temperature $T_2$, when the engine performs a complete cycle.

The terms $Q_1/T_1$ and $Q_2/T_2$ were called by Clausius the change of *entropy* of the working substance. When heat, $Q$, is added to a substance at constant temperature, $T$, there is said to be a gain of entropy, $Q/T$; when heat is subtracted there is a loss of entropy.

In a reversible cycle the change of entropy of the working substance, $(Q_1/T_1)-(Q_2/T_2)$, is zero. But in a non-reversible engine the working substance absorbs a larger quantity of heat from the source than in a corresponding reversible engine and, in its case, $Q_1/T_1$ is greater than $Q_2/T_2$. Hence the change of entropy during each cycle, $(Q_1/T_1)-(Q_2/T_2)$, is a positive quantity. Indeed, in all the irreversible changes in nature the entropy increases. When a hot body loses heat to a cold body there is an over-all increase in entropy because $Q/T$ is greater for the cold body than for the hot.

Clausius stated the second law of thermodynamics in the alternative form: *the entropy of the world tends to a maximum.*

Exception could be taken to this statement because it is hazardous to extrapolate generalisations obtained from terrestrial experiments to the world or universe as a whole. To overcome the objection the law could be stated in the form: the entropy of a closed terrestrial system tends to a maximum.

Lord Kelvin also pointed out that the inevitable consequence of the tendency of heat to pass from a higher to a lower temperature, and hence to become degraded, is that the universe is slowly running down and that eventually all energy will be at the same uniform level of unavailability, unless there is some undiscovered counteracting process at work.

Such a counteracting process has been suggested in the continuous creation throughout space of hydrogen, which eventually condenses into new galaxies. Under such conditions the universe would not run down but would be a steady-state system. The continuous-creation theory requires a uniform distribution of galaxies, whereas the rival theory of a single creation followed by an expansion of the universe requires a thinning out of the galaxies at the observational confines of the universe. Observation at present favours the single creation theory.

**Statistical mechanics**

Thermodynamics, as developed by Carnot, Clausius and Kelvin, dealt with macroscopic rather than with microscopic phenomena; it ignored atoms and molecules, being concerned with quantities of heat met with in everyday life. The application of the concepts of thermodynamics to the world of atoms and molecules by Maxwell and Boltzmann proved extraordinarily fruitful.

According to the kinetic theory of gases, a gas consists of molecules whose average velocities are greater the higher the temperature of the gas. The molecules are continually colliding, with the result that they do not all have the same velocity; a small fraction are moving more quickly than the average and another small fraction are moving more slowly. Maxwell perceived that this picture of a gas provided a loophole for a violation of the second law of thermodynamics.

Imagine two gases at different temperatures separated by a partition having a frictionless trapdoor operated by a 'sorting demon'. The trapdoor will be bombarded by molecules on both sides. Suppose that the demon opens the trapdoor to allow the fastest molecules from the cold gas to enter the hot gas and the slowest molecules from the hot gas to enter the cold gas. In this way heat will pass from the cold gas to the hot gas without the expenditure of work, thus violating the second law of thermodynamics. Even without the assistance of the demon such a sorting of the molecules could conceivably occur by chance, although the billions of molecules involved make the chance infinitesimal.

Thus the second law of thermodynamics is a statistical law. When heat flows from a higher to a lower temperature, rather than in the reverse direction, the molecules are merely changing from a less probable to a more probable state. Maxwell initiated the science of statistical mechanics in which the laws of chance were used to predict the statistical behaviour of a system consisting of a vast number of molecules. His work was continued by Boltzmann, who deduced the generalisation, revealing the deeper significance of entropy, that the entropy of a state of a system is proportional to the logarithm of the probability of that state.

### Entropy and disorder

Heat may be regarded as disordered energy, and the quantity of disorder is measured by entropy.

Suppose that a mass of gas is continuously cooled at constant volume. The entropy decreases, heat being withdrawn, and the disorder of the molecules likewise decreases because their thermal motion, the cause of the disorder, becomes less. Below the critical temperature the disorder has been reduced sufficiently for the gas to be liquefied by pressure alone. There is a sudden decrease of entropy when the gas liquefies and the latent heat of vaporisation is given up; there is a corresponding decrease in disorder of the molecules as they change to the liquid state. There is another abrupt decrease in entropy and disorder when the liquid solidifies; the latent heat of fusion is released and the molecules take up definite positions.

The decrease in disorder as substances are cooled reaches its culmination at the absolute zero when all substances are in a state of perfect order. This, in effect, is the third law of thermodynamics, which is the chief guiding principle of low-temperature research. One way of stating the law is as follows: at the absolute zero the thermal motion of the molecules is so small that there is only one configuration possible and this is the greatest order of which the system is capable.

### QUESTIONS

1. (a) What are the conditions that a heat engine should be reversible?
    (b) Prove that a reversible engine is more efficient than an irreversible engine.

2. (a) Explain, with a $p$–$v$ diagram, what is meant by a Carnot cycle.
    (b) What factors cause the efficiency of a steam engine to be less than that of a Carnot engine?

3. (a) What is the efficiency of a Carnot engine operating between 100 and 0 °C?
    (b) Under what conditions can a Carnot engine have an efficiency of 100%?

4. A Carnot engine operates between temperatures of 227 and 127 °C. By how much would the efficiency increase if (a) the higher temperature were raised by 100 °C, (b) the lower temperature were lowered by 100 °C?

5. A reversible engine operating between 300 and 200 °F develops 8 h.p. How much heat is (i) absorbed from the hot source, (ii) rejected to the cold source?
   (1 Btu = 778 ft lb.)

6. (a) How does the cycle of an internal combustion engine depart from a Carnot cycle?
   (b) Why does the efficiency of a petrol engine increase with increasing compression ratio?

7. (a) Describe the principle of a refrigerator.
   (b) Explain whether a room can be cooled by leaving open the door of a refrigerator in the room.

8. Distinguish between a refrigerator and a heat pump. How do their coefficients of performance differ?

9. A heat pump, operated by electric power, extracts heat from a lake at 4 °C and delivers it to a house at 27 °C. Compare the costs of heating the house by the heat pump and by coal fires, if the cost of electric power is twice that of coal of equivalent power. (Assume the heat pump to be 100 % efficient.)

10. Define Kelvin's absolute scale of temperature and show that it agrees with the scale of the perfect gas thermometer.

11. Distinguish between isothermal and adiabatic changes.
   A constant mass of ideal gas is taken round a cycle represented by ABCD on a pressure–volume diagram. AB and DC are isothermals at 150 and 27 °C respectively, and AD and BC are adiabatics. If the volumes at A and B are respectively 20 and 50 l. and the pressure at A is 10 atm, calculate (a) the heat entry along AB, (b) the net work done by the gas during the complete cycle. Assume 1 atm = $10^6$ dyn/cm². Take $\log_e 10 = 2.30$.
   (N.)

12. Explain the terms *an ideal heat engine* and *efficiency of a heat engine*.
   An ideal heat engine absorbs heat at 100 °C, which is supplied by the condensation of steam, and rejects heat at 0 °C, the heat rejected being used to melt ice. It is found that for every gram of steam condensed, when the engine is running, 4·952 gm of ice are melted. Calculate the temperature of the ice-point on the absolute thermodynamic scale.
   (Latent heat of condensation of steam = 538·7 cal/gm. Latent heat of fusion of ice = 79·63 cal/gm.)
   (O.S.)

13. What is meant by the efficiency of a heat engine?

Derive an expression for the efficiency of a Carnot engine, having a perfect gas as working substance, in terms of the temperatures of the source and sink.

A Carnot engine, having a perfect gas as working substance, is driven backwards and is used for freezing water already at 0 °C. If the engine is driven by a 500 W electric motor, having an efficiency of 60 %, how long will it take to freeze 9 kg of water?

(Take 15 and 0 °C as the working temperatures of the engine, and assume that there are no heat losses in the refrigerating system. Latent heat of fusion of ice = 80 cal/gm; $J = 4.2$ J/cal.) (C.S.)

14. Distinguish between internal energy and entropy. A perfect gas is heated at constant temperature so that it does work by expansion. Explain whether there is any change in (a) its internal energy, (b) its entropy.

15. Calculate the change of entropy
   (a) of 1 gm of water at 0 °C when it is converted into ice at the same temperature;
   (b) of 1 gm of water at 100 °C when it is converted into steam at the same temperature.

16. An electric current of 2 A flows through a wire of resistance 4·2 Ω and it is kept at the constant temperature of 27 °C by a flow of water. What is the change of entropy in 1 sec (a) of the wire, (b) of the universe?

17. One statement of the second law of thermodynamics is as follows: 'it is impossible for a heat engine to produce net work in a complete cycle if it exchanges heat only with bodies at a single fixed temperature'. Discuss this statement in terms of (a) Carnot's cycle, (b) entropy.

# ANSWERS TO QUESTIONS

## CHAPTER 1 (page 15)

**13.** $-145\ °C$.      **14.** $-277\ °C$.      **15.** $197\ °C$.

## CHAPTER 2 (page 35)

**4.** $0·09$ cal gm$^{-1}$ deg$^{-1}$ C.      **5.** (b) 7 min, 38 min.

**6.** 50 cal gm$^{-1}$, $0·070$ cal gm$^{-1}$ deg$^{-1}$ C.      **8.** $0·54$ cal gm$^{-1}$ deg$^{-1}$ C.

**9.** (c) (i) 88 cal min$^{-1}$, (ii) $1·4\ °C$ min$^{-1}$.      **10.** (b) 67 cal gm$^{-1}$.

**12.** 2290 J gm$^{-1}$.      **13.** (b) $0·12$ cal gm$^{-1}$ deg$^{-1}$ C.

**14.** (b) $0·727$ J gm$^{-1}$ deg$^{-1}$ C.      **15.** (b) $4·2$ cal gm$^{-1}$.

**16.** $32·0\ °C$, $0·50$ cal gm$^{-1}$ deg$^{-1}$ C.      **17.** $0·51$ cal gm$^{-1}$ deg$^{-1}$ C.

**18.** $37·5$ gm, $1003·4$ c.c.      **19.** $106·8$ cal gm$^{-1}$.

**20.** $50·7$ cal gm$^{-1}$.      **21.** $15·2$ min.

## CHAPTER 3 (page 49)

**2.** 410 ft lb sec$^{-1}$.      **4.** 310 Btu.      **5.** 1470 cal.

**6.** 230 gm sec$^{-1}$.      **7.** 350 m sec$^{-1}$.      **8.** $0·17$.

**9.** $4·1$ J cal$^{-1}$.      **15.** $51·6\ °C$.      **16.** $0·53$ cal gm$^{-1}$ deg$^{-1}$ C.

**17.** $0·71$ l. min$^{-1}$.      **18.** $64\ °C$ sec$^{-1}$.      **20.** (b) $17·3$ MeV.

**21.** $0·215$ a.m.u.

## CHAPTER 4 (page 68)

**1.** (b) $8·32 \times 10^7$ ergs mole$^{-1}$ deg$^{-1}$ C.      **2.** (b) $767·5$ mm.      **3.** $62·2$ cm.

**4.** 160 cm of mercury.      **5.** $\frac{10}{7}\,p$.      **7.** 107 cm of mercury, $139\ °C$.

**8.** $160\ °C$.      **10.** $36·7$ J.      **12.** $\frac{4}{3} \times 10^{12}$ dynes.

**13.** (c) $2·04$ J gm$^{-1}$ deg$^{-1}$ C.      **14.** $4·1 \times 10^7$ ergs cal$^{-1}$.

**15.** $0·98$ cal gm$^{-1}$ deg$^{-1}$ C.

**16.** $6·2$ cal.      **17.** 35 atm.      **18.** 22 cm of mercury.

**19.** 988 m.      **21.** $2·12$ h.p.

**22.** $166\ °C$, $69·8$ lb wt in$^{-2}$.      **24.** (a) $160\ °C$; (b) $2·0 \times 10^{10}$ ergs.

**25.** 457 cm$^3$, 379 cm$^3$.      **27.** $7·4\ °C$.      **29.** $\gamma = 1·40$.

**30.** $1·22$ atm.

**31.** $l = \dfrac{V}{a}\left\{\left(\dfrac{p+p_0}{p}\right)^{1/\gamma} - 1\right\}.$

     K.E. $= \dfrac{V}{\gamma-1}\left\{p_0 + p - p\left(\dfrac{p+p_0}{p}\right)^{1/\gamma}\right\}.$

**32.** $307\ °C$.

## CHAPTER 5 (page 90)

**3.** (*b*) $6.9 \times 10^4$ cm sec$^{-1}$.

**6.** (*a*) 0.75 and 1.25 cal gm$^{-1}$ deg$^{-1}$ C;

(*b*) 0.18 and 0.25 cal gm$^{-1}$ deg$^{-1}$ C.     **10.** 2500 °C.

**11.** $1.510 \times 10^{26}$ molecules, $1.346 \times 10^5$ cm sec$^{-1}$, 1.003 kg.

**12.** $4.73 \times 10^4$ cm sec$^{-1}$.     **14.** (*a*) 0.985; (*b*) 0.589.

**16.** $0.986 \times 10^6$ dyn cm$^{-2}$.     **17.** $1.2 \times 10^{22}$ mol sec$^{-1}$.

**18.** $1.305 \times 10^5$ cm sec$^{-1}$, 20000 °K.     **19.** $2R/J$.

**20.** 1.53, 430 °K.     **21.** $6.06 \times 10^{23}$.

## CHAPTER 6 (page 111)

**11.** 66.5 °K.

## CHAPTER 7 (page 127)

**6.** 80.8 cm of mercury.   **7.** 49.1 c.c.     **9.** 11.3 cm.

**13.** 37 cm.     **17.** 9.6 gm.     **21.** 77.2 %.

**22.** 52.6 %.   **24.** 27.0 cm of mercury.   **25.** 228 mm of mercury.

**26.** 0.94 cm of mercury.   **28.** 0.16.     **29.** 1190 gm.

## CHAPTER 8 (page 146)

**3.** (*b*) 2660 Btu ft$^{-2}$ hr$^{-1}$ deg$^{-1}$ F in.   **4.** 105.4 °C.

**5.** 0.087:1.     **6.** 0.002 W cm$^{-1}$ deg$^{-1}$ C.

**7.** 10.7 °C.     **11.** 0.0025 cal cm$^{-1}$ sec$^{-1}$ deg$^{-1}$ C.

**14.** $4.72 \times 10^{-4}$ W cm$^{-1}$ deg$^{-1}$ C.   **15.** From 2.7 to 1.5 kW.

**16.** $5 \times 10^{-4}$ cal cm$^{-1}$ sec$^{-1}$ deg$^{-1}$ C.   **19.** 2.6 cm.   **20.** 13 °C.

**21.** $4.6 \times 10^{-4}$ cal cm$^{-1}$ sec$^{-1}$ deg$^{-1}$ C.   **22.** 16.8 kW, 0.622 kW.

## CHAPTER 9 (page 168)

**16.** $5.73 \times 10^{-5}$ erg cm$^{-2}$ sec$^{-1}$ deg$^{-4}$ C.     **18.** 4.35 °C min$^{-1}$.

**19.** 240 W.     **20.** 0.38.     **21.** 774 °C.

**23.** 6030 °K.   **24.** −6 °F.   **25.** 5820 °K.   **26.** 280 °K.

**28.** 66 °C, −39 °C.

## CHAPTER 10 (page 188)

**4.** Efficiency changes from $\frac{1}{5}$ to (*a*) $\frac{1}{3}$, (*b*) $\frac{2}{5}$.

**5.** (i) 43 Btu sec$^{-1}$, (ii) 37.3 Btu sec$^{-1}$.     **9.** 1:6.

**11.** (*a*) $1.83 \times 10^4$ J; (*b*) $5.32 \times 10^3$ J.   **12.** 273.1 °K.   **13.** 9.23 min.

# INDEX